SIGN OFF

Other Books by Edwin Diamond

Jimmy Carter: An Interpretive Biography (with Bruce Mazlish)

Good News, Bad News

The Tin Kazoo: Television, Politics, and the News

The Rise and Fall of the Space Age

The Science of Dreams

Five Worlds of Our Lives (Contributor)

SIGN OFF

The Last Days of Television

Edwin Diamond

The MIT Press
Cambridge, Massachusetts
London, England

Second printing, September 1982
© 1982 by
The Massachusetts Institute of Technology

This book was set in Baskerville by Achorn Graphic Services, Inc., and
printed and bound in the United States of America.

Library of Congress Cataloging in Publication Data

Diamond, Edwin.
    Sign off: the last days of television.

    Includes bibliographical references and index.
    1. Television broadcasting of new—United States.   2. Television
broadcasting—United States.   I. Title.
PN4888.T4D48   070.1′9   82-230
ISBN 0-262-04069-7   AACR2

CONTENTS

PART III
Illusions of Power

INTRODUCTION

In May 1981 RCA, parent corporation of the National Broadcasting Company, announced that it was going into the cable
television business. Thus RCA became the last of the big three
broadcasting entities to enter the growing field of cable-
programming suppliers, or software makers. Both the American
Broadcasting Company and the Columbia Broadcasting System
had earlier begun corporate ventures into cable programming
for the cable-system operators in the United States. ABC Arts, a
cultural cable service, planned to be on air—or, on-line—in the
late fall of 1981, followed by ABC Beta, billed as a cable service
for women. By early 1982, too, CBS Cable promised to be
transmitting a cultural service featuring such artists as Leonard
Bernstein, Count Basie, Carly Simon, and Twyla Tharp. These
cable services began soliciting advertising in the spring of 1981,
which meant, of course, that they were competing with the over-
the-air services of ABC, CBS, and NBC for the revenues that are
the lifeblood of traditional broadcasting.[1]

RCA's belated crossover from traditional broadcasting technology to the new, wired technology of cable is as good a date as

any to mark the end of the present era of television in the United States and the birth of a new era. Traditional television of the period 1950 to 1980 was shaped by a major technological factor—the limited electromagnetic spectrum produced a system based on scarcity of channels; no more than six or seven voices could be heard on the VHF dial. Developments in cable technology, plus space satellite transmissions, can bring a system of abundance, quantitatively at least: not six or seven but sixty or a hundred channels of information/entertainment/data services can be carried, with the only practical limit on the number of voices being the ingenuity of the software makers and the interests and time of the audience.

The broadcast era that is ending with the move to cable technology has been dominated by the Big Three networks. In the new era there will still be an ABC, a CBS, and an NBC, for it is premature to write the obituary of companies that continue to show such strong earnings even in "bad" economic years (in 1980 NBC, the lagging network, earned pretax profits of $75 million). But the economic basis of broadcasting will be shifting. Cable audiences will be paying for programs that they have been getting free (the cost of the programming now charged to advertisers is passed on to consumers as part of the cost of the advertisers' product). For their part advertisers will aim at ever smaller special interest audiences, as is done by magazines these days. It will take several years for all this to happen; like the Cheshire cat, over-the-air broadcasting will gradually fade until there remains the smile that only forty years of creamy profits can bring.[2]

For now, the 1980s, television is still in its prime time and hearing the first intimations of mortality. What we see now on the air is what the medium of television is able to do at the top of its form. This book, then, is mainly an examination of the mature institution of television, a study of television's performance in its prime years, using the tools of reporting and analysis. Because television does not operate alone in society, other institutions, newspapers, magazines, and radio, are also examined when appropriate. Throughout, the focus is on how the institution of television and, more generally, the institutions of the media present other major institutions of American public life. This means a concentration here on news and informational programming, although other program formats, for example, prime-time entertainment shows, soap operas, and commercials, are also discussed.

The materials in this book came from interviews conducted by me and my associates in the News Study Group, Department of Political Science, Massachusetts Institute of Technology. The News Study Group began its work in 1972, studying press coverage of the Nixon–McGovern presidential race. We made two early—and, it turns out, wise—decisions. First, we concluded that the then-emerging technology of videotape would make possible the recording and analysis of public events and institutions as they were presented on television. That made possible, in turn, the rigorous study of what had been until then an evanescent subject. Second, the NSG decided to involve both graduate and undergraduate students in its work. The videotape technology provided a fresh method—reliable, storable, recallable—for studying television; the students provided an intelligent, energetic pool of talent.

With modest initial help from the Markle, Ford, and Sloan foundations, and with continuing support from MIT, the NSG has been able to expand its work. In 1975 I published the first results of the NSG work, *The Tin Kazoo: Television, Politics, and the News* (The MIT Press). *The Tin Kazoo* used video materials to look at major news events of the 1960s and early 1970s, including the Vietnam war, the 1968 and 1972 elections, Watergate, and the Nixon impeachment proceedings. In 1978 I published *Good News, Bad News* (The MIT Press), the second volume based on NSG work. It focused primarily on the 1976 presidential campaign and the performance of all the news media, print as well as broadcasting.

Since 1976 the NSG has widened its studies to include analysis of press treatment of other major institutions in American society; this analysis is the basis for this present study, *Sign-Off: The Last Days of Television*.

There are now well over 1,000 hours of catalogued videotape in the NSG archives at MIT. They are organized in such categories as Presidential Debates (Kennedy–Nixon, Ford–Carter, Reagan–Carter); Political Commercials, some dating from the early 1950s and from city, state, and congressional races as well as presidential campaigns; Religion on Television (from early Oral Roberts to late Jerry Falwell); News and Documentary programming (local as well as network, non-American as well as American); Children's Programming and Special Events Coverage (among these, election nights, Mideast wars, and the Three Mile Island crisis). The NSG archives are available to students, faculty, and researchers at MIT and elsewhere. The videotapes are used just as library books are used: as a historical record; as source materials for press critics and specialists doing critical analysis (such as this series of The MIT Press books); in the writing of graduate and undergraduate papers; in the classroom as a supplement to the readings and lectures.

In addition to the resource of NSG videotapes, I also used the more traditional reporting and research tools for this study. When sources are quoted, they have been interviewed by me, or by one of my associates in the NSG. In the few cases where materials are from sources other than our own reporting and research, I indicate these credits, along with further references for any one interested in pursuing various points.

Why subject television to serious analysis, especially at a time when it is about to undergo major change? This question is usually asked from one of two points of view, each equally erroneous. One attitude, apocalyptic in nature, is that television is so harmful and/or misleading in its slick, superficial, mass-oriented ways that it demands an absolute, automatic rejection: TV is not for grown-ups and should be kept out of the reach of children and gullible adults. The other attitude more coolly holds that, because the old order is dying, all our energies should be poured into working on the blue sky, the tabula rasa, of the new cable-satellite information order.

Those who profess to see nothing worth thinking about in television fail to recognize that our media reflect our culture and politics: to understand the what, how, and why of television is to begin to understand the complex, contradictory, confusing workings of our society, particularly of our public life. Those who, in the second instance, eagerly anticipate the new information order forget that the same culture and politics and society that shaped television in the old days will also be shaping the new technology. It shouldn't be necessary to remind people that there is nothing magical or mysterious about television. It is an artifact of popular culture. To look at television is no more, or less, than to look at ourselves, today and tomorrow.

Portions of this book appeared in different form in *American Film* magazine, the *New York Times*, *Next* magazine, *Panorama* magazine, *TV Guide*, and the *Washington Journalism Review*. I wish to thank in particular the following editors for their help and advice: Hollis Alpert, Roger Kranz, Gene Lambinus, David Sendler, Andrew Mills, Robert Smith, Ray White, and Roger Youman. A number of other editors and journalists also contributed to my understanding, including Jules Bergman, Mervin Block, Clay Felker, Lee Hanna, David Laventhol, Bill Moyers, Tom Morgan, Sasha Norkin, Michael J. O'Neill, Judith Parker, Ken Peirce, Frank Van Riper, Earl Ubell, and Stuart Zanger. Last, I owe a major debt to the faculty and staff of the Political Science Department at the Massachusetts Institute of Technology and to the students from MIT, Harvard, and Wellesley who worked with our News Study Group at MIT. Many people helped, but particularly Paula Cassidy, Hugh Donohue, Erika Max, Mary Miller, Dean Phillips, Ithiel De Sola Pool, Leigh Passman, Vivian Reifberg, and Clive Smith. I wish to thank Jane Grossman and Ann Fryling, also from MIT, and Steven Scheuer for their support of the News Study Group.

All opinions and conclusions expressed here are, naturally, my own.

FORMS

PART I

CHAPTER 1

Fifty-three years ago the American philosopher George Herbert Mead suggested that there are two models of journalism. One form he called the information model. Information journalism reported facts, such as election results; it emphasized the truth value of news. The other journalistic form Mead called the story model. Story journalism emphasized the enjoyability and consumatory value of news; story news was presented in such a way as to create satisfying aesthetic experiences and to help people relate events to their own lives. A refreshing as well as an original thinker, Mead rather approved of story journalism; he thought it was natural that popular newspapers sent out their reporters to get a story rather than just the facts.[1]

There was no way, of course, for Mead to be able to foresee that practitioners of the story form in the late 1970s would be pursuing enjoyability so much that they approached a model of journalism that was practically all entertainment and practically zero information. This new form, most instantly recognizable on certain television news and public affairs programs but also plain to see in print, emphasizes style over substance. Programs must have pace, as they say in television news. On-air talent must be contemporary-looking people. What is said—the reporting and narration, the content—becomes less and less important; what counts is how people look when they are saying it. There are lights, action, bright colors, pulsing music, a fast beat, and overall a general mindlessness in the total picture. Dim your eyes a bit, and you're in a familiar *now* place. This is *disco news,* a beat heard on television but also influential in print. When the big Janet Cooke story hit in April 1981, an avalanche of words were spilled out about journalistic excess, hyped-up quotes, and dramatic fiction passing as fact. The *Washington Post,* the paper of Watergate, had published a made-up story and the Pulitzer Prize board, arbiters of journalism's most prestige-laden award, had honored it. Everyone called the episode a scandal (properly so) and piously assured each other that the Cooke story had been an "aberration," an accident. I was as shocked as the next hand wringer, but I was not surprised, for Cooke's fiction was the extension into print of disco news.[2]

But we're getting ahead of the story. Mead was interested in the newspaper journalism of the 1920s. Contemporary consumers of the media have no difficulty relating his models to our current experience. A serious newspaper model of the 1920s, the *New York Times,* is an even better practitioner of information journalism today, and the *Times* has been joined by other serious newspapers, such as the *Washington Post,* the *Boston Globe,* the *Chicago Tribune,* and the *Los Angeles Times.* Since the 1920s the popular newspapers, in Mead's terms, have been paying more attention to information and fact reporting (see, for example, the changes in the last decade or so at the New York *Daily News,* the largest circulation daily in the country). But as newspapers have moved toward fact models, the story-telling model has been largely taken over, first, by the news magazines and, more recently, by television news.

It is hardly news to anyone that the big journalistic success stories of the last decade involve practitioners of the story model—*People* magazine in print and CBS News' *60 Minutes* on television. *People* ought to be studied by the high-brow critics, because they would realize how it has been designed to look like undemanding, consumatory, enjoyable television—big pictures, small news, beautiful people. *People* and *60 Minutes* package the news into entertaining and smoothly consumed stories, and, because success breeds imitation, *People* and *60 Minutes* are being widely copied. The *People* influence can be seen in clones like *Us* magazine as well as in the pages of the old-line news magazines, *Time* and *Newsweek*. The *60 Minutes* model is echoed in television shows such as NBC's *Magazine* (formerly *Prime-Time Sunday*) and ABC's *20/20* program.

What is news, however, is the extent to which the journalists who engage in story-form news are unaware of how pervasively certain aesthetic values—for example, considerations of pace, the look, the feel of it all—rather than news values shape their work. A few critics and commentators have sniffed around the edges of this development when they wrote worriedly of the coming of a television generation. Such talk was always done in a despairing way about its awful effect on youth who never learn to read and write properly and grow up to take charge of the world. It was as if barbaric hordes were at the city gates, or had infiltrated and were taking over. Present-day television, in fact, is in a transitional period from the story model to the form that I call disco news.

Obviously, disco news is an exaggeration and in itself a kind of journalistic hype almost as outrageous as the form it seeks to criticize. CBS News will always deliver the news goods straight, in a serious, responsible fashion. Walter Cronkite, Dan Rather, Charles Kuralt, or whoever sits in the anchor chair will continue to uphold the standards. John Chancellor or Roger Mudd will retain a calm, professorial mien. We'll never see Frank Reynolds, Max Robinson, Peter Jennings, or Barbara Walters in disco news blazers or designer jeans.

But can we really be sure? Cronkite, Chancellor, Reynolds, and the executives who have nurtured them over the last thirty years represent the first, or 1950s, television generation. Almost all these men and women came from newspapers, wire services, or magazines. They were trained in the print information model. The transitional generation of television journalists is made of 1970s figures like Tom Snyder, Tom Brokaw, and the younger men and women who produce programs like *20/20* and the *Today Show*. Their experience is almost solely in broadcasting; their reporting and writing experience is somewhat limited. The world of the fast-paced, two-minute standupper and the ten-second react may be the only world they know. They may have keen eyes for format but no real ear for content.

I had a chance to observe this tone deafness a while back in what turned out to be an instructive experimental setting. It didn't start that way. I had invited a highly intelligent, sensible television producer to a class to show some videotape samples of the network news program she worked on. Proudly, she played for the students the videotape cassette of an economic report that was the lead (the top of the show) of the newscast the previous night.

We saw the anchor wishing us good evening . . . cut to the Washington reporter with the latest inflation bad news . . . then quickly three consumer reports from around the country . . . then a U.S. map with graphics showing cost-of-living rates . . . back to the anchor and then the Washington reporter, followed by tape and sound bites (15-second quotes) from congressional leaders and cabinet officers . . . finally, the Wall Street reaction . . . and then break for commercial. In all, no more than three minutes had elapsed.

As the various tape, sound, and graphics elements in the economics package gave way to each other, the producer, who was sitting alongside me, snapped her fingers and softly whispered, "Hit it"—right in time with each element. She was proud of her network's handiwork. But the students in the classroom shot up their hands. What was that all about? What did it mean? What are you trying to tell us about the economy? Many college students naturally enjoy deflating establishment (in their eyes) types; and, if the guest is a friend of the professor, so much the better. But when we all watched the videotape once again from the viewpoint of the audience—people who know little about the effort that goes into the smooth mingling of tape and sound and videofonts and slides, and care even less—we had to admit that it was difficult to grasp, sort out, and understand the news somewhere underneath all the production.

I am more empathetic of television than the students. James Snyder, a television news executive of the old school, once told me that producing a daily news program for television was like wrestling with a big bear. The challenges of bringing the human and technical problems together are prodigious. Another old school journalist, Bill Moyers, uses a different, but equally vivid, figure of speech. After completing a twenty-six-week series of his *Journal* on public television, he dryly observed that Christopher Columbus and television producers have a lot in common: "Columbus didn't know where he was going, didn't know where he was when he got there, and didn't know where he had been when he returned, and television producers find themselves in that same boat week after week."

Snyder, Moyers, and others of television's older generation of journalists are perhaps more modest about their accomplishments than the newer breed and more sensitive to the prospects of story-form news becoming disco news. Once you've been to the disco, it is hard not to get caught up in the beat. Not too long ago, someone asked me what I thought of a particular presidential speech on television. "Well," I began, "I thought Reagan *looked* good." The question, But what about what he *said*, what about his proposals? sharply brought me out of the disco mode.

In any argument about the entertainment gloss on the news, someone can always say, reassuringly, that show business values won't really take over. The main line of resistance must be drawn by editors exercising good judgment, taste, news values. But too often, in television news organizations an editor is someone who cuts film or videotape on demand, like a pantsmaker in the garment industry. The managing editor title may actually belong to the head of the assignment desk. While these are key jobs, they are not normally occupied by people with power to say to a newsgatherer or a documentarian, "You haven't done it right. The pattern isn't any good."

The downgrading of editing and editors follows in part from the fact that television has become a star medium. One popular highly acclaimed television newsperson was given the nickname Gorilla by his colleagues (after the joke that goes, "What can an 800-pound gorilla do? the answer, Anything he wants to do."). So, too, as popular print journalists begin to attain the star status of television journalists, they will be doing just about anything they want to.

In some cases strong personalities do involve themselves in the editorial process. Bill Moyers, for example, played a dominant role in every step of the production of his *Journal*. It was indeed, Moyers's journal. Yet, Moyers brought an experienced editor's news judgment and sensibility to the program. On Moyers's program a moral issue was joined when Moyers and the writer Garry Wills talked about Thomas Jefferson. On a star vehicle program, such as NBC's disastrous *Prime-Time Sunday,* with the parajournalist Tom Snyder, the idea of a moral discussion involved two parish priests arguing about whether slain underworld figure Carmine Galante should be accorded a Catholic Church burial.

One hindrance to editing in television is related to the limited amount of time available in a complex technology. Most print reporters collect and write their stories and hand them to subeditors who either read through the copy for errors or, as is often done nowadays, scan it on video display terminals. In television one person may gather the story, a second person edit the film or tape, a third person prepare the script introductions and cues, and a fourth person do the narration. The production process itself is so costly that it takes on an existence of its own; producers are likely to say, when a story is questioned, "Hey, think how we killed ourselves to get that footage. Let's use it." But the footage might not be appropriate, and often no one has the time to look carefully at how the parts fit. When the critics savaged the ABC newsmagazine *20/20* after its premiere in 1979, ABC News President Roone Arledge, by way of defense, explained that he had prescreened the individual segments but not the whole program. For almost ten years, as an on-air commentator for news programs broadcast from Washington, D.C., I spent one day a week in a working television newsroom where news programs were produced morning, noon, early evening, and late night. Even in this operation, one of the best I have observed, the news director and the executive producer, serious professionals who were making prodigious efforts to supervise the preparation of copy and edited tape, were able to see the completed program for the first time only along with home viewers.

Another reason that television is underedited derives from television's self-image, or what may be its self-deception. Some television producers, though certainly not all, really believe it when they say that the camera doesn't lie, or more important that the camera can record what's really there, if only outsiders, kibitzers, and anyone who wasn't there when the camera rolled would just stand aside. Such people often see themselves as documentary artists rather than broadcast journalists. The first generation of television journalists, the Moyerses, the Cronkites, the Chancellors, came from newspaper or magazine backgrounds. The newer television generation journalists tend to act as if they were standing above and beyond print journalists (with their fussy, too-literal regard for the facts and sober reportage).

The information-model standards of print and of the traditional broadcasters may seem old-fashioned to today's news-gatherers. They can do better. In the mid-1970s CBS News experimented with an in-house memo intended to take a second look at news performance. The memo's author, the veteran journalist Merv Block, drew attention to details of grammar, besides offering criticism of stories. It was all mild enough, but, admirable as it was, the idea expired after just a few issues, reportedly because it made too many stars unhappy.

It is useful to look at two recent examples of underediting in supposedly major league television. In 1978–79 the National News Council, a private foundation-funded group that investigates complaints about unfair or misleading journalism, upheld charges brought against two televised documentaries (the council has no power to punish, only to publicize its decisions).[3] One complaint involved the independently produced *Bad Boys*, first broadcast in October 1978 on public television. The other involved the NBC News documentary *I Want It All Now*, broadcast in July 1978. *Bad Boys* was produced for WNET, New York, by the husband-and-wife team of Alan and Susan Raymond. The Raymonds shot eighty hours of tape and edited this into a two-hour program, of which about thirty minutes focused on the students of Bryant High School in the New York City borough of Queens. *I Want It All Now* was intended to be about life in California's Marin County. Both programs had an editorial point to make. *Bad Boys* looked at school truancy and its relationship to delinquency in later life. *I Want It All Now* was intended to show Marin County's laidback, Cuisinart-and-hot-tub society, the landscape so deftly sketched by Cyra McFadden in her book *The Serial*.

Without getting into the merits of the argument about the causes of delinquency or what may or may not be decadence in

Marin County, it is possible to look at the complaints against these two programs and see how easily they could have been averted by a firm, knowing editorial eye.

For example, according to the council's report, the producers of *Bad Boys* spent several weeks at the Queens high school visiting various classes. Yet, *Bad Boys,* as broadcast, concentrated on only one class—a typing class for problem students with learning difficulties. Students in crowd scenes outside the school were described as truants, though some were waiting to go to class or had finished class. On NBC's *I Want It All Now* the program opened with an apparently nude woman, named Beth Furth, being stroked by peacock feathers wielded by two handsome young men at a massage service for women called Secret Garden. The program went on to quote figures about Marin County's 75 percent divorce rate, to characterize the Marin County suicide rate as twice the national average, and otherwise to fill out the picture of overly indulgent, decadent life-styles. In fact, the Secret Garden scene was a re-creation of a massage Beth Furth had received in San Francisco, across the bay from Marin; also the divorce and suicide figures quoted by NBC were inaccurate. A questioning editor in each case could have saved the documentary makers, the Raymonds and the NBC crew, the embarrassments of their mistakes.

As soon as someone suggests tough editing, others smell censorship and a challenge to relevant, strong journalism. Censorship and editing are not that hard to distinguish. There is no conflict between good journalism and good editing by editors so designated. *Bad Boys* was made by independents in association with WNET, and just as independent producers are entitled to make their own documentaries, so too are station managements entitled to select, reject, and supervise—in a word, edit—the programs they broadcast. Supervisory editors cannot substitute their own viewpoints for those of the reporter or documentarian; no reputable print writer would allow an editor to do that, nor should broadcast journalists. The main point, however, is that in every medium there is the need for an editor, a second pair of eyes.

More than two decades ago the broadcast team of Edward R. Murrow and Fred W. Friendly combined to produce excellent and, on occasion, highly courageous television programs. As Friendly recalls it, the collaboration of the star and the producer was built on the principle of editing. "There was a piece that Murrow never forgave me for when I wouldn't allow it to run," Friendly remembers. "But Ed and I could say no to each other and continue to respect one another and to work together." That's the key: editors are paid to say no. Who else can help turn down the sound and lights of disco news?

HYPES, NEWSBREAKS, TEASES, GRABBERS

CHAPTER 2

A question has been nagging at reasonably attentive television viewers over the past few years: Has our public news become more dramatic, more exciting, more frenetic, more portentous, the most, the first, the best, the biggest, the greatest—or has the coverage of our public news become more dramatic, exciting, frenetic, portentous, etc., etc., etc.? To put the problem in the marketplace, are we being sold the sizzle rather than the steak as events are hyped beyond their news substance?[1]

It is not a new question. Almost a century ago, Lincoln Steffens wrote about how Theodore Roosevelt, when he was police commissioner of New York City, complained about newspaper reports of a crime wave sweeping the city. Roosevelt argued that the New York crime rate had actually dropped under his regime. What had happened to Roosevelt is a now familiar story: there was an increase, not in crime but in newspaper reporting about crime, to hype street sales. Nor is the news hype we see on television as blatant as the practices of the advertising industry, book publishing, or motion picture makers. These hypes for toothpastes or bad novels, however, are amiable free-enterprise excrescences involving no more, and no less, than the separation of a few dollars from consumer's wallets. When hype comes to the news, something more is at stake; news hype affects our politics, our public dialogue, our ways of perceiving the world. A different level of danger is involved when bad movies succeed than when bad candidates succeed. Our public news doesn't need any more heating up.

When Walter Cronkite told his CBS audience watching the Republican National Convention on the night of July 16, 1980, that there was a definite plan for a Ronald Reagan–Gerald Ford ticket—"an unprecedented, unparalleled, unprecedented situation"—Cronkite wasn't just getting the story wrong. He was also creating an aura of self-importance for the television process. In this hothouse atmosphere the hype lives on after the story dies. *Newsweek* magazine's superheated account of the television coverage of the Reagan–Ford mismatch went beyond "unparalleled" and "unprecedented" to declare: "The Veepstakes set off a media stampede that may have changed history." History? Well, Ford didn't become the vice-presidential candidate because he asked too much of Reagan, who offered the job to Bush, and so, if the Republicans win (as they did), and if Reagan dies in office, then Bush becomes president, and, if Bush responds to some crisis in a different way than Reagan would have, then history has been changed, get it? That's how hype works.

What makes news hype of immediate concern is the way it has taken hold and proliferated, kudzu vinelike, in the medium of television. While newspaper front pages have generally become more responsible, even sedate, the yellow journalism style that so upset Theodore Roosevelt flourishes on the nightly news. Press lord William Randolph Hearst, the story goes, used to describe the kind of reaction he sought in his paper, the *New York American:* "You look at the first page and say, GEE WHIZ! You turn to page two and say, HOLY MOSES! You move to page three and say, GOD ALMIGHTY!" Now, an evening of television news watching produces the same reactions.

News hype, I think, grows out of four factors, each interrelated but still possible to discuss separately. First, there is technology. Newsgatherers and news producers now have equipment that enables them to do more to the news, to make news presentation as exciting as the content, or more exciting. In the old 1960s style of newsreel television, the technical story form was fairly rigid: anchorman introduces news film, received by packet from overseas or Washington and edited on movieola, of dignitary descending airplane steps; anchorman then reads short items before introducing next film. Today live broadcasts via satellite, split-screen hookups, and computer graphics make the television screen more visually stimulating. We are there, live, as the plane lands and dignitary descends (the steps down from the plane are still the same). A dull Gallup poll that may reveal nothing more than that one-third of the electorate is still uncertain about its presidential choices—the kind of item that would have been read in 15 seconds in the old days—suddenly comes to life as numbers spin out on screen and bar graphs are generated before our eyes. Lightweight cameras, the shift from film to easily processed videotape, and the availability of satellite transponders for live transmissions have speeded up the news process. As it becomes possible to get stories on the air faster, there is less time for editing and organizing the news; thought becomes less important than speed and technical skill. Thinking, in fact, sounds musty, the enemy of television-style action.

It's possible to make out the future of television news in the style of Ted Turner's Cable News Network, which began operation in June 1980. CNN introduces us to the possibilities of new multichannel information and entertainment cable-casting systems in the United States. Cable technology and space satellites make possible the Turner network, which brings news programming into millions of homes twenty-four hours a day, seven days a week. Now no one has to wait until 7 P.M., or even the hourly newsbreaks, for the latest happenings. Early in CNN's infancy, for example, one of the anchors appeared around 9:30 P.M. after a commercial to tell CNN watchers, "Bottles were thrown at the press bus during President Carter's visit to Miami [the Liberty City area, scene of black riots in late May]. . . . Here is what it looked like, the unedited film. . . ."

Next, viewers saw scenes of surging crowds and running police. The videotape appeared to be shot out of an accelerating bus from the looks of it, with some of the tapes recorded as the camera operator crouched on the bus floor. It was exciting stuff certainly; but there was no accompanying narrative to tell us of injuries, arrests, and, most important, the denouement, the results. There were no facts or comments to help us make intelligent sense of the wrenching visceral thrills. On the contrary CNN seemed proud of the raw reality presented ("here is the unedited tape"). The coverage turned traditional ideas of journalism on its head. It was not: *here is the story as selected, shaped, and edited by our competent trained news processors, given the familiar constraints of time and space* . . . But: *Here it is, right off the satellite transponder, get the news while it's still sizzling, courtesy of technology . . . Hot enough for you? . . . Have an exciting day* . . . break for commercial.

The second reason we may be seeing more hype involves the element of time. Not only does television news today come at us faster, but there is also more air time for the news. Even leaving aside Ted Turner's around-the-clock operation, local station newscasts now run as long as 2 hours in the early evening in some cities. ABC News has added *Nightline*, a thirty-minute late night newscast. When the morning informational programs, such as *The Today Show* and *Good Morning America*, and the evening magazine shows, such as *PM Magazine*, are added, a typical station may be offering as much as five hours of news a day. This programming is not necessarily done out of the belief in the need for a more informed society. Rather the news has become a moneymaker in recent years, less expensive to produce than prime time entertainment. It cost $500,000 in 1981 dollars to make a half-hour situation comedy episode and about one-fifth of that to put on an extra half hour of news like *Nightline*.

The news gets more time because it has become more popular, which means more profitable—the third reason for hype. CBS News' *60 Minutes* was the top-rated regular series in the 1979–80 season. With the news, television sees itself delivered from mediocre entertainment, schlock story ideas, and writing by hack committee—as long as the news programs can be made lively and interesting, as long as the news can be more entertaining than the entertainment shows. But the news producers aren't willing to depend entirely on reality, the quotidian events that make news, to be exciting—any more than entertainment producers can depend on their writers to be Chekov every week. Provision has to be made for slow news days; procedures have to be developed to carry along interest on moderate news days. Audience attention has to be flogged even on big news days; having yelled hype! hype! often, television has to have alerting devices when there appears to be a real wolf at the door. Along with the usual dramatic devices of deepening voice modulation and serious facial expression, television has borrowed from the carnival midway the barker's tease: "Coming Up Next: a Perfect 10" (Sex? Bo Derek? No, the weatherman comes on to say tomorrow will be nice). But the real breakthrough in the 1980s has been the newsbreak.

The newsbreak is an art form in itself—a thirty-second package consisting typically of two ten-second news items wrapped around a ten-second commercial, usually run in the prime-time hours between the early and late evening newscasts. Do the news producers think we cannot wait from 7:30 P.M. to 11:00 P.M. to find out what happened after Dan Rather or John Chancellor signed off? Were they worried we would switch to CNN? Perhaps, but they also realized that the thirty-second newsbreak idea gives both the networks and the local stations another program in which to insert commercials.[2] Granted, it is a sci-fi mutant of a program, an incredible shrinking newscast, like *The Incredible Shrinking Man* who, as Tom Wolfe once observed, doesn't shrivel but grows smaller and remains perfectly formed and smartly dressed. Very smartly dressed. One Boston station manager told me that he carved out his own minute around 9 P.M. and sold the commercial seconds to bring in $1 million a year for his station.

The benefits that ten-second mutant newsbreaks bring to the viewer are mixed. These headlines presumably can inform us, or move us to the late news where more information may be forthcoming. But, more and more, the 9:00 P.M. newsbreak leads to a 10:30 tease that leads to a 11:02 grabber that does nothing more than set our antennae quivering: CHEMICAL FIRE IN NEW JERSEY . . . MISSING GIRL'S BODY FOUND . . . HIJACK IN PROGRESS IN KUWAIT . . . from hype to hype to hype, a lethal double play combination on the playing fields of our nervous systems.

In seven places out of ten, if the above proposition were to be put to the people who produce the news, they would dismiss me as some sort of cranky traditionalist from print or from 1960s television. The three exceptions would be the networks, where older, print-influenced producers still have a foothold, though a fast-slipping one.[3] Hype comes naturally to the new generation of television producer—the fourth element in the equation. It's part of that disco beat of the visual over the analytical, of excitement over explication, of stimulation over talking heads. Form-oriented disco newspeople only half attend to content under the best circumstances. Facts, the hard nuggets of the news, have relatively less interest for this generation than for earlier generations of journalists. In the 1950s and 1960s there was a commitment to some principles, some of them perhaps wrong-headed principles but ideas nevertheless (Democracy, the Free World, Consumption, the Cold War). The television of the late 1970s and early 1980s concerns itself with *tv qua tv*. When young producers want to praise a piece, they say, "It's good television!" not "This will rattle them at city hall!" From good television to hype is little more than an automatic shift.

Boston, for example, is the sixth largest television market in the country and a not unsophisticated city. The age of the active news producers in Boston, older father figure anchormen excepted, probably averages around thirty-one. These people are bright, fast, tough, noncerebral—don't expect to discuss Graham Greene, or even Tom Wicker, with them. But rely on them to produce fast-paced, entertaining news, so disco beat that it disorients. Not too long ago you may remember that a homosexual young man in Rhode Island decided to take another young man as his date to his high school prom. Boston television stations treated the story as if it were the first lunar landing adventure:

It's one week to the prom and . . .
For tomorrow's prom the school principal plans . . .
Tonight's the prom. Our reporter is on scene . . .
Rhode Island prom . . . details at 11 P.M.
Here's a special report on the prom . . .

What happened at the prom? Nothing much: the young men attended and left. For television to turn such tricks with the news for ratings is a form of prostitution but hardly a victimless crime. News hype inflames an already confused, complex, disoriented society.

For a cynical viewer to say that the prom story was hyped for the sake of ratings during a slow news time is to miss the real cause for cynicism: the disco news producers really think it's good television. So in the end news hype exists because the news producers have a cynic's view of their audience. The television-producing generation of the 1980s, for all its contemporary disco news ways, pictures a 1950s audience out there: short attention spans, low political interests, unschooled in visual techniques. This doltish audience, it is said, has to be teased, tickled, jerked off and around. Around newsrooms there is a certain kind of story known as the grabber. In his study, *The Whole World Is Watching,* the Berkeley sociologist and former student activist, Todd Gitlin, recounts how in the mid-1960s the story of the radical Students for a Democratic Society (SDS) was handled by the television networks. Stanhope Gould, a young, long-haired, brash producer for Walter Cronkite at CBS News, proposed going with a grabber. Gould wanted to do the story of SDS in the high schools, expecting to draw the reaction, "What? Those f—— are in the high schools?" Gould, says Gitlin, "wanted to stoke up public anger, thinking that whatever 'punched through' the public apathy would produce a *reasoned* anger."

Back in the 1960s Gould had a political purpose and a journalistic one: he wanted to make people think. Whatever his politics—he had long hair!—his news instincts were true: punch through to the brain. Today's apolitical newsroom generation aims at punching through no higher than the groin, or the gut.

The hype producers are wrong about the audience. The average thirty-year-old viewer has been watching television for twenty-five years now and is not dumb. No one took to the streets of Rhode Island on prom night except the TV cameras. No amount of news hype on television about the presidential campaign—another big story of 1980—could get people excited about Ronald Reagan or Jimmy Carter. A year after the Three Mile Island media overkill, polls showed that a majority of Americans would accept nuclear power as a transitional energy source. On prom night in Rhode Island, the fabric of society did not fray. Only television became unraveled.

The misreading, and misrepresentation, of the audience by the media experts shows no signs of slackening. The 1970s, we heard, was the Me decade (self-centered people into jogging, Scarsdale diets, and EST), or the passive years (lots of eastern religion and Hari-Krishna chantings in the streets). When the pop psychologists look to the 1980s, they see more inward turning. Robert M. Teeter, the pollster and Ronald Reagan adviser, recently pointed out that of the 75 million young Americans who have reached voting age since 1960—roughly today's young adult generation of 18-to-40-year-olds—some 50 million have not even bothered to register to vote.

Yet, when we look critically beneath the catch phrases and the statistics, certain doubts arise. Are young adult Americans of today any more selfish, or more bored, or more alienated, than earlier generations of Americans? "Every decade is a Me decade," the Columbia University sociologist Herbert Gans reflected to me recently. "All generations since time began, we have to say, were self-centered, in the sense of putting their own interests first." How do social scientists measure a quality like passivity? The decision not to vote, for example, may spring from an active decision, a conscious verdict on the political system or the caliber of the candidates rather than from feelings of alienation or apathy.

Yet the notion of a Me generation somehow qualitatively different from previous generations exerts a great deal of attraction. It sounds sinister and feeds fantasies that something new and altogether unprecedented is happening to us or to our society. At Harvard the psychologist, Howard Gardner, has been studying what he calls the TV child. His work proceeds from the fact, undeniable, that today's average teenager has spent more time in front of the television set than in a school classroom. But what do those hours add up to? Gardner himself, reviewing the major study on television and human behavior, a monumental report on more than 2,500 separate reports, finds that there is little hard evidence about the effects of television on children.[4]

Millions of research dollars, for example, have been spent over the last twenty years studying two controversial issues— televised violence and its effects on children, and the effects of commercial messages on children. After all this money and effort Gardner finds that the conclusions are about what the researchers' proverbial grandmother would have expected: (1) Some younger children under some conditions tend to imitate the behavior, violent or prosocial, they see on television, and (2) the younger the child, the more likely he or she believes what the commercials say about Kellogg's Corn Flakes or Mattel Toys. As the child who shares your room and board might say, Big deal!

Yet Gardner still believes in generational labels, and in the ability of the genie of research to make them tangible. A younger generation of experimenters, reared on television and McLuhan, he says, have been probing how the mind of the TV child differs from the mind of the print-oriented child (the kid who reads books). Gardner holds that television's jump cuts, zooms, fast tempo, and other visual elements produce in children a different kind of imaginative power—a quick-cut TV mind, no less—than is produced by the experience of reading books. By inference it is a weaker mind, though Gardner, after scaring us, makes an elaborate point of pretending that he is not taking sides.

But where Gardner stops, other speculative research takes off. In addition to their supposed effects on young imaginations, television's fast pace and visual orientation are said to shorten the attention span of children and impair their ability to reflect on events. Moreover, it is claimed that television over stimulates their appetite for novelty and lively action. No wonder they are de-politicized when they grow up: they can't concentrate on substantive materials, and serious political discussion is too static (that deadly TV turn-off—talking heads).

The two researchers associated with the short attention span idea are Drs. Jerome and Dorothy Singer of the Yale Family Television Research and Consultation Center. In their work they contrast the responses of one group of children to the fast-paced Sesame Street program with another group's responses to the low-key *Mister Rogers' Neighborhood*. According to the Singers, the *Sesame Street* kids kept their eyes glued to the sets, mesmerized by all the visual stimulation—five dogs, five cats, five cookies; the kids watching the relaxed Mister Rogers, meanwhile, wandered around the room and showed more imaginative play and more positive emotional reactions to other kids.

By this account the results should be enough be bring Mister Rogers back to television, or to tie down Big Bird. But when Professor Gerald Lesser of Harvard, an adviser to *Sesame Street,* looked at much of this same research, he found little basis for the alleged bad effects of fast pacing; for that matter he didn't find any evidence of shortened attention spans or of the television child's desire for new and noisier sensations.

Do young minds wander in high school chemistry lab or during family time at the dinner table? Wasn't it ever thus? But if more objective yardsticks are needed, we can look at motion pictures, rock concerts, records, and other pop culture activities that engage adolescents and young adults. Movies today are longer in actual minutes than the movies of the 1930s and 1940s. The music of the big band era specialized in sprints of three or four minutes; contrast that with the marathon sets of rock groups today. Mass market writers who appeal to contemporary readers, like John Irving (*The World According to Garp*) or John Barth (*Giles the Goat Boy*) aren't noted for their brevity. None of this, of course, is an argument that longer is better (I'm a James Joyce *Dubliners* man myself). It is an argument that there is no real evidence, in life or literature, that young Americans have developed quick-cut TV minds, or other afflictions that may spell the imminent decline of western civilization.

About this point in any discussion of television's effects, someone usually jumps up and impatiently waves away talk of pop-culture tastes. The objector wants to know, What about the falling SAT (Scholastic Achievement Test) Scores? Or alternatively, What about IQ test scores? Johnny and Jane can't read, or write or add 2 and 2; watching the tube, they don't have to. In fact, a lot of college admissions officers will acknowledge that the SATs may test nothing more than the ability to take tests. As for the IQ curve, the whole subject is notoriously suspect, but at least one respected study suggests that on the average, adolescents today score ten points higher on IQ scales than did the generation of the pre-TV 1930s.

Anyone over forty with a good memory can recall tales about the harm done to the youth of America by 1940s comic books, or in the 1930s radio age, "How terrible, doing home work with the radio on!" If we wanted to find an American environment where cultural conditions most clearly contrast with today's, we would have to go back past the 1940s—and the 1930s and the 1920s—before radio and national magazines and low-cost books to a pre-World War I America that was largely rural, isolated, puritanical, where children were still bound by rigid codes of conduct at home and at school. If the country has been going to hell, it has been going for a long time.

But if we can't find a television generation that is culturally or intellectually distinct, then surely there must be discernible moral or emotional differences. Most people, I would guess, would agree that there has been enormous attention lately to having/ cultivating/expressing feelings. Talk show guests, touring authors, and gurus of all kinds urge us to get in touch with our feelings. When the public opinion samplers carefully listen to what people are saying, however, they find many of these feelings are quite traditional ones. A recent *Washington Post* survey reported that almost three in every four Americans consider themselves very religious or somewhat religious and that almost one in every three young Americans says that religion is more important to them than it was to their pre-TV parents.

There is one feature of contemporary culture that does distinguish it from the culture of past generations. The birth of rock music in the early 1950s, as *New York Times* music critic John Rockwell observes, marked "an unprecedented free expression of adolescent sexual and aggressive energy." Though it can be argued that the Rolling Stones, urgently singing about not getting any satisfaction, had the same thing on their minds as did Frank Sinatra or Bing Crosby warbling about their desire to get the girl on a slow boat to China, it's nevertheless true that the explicit has replaced the bland in pop music; Elvis Presley's pelvis made points that the crooners only implied. At a rock concert it *looks* and *sounds* as if there is a great teenage Saturnalia loose in the land. But not only does this have little to do with TV minds, it also contradicts the notions of self-centeredness. Peter Townshend, the guitarist and chief songwriter for The Who, a premier rock group, once explained that "the whole purpose of a rock concert is for people to forget themselves, to lose their egos in the crowd and to disappear—a temporary sort of flight."

We are left, then, for proof of generational differences, with the voting statistics and similar outward signs of the rejection of public life and political affairs. The voter registration numbers for 18-to-40-year-olds are depressing. They should be tempered, however, by some familiar facts of politics. While younger people traditionally vote less than older people, as men and women acquire a stake in their communities, typically through home owning, they get more interested in politics. Other non-media elements influence participation. When an American Bar Association committee recently looked into the reasons for nonvoting, it singled out these factors, among other things: political mistrust; the decline of allegiance to political parties; a widespread feeling of helplessness, particularly among the poor and the poorly educated, about changing anything by voting; the remaining mechanical barriers to voting and the complexities of the absentee ballot voting system at a time when people were moving from one place to another as never before.

It is rather dry stuff, that ABA report, not really sexy, not something that can be told very well in a ten-second newsbreak. The TV children, I fear, mainly live and work in television news.

CASES

PART II

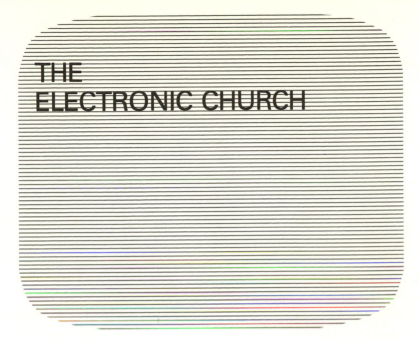

THE ELECTRONIC CHURCH

CHAPTER 3

It's pledge month. The mistress of ceremonies, an almost forty-ish blond whose bubbly manner and pert good looks remind the viewer of a younger Debbie Reynolds, admonishes the television audience: "This is the time of year when we've got to raise the budget." The toll-free number is superimposed on the screen as she explains how a "$15-a-month partnership pledge will help keep PTL on the air in your area. . . . Sixty telephone operators are standing by. . . . Some people are writin' us and tellin' us that they're watching television and can't find us, and we have to explain that without money we can't stay on the air. . . ."

The studio band riffs into upbeat music. The phones ring; a floor producer signals for studio applause. The Debbie Reynolds look-alike—her name, in fact, is Tammy Bakker—beams over the gifts that a partnership pledge will bring: a PTL stickpin, the PTL newsletter, a PTL Bible, and, for a one-time gift of $1,000, an Heirloom Bible, illustrated, with a stamped antique gold cover and the donor's name printed on it.

PTL is not the public television station in Louisville, despite Tammy Bakker's down-home accent and the all-too-familiar sound of the pledge month pitch. PTL stands for Praise the Lord, a television production and distribution service run by a former tent preacher, and Tammy's husband, named Jim Bakker. Jim Bakker, Tammy Bakker, the PTL singers, and the PTL pledge operation are all part of the biggest, arguably strangest, and until recently, least-discussed new development in our popular culture—God's television.

God's television manifests itself in many forms around the dial: Bakker's song, dance, and prayer PTL Club, beamed by satellite to scores of stations in the United States and Canada, reaches 4 million homes with cable and is carried on 225 television stations (not all the cable homes, of course, watch PTL). Then there are Oral Roberts's evangelical Bible-teaching sessions and prime-time variety specials; Robert Schuller's *Hour of Power* from Garden Grove, California, with its inspirational message of possibility thinking; and Pat Robertson's fast-paced *700 Club* from Virginia Beach, Virginia, part of the Christian Broadcasting Network (CBN) that also uses satellites to reach Robertson-owned stations in Atlanta, Boston, Dallas, and Norfolk, as well as other television markets. CBN also reaches cable systems with 8 million subscribers. And there is the Reverend Jerry Falwell of the Thomas Road Baptist Church, Lynchburg, Virginia, and the *Old-Time Gospel Hour,* which claims it reaches an estimated 18 million television viewers each week.[1] In 1979 Falwell extended his television ministry by starting the political action group Moral Majority with its fundamentalist message of pro-life, pro-free enterprise, and pro-national defense. (More on Falwell and Moral Majority later.) There are also Rex Humbard, Jimmy Swaggart, Ernest Angley, and a host of others, small-town evangelicals and UHF preachers, often known no further than the modest range of an ultra-high frequency television signal from a heartland station. The association of national religious broadcasters claims some 1,000 members, and a recent survey indicated that 38 television stations and 66 cable systems across the United States, as well as 1,400 radio stations, specialize in what the FCC counts as religious broadcasting.

Bakker, Roberts, Schuller, Robertson, and Falwell are the Big Five of Christian television; they are in the major television markets, with yearly broadcast budgets of up to $50 million or more. Oral Roberts, the founding father of God's television, is now sixty-one. He began his television faith healing and Bible preaching in 1954, in television's infancy when, he says, "I could buy prime time every week, whenever I wanted it." Today, Roberts's large staff says it needs $10 million a month to operate the Oral Roberts University and the Oral Roberts City of Faith medical complex, all in Tulsa.

Pat Robertson began broadcasting in 1961 with one UHF station in Virginia. Today, he boasts, his Christian Broadcasting Network (CBN) is America's largest syndicator of programs via satellite. Jim Bakker, who used to work for Robertson, started his own television program just five years ago, borrowing a sound-alike name and the similar variety show format from Robertson. "Our broadcast budget in 1974 used to be $20,000 a month; now it's a million dollars a week," Bakker says. Fifty-two-year-old Robert Schuller, the only mainstream minister of the Big Five—he belongs to the Reformed Church in America—organized his first congregation in 1955, using a drive-in theater for six years. Schuller now says his *Hour of Power* is on 142 stations in the United States and Canada, plus the 82 outlets of the armed forces network. The Reverend Jerry Falwell, according to *Newsweek*, didn't get religion until a wintry Sunday in 1952 when he went to church in search of girls and found both Jesus and a pretty organist named Macel Pate. In 1956, after playing the part of BMOC at a Bible college in Missouri, Falwell went to Lynchburg to found his own independent Baptist church in an abandoned pop-bottling factory and to continue courting Macel Pate, whom he later married. Six months later he aired his first religious show on local television. By 1980 his hometown church claimed 17,000 members, more than a quarter of Lynchburg's population, and more of the faithful listen to his broadcast sermons every week and support his pyramid of enterprises. Falwell's Sunday service, the *Old-Time Gospel Hour,* is carried by 681 television and radio stations. The yield from this and other fund-raising operations, estimated by *Newsweek* to be $1 million each week, supports what is, in effect, Falwell's own Christian denomination, including a children's academy, a Bible institute, a correspondence school, a seminary, and Liberty Baptist College, yet-to-be accredited, with nearly 3,000 undergraduates.

God's television—the phrase was used on one of Robertson's programs—seldom caught the attention of the critics for the *Washington Post,* the *New York Times,* or the other major league media until the 1980 political campaign and Falwell's efforts to defeat undesirable, that is, liberal Democratic, politicians. (One exception to this critical neglect was Elizabeth Hardwick, who wrote about evangelical television for the *New York Review of Books.*[2]) But long before the 1980 campaign God's television was a big, booming industry, one that today may be changing traditional notions of television and of religion.

Since its inception, television has been in the business of crowd collecting, normally for the sake of advertisers who want to reach specific audiences. Over the years television served certain audiences, for example, the consumers of comedy, or sports, or children's programs, or news and public affairs, or *Masterpiece Theatre,* or old movies. But it apparently was ignoring the interests of other audiences. About the time of candidate Jimmy Carter's rise from southern obscurity in 1976, the political experts and cultural savants did a double take. From the vantage point of midtown Manhattan, *Time* magazine had already proclaimed that God Was Dead. But God was not dead for the 55 million Americans who were born-again Christians with a fundamentalist belief in the Bible. It turned out that popular culture was ignoring 20 percent of the population, an overlooked demographic group, if you please. These fundamentalist Christians had special meaning for television, our most pervasive medium for popular culture.

From the first days of radio, religion has been a staple of broadcasting. Of the 4,600 AM radio stations in the United States, an estimated 500 currently (1981) devote themselves mostly to religious broadcasting. By the late fifties, although television had displaced radio as our chief attention getter, the evangelists and faith healers had not yet moved in force into the new medium. The audience was there, however. "By the mid-seventies it was clear that there were many people out there who weren't interested in *Charlie's Angels* or the *Super Bowl* or rock 'n' roll stars or show business talk on *Merv Griffin*," says Stuart Zanger, a documentary filmmaker in Memphis, Tennessee, and among the first journalists to explore the world of God's television. "These people wanted sincere, fundamentalist Christian programming, and now they're getting it."

The matter of sincerity immediately occurs to any skeptic who watches the big five of God's television. Their programs are so slickly produced in the most glitzy Hollywood variety show manner; the performers—the star preachers, gospel singers, guest healers, and inspirational figures—are so neatly turned out in their blow-dry hair, capped teeth, thousand-watt smiles, banker's gray suits, and flowing robes; the format is so artfully stage managed (one black face invariably integrates Tammy Bakker's backup singing group or Robert Schuller's massed choir), the pledge numbers and pay-for-prayer messages so insistently presented, that God's television inevitably evokes images of the charlatan preacher, of the Elmer Gantrys and the Reverend Ikes: I wear $400 suits because the Lord wants me to wear $400 suits.

I met Stuart Zanger when he was filming a documentary on God's television for Scripps-Howard Broadcasting. The documentary was, in fact, objective and nonjudgmental. But off-camera, Zanger thought it was wrong to view these programs as, strictly speaking, religion. "They're a hybrid," he said, "a combination of gospel values and television values."

In his inspirational story *Move That Mountain,* Jim Bakker ingeniously captures that strange combination:

. . . the moment that I stepped before a television camera at CBN, God began to anoint me to raise money for Christian television. I realized it the night I wept during the first *700 Club* telethon. Many times since then, God similarly anointed me. But one August night in 1967, while hosting the *700 Club,* I felt the Lord urging me to raise money for CBN to purchase color cameras. Earlier Pat (Robertson) and I had talked about the station going color. He told me that RCA had two 141-C color cameras, the last two of that model, and would sell them for $70,000. Normally, a single 141-C sold for $70,000. We could have them for half price. The only problem: We had to have a 10 percent down payment within twenty-four hours to hold the cameras. I went on the air that night and presented it to the people. The viewing audience responded generously, and, before the show left the air, the down payment had been raised.

In fact, the physical church has been all but abandoned on God's television.[3] PTL, the *700 Club,* and the Oral Roberts program all take place not in churches but in television studios with sweeping stages, banked seats for the audience, an orchestra stand, conversational sofas (in the manner of Johnny Carson and Merv Griffin), and cameras that dolly, zoom, and do close-ups and deep-focus shots just like the cameras on a Bob Hope special. If steeples and stained glass are symbols of traditional religion, then God's television is distinguished by satellite transponders, phone banks, and direct-mail, follow-up letters. Viewers who phone or write become part of computerized mailing lists, which can be used for further solicitation of funds or for marketing a whole line of Christian consumer goods, like the Heirloom Bible, as well as for political mailings on behalf of New Right causes. The computer lists themselves may also be sold to other organizations in the manner of modern direct-mail selling. The $5 and $10 pledges add up; but so do the expenses for production, for satellite time, for staff and phone counselors and letter answerers. On God's television yearly budgets range from $15 million for Schuller to $50 million for the Christian Broadcasting Network.

Religion, of course, is not exactly a stranger to production values or to business values. For centuries churches have understood the appeal of soaring cathedrals and the full sensorium of sermon, ritual, music, lights, and incense. The collection box is older than America. So the question of sincerity versus shuck has to be answered individually for each preacher. While Jim Bakker in Charlotte, North Carolina, for example, has been the subject of an FCC investigation and articles in the *Charlotte Observer* about possible diversion of funds in his television empire, out west Robert Schuller has been riding high and handsomely. The architect Philip Johnson designed Schuller's new Crystal Cathedral, a spectacular, $15-million, all-glass studio for the *Hour of Power*.

Perhaps the more appropriate questions about God's television might be: What is the content of these programs, and what images come across on the screen, explicitly and implicitly? What do viewers get from these programs, and what does this tell us about ourselves, as a television audience and as a society?

First of all, God's television presents a cluster of mythical stories involving faith, folksiness, struggle, and family. One image we see on the screen is the American ethos about the poor boy who makes good through hard work and the love of his wife and children. Jim Bakker is the poor kid from Muskegon, Michigan, who went on the road for the pentacostal Assembly of God. Oral Roberts is the poor kid from Oklahoma who founded and named a university after himself and now lives the millionaire's life in Palm Springs, on the edge of a golf course. (His son, a Pat Boone look-alike, serves as emcee on the program and introduces him as "author, educator, evangelist, and my father.") Jerry Falwell is the poor kid from the other side of the tracks, whose father killed a relative in a family feud and later died from alcoholism.

While Robert Schuller is the only one of the Big Five who belongs to a mainline Protestant denomination, he, too, presents himself as the indigent farm boy from Iowa. Schuller tells how, twenty-five years ago, he came to California with $500 in cash and an organ in a rented U-haul trailer, went door to door in search of a congregation, and finally started his drive-in church. Even Pat Robertson, son of the former U.S. senator from Virginia and a Yale graduate, had to become poor again in order to begin to serve God. His saga is that of the secularist who moved out of his Manhattan apartment, with its wealth but emptiness, eventually to go back to Virginia to study the Bible.

A second image is one of brisk, no-apologies materialism. It's not just that everyone on God's television looks so television-commercial squeaky clean and expensively turned out. Nor is it just that so much attention has been lavished on production values like the studio sets and the multiple cameras and the lighting. It is that on God's television one prays for God's help to get a new car or a higher paying job or a better apartment, and that the unremitting faith in getting the world's goods often makes these programs resemble *The $20,000 Pyramid* or other television grab shows. A game show host like Bob Barker appears interchangeable, in looks and manner, with gospel show hosts Bakker or Robertson.

Jim Bakker is up front about making it. He wanted to get ahead in the world, and he thinks that good Christians should have the riches of the world as much as anyone else. "Diamonds are made for Christians, not Satan," he says. Here is another passage from *Mountain*:

Later, on our way back home, I spoke in a Presbyterian church in Charlotte and told the wonderful story of praise. God's blessing on our trip to Atlanta excellently illustrated the value of praise.

Afterward a man and his wife walked up to shake my hand. "Jim," the man said, "the Lord spoke to us while you were speaking, and we'd like to buy you a new wardrobe. Can you go with us tomorrow to take care of that?"

"Yes, sir, I certainly can," I answered.

And sure enough, they drove me around the next day in their custom-built Lincoln and purchased an entire wardrobe of clothes for me—shirts, shoes, coats, socks, pants, the "works."

That praise story brought blessing after blessing to all who heard it, including me! In every situation, the child of God can praise and thank Him when he knows it's all working together for his good.

Not surprisingly, God's television emphasizes happy endings, just like prime-time television. Like television commercials, it stresses getting things. On God's television there is no virtue in solitude, or poverty, or humility. This is a worldly Christianity. Its motto could be lifted directly from a beer commercial: "Go for It."[4]

When Schuller, who keeps his mouth turned up in a perpetual Kewpie doll smile, interviews Ray Kroc, the founder of McDonald's, it sounds like Hope and Crosby, or Carson and McMahon, each comparing his various successful business enterprises:

Schuller: What do you think people know about you?
Kroc: Hamburgers . . . ?
Schuller: You started with $1,000 . . . and you've grown since then?
Kroc: Quite a bit.
Schuller: How many retail outlets do you have?
Kroc: Five thousand.
Schuller: All over the world?
Kroc: All over the world. Japan, Hong Kong, Germany, Austria, Holland, Sweden, New Zealand.
Schuller: How old are you?
Kroc: Seventy-six. How old are you?
Schuller: Well, I'm fifty-two.
Kroc: Well, you've started something, too (laughter and applause).

Schuller then asks Kroc the secret of his success, and Kroc replies that he had good parents, that he worked hard, and that America is the greatest country in the world. Sure enough, we're just poor little old boys up here, but we know how to make that buck by satisfying our customers. Or, in the words of the Fats Waller song, "Find out what he wants and give it to him just that way." Waller is the spiritual father of modern marketing strategies, with their focus groups and demographic research aimed at identifying audience interests in order to raise sales or ratings. And Schuller is in the same ministry: "Find the hurt and heal it," he says.

The dominant image of God's television, then, is that of entertainment: rich, visual pleasures; simple story lines, Christian success driving away Satan's worry. If there is adversity in life, a cancerous growth, or a meddlesome FCC, then that's part of God's story line, too: every situation must have complicating action before the dramatic resolution. ("If I weren't a Christian, the FCC would have driven me out of my mind," Tammy Bakker lamented during the time of the troubles.) But, above all, every television show must have a star, and Roberts, Schuller, and their brethren are consummately telegenic.

A producer connected with fundamentalist television programming once told Stuart Zanger that any number of ministers had come to him and pleaded, "Get me on television." They had seen Oral Roberts's great success on television, and they figured, "What worked for him will work for me." But the producer says he told the would-be performers that the field was overcrowded. Then he reflected to Zanger, "Think about it. Why are these men on and not others? It's not their great deeds or their great intelligence. How can they be worth a $50-million-a-year operation? The answer is, because they're great television performers."

Viewers of a certain kind are entertained by the fundamentalist Big Five performers and the gospel beat, just as some viewers are entertained by *Saturday Night Live,* Bogart movies, or Las Vegas comics. When Zanger talked to viewers round the country, they told him, in effect, that they go to church on Sunday morning and to prayer meeting on Wednesday night, but that isn't enough. They want the Christian message in between times as well, from the television set if necessary. They feel the need for God's television as surely as they need food or sleep.

The Big Five and the smaller regional ministries take aim at this spiritual hunger (as well as at materialistic and entertainment cravings). Oral Roberts, until recently, called his program *Oral Roberts and You.* A recent Rex Humbard prime-time special was called "You Are Loved." Pat Robertson's *700 Club* reminds viewers that "telephone counselors are standing by to talk to you because you are important." God's television makes many viewers, perhaps most viewers, believe that they are not alone, that somebody likes them Up There—and down here, right here, on television. Zanger, for one, thinks that God's television, with its offerings of Christian love and spiritual entertainment, does some people some good. Whether it is the good that formal religion aims at is another matter. Whatever the judgment, it's clear that millions of Americans haven't found, or can't find, love in their own everyday lives, or need more than they're getting.

Are the Big Five just another form of special audience programming? In that sense, I suppose, a lot of God's television is "sincere." The fundamentalist reads the Bible and hears the command to go forth to the corners of the earth and preach the gospel. What better way to carry God's message than by the medium of television, linked to satellite transponders and direct-mail campaigns? Is no harm done even if, in carrying out the biblical command, a few of God's messengers happen to enrich themselves a bit? In mainstream religion, contributors help pay for the parish house, the organ, and the clergy. On God's television the pledge dollars go for satellite time, telephone lines, the studio set, and the producers' salaries. Isn't it all the same?

Such a benign vision is in keeping with those pluralistic notions of American society so beloved by the political scientists: feed and let feed. When I finished my research and viewing on televangelists in the early spring of 1980, I felt less confident about the implications of the new prime-time religion than others, Stu Zanger for one. I observed in my article for the *American Film* magazine: "Some star performers on God's television now face the temptations of wider audiences. Some evangelists want to organize around Pat Robertson for political action. Robertson's Christian Broadcasting Network already offers a newsletter, *Perspectives*. The sincere-looking pitchman on CBN's television commercial promises us that "*Perspectives* relates current events to the Scriptures."

And I concluded: "The tent preacher or sawdust-trail evangelist who aspires to a more powerful pulpit has long been a staple of the American novel and melodrama. Soon you may be watching it on the dial, in real life. In the thirties, a time of great unrest and social change, the demagogic voice of Father Coughlin, the radio preacher, came out of the midwest with its mixed messages of populism, faith, and hate. The eighties may be a time of change and unrest once again, with more people pursuing fewer resources. In an uncertain time of energy shortages and inflationary pressures, oversimplistic appeals from telegenic operators may take hold and grow in the darker ground of the American spirit."

The eighties arrived a lot faster than I expected. The Reverend Jerry Falwell's Moral Majority, organizing at the political precinct level, entered the periphery of our national vision by winning control of the Alaska delegation to the Republican National Convention in Detroit in July, 1980. On the floor of the convention, it turned out, Moral Majority members were one of the largest and most disciplined voting blocs. They were very much in the Republican majority as the convention adopted a whole series of far-right conservative stands, among these on abortion (against), on the strategic arms limitations talks, SALT (against), on school prayer (for), on the Equal Rights Amendment (against), on national defense (for). On election day, 1980, the voice of Falwell and his Moral Majority supporters were also heard. He had his own hit list of liberal Democratic senators:

George McGovern of South Dakota, Frank Church of Idaho, John Culver of Iowa, Birch Bayh of Indiana, among others. The Moral Majority said that they had to go, and they did. The liberals probably would have lost anyway, but the legend of Moral Majority money, effort, and voter-registration and education drives was born, or born-again.

For 1982 Falwell has another hit list of liberals, including Senator Edward M. Kennedy of Massachusetts and Senator Daniel Patrick Moynihan of New York. In the meantime Moral Majority found an interim campaign to wage—and to keep the dollars and contributions flowing. Falwell linked up with the Reverend Donald Wildmon, who wants to clean up television entertainment, and rid it of "sexual innuendo and pornography." After a show is monitored and found "dirty," a letter-writing campaign to the advertiser will be conducted. The goal is noble, the method hardly new. Other pressure groups have been writing advertisers for years to complain about sponsorship of undesirable programs. Each group, from left to right, of course, has a different definition of what is undesirable and of what should be censored.

All pressure groups, though, have one thing in common. Their crusades keep them in business. If viewers listen carefully to the television pitches of the new prime-time religion, they are likely to hear the television version of the fine print in legal documents. We are told that money raised from all those $5 and $10 contributions goes for the specific project being pitched and, in the fine print, "other operating costs of the ministry." Falwell, for example, has a $50 million a year operation to keep going.[5] A Lynchburg banker told a *Newsweek* reporter: "He [Falwell] can't stop raising money; if he does, it all falls apart."

Feed and let feed, indeed.

THY NEIGHBOR'S
CHANNEL

CHAPTER 4

One of the duties of a television newswriter is to produce the
grabbers, or teases: Near Miss at LA Airport . . . Details at 11:00
. . . Archie Gets a Surprise Visitor . . . Stay Tuned . . . As with a
strip tease, so with the television tease; the promise of something
big to come. When the ABC newsmagazine *20/20* took up the
subject of "Sexual Fantasies" not so long ago, its tease, appropriately enough, was some strobe-lighted footage of a blonde exotic
dancer writhing away in flowing white robes. If you watched
closely enough in the microsecond she was lit, you might have
seen some frontal nudity, or merely fantasized seeing nudity as
the teasing voiceover implored you to stay tuned to hear more
about the sexual revolution that's changing America. The *20/20*
sexual fantasy sequence was equally evanescent, a tease in its
own way about the larger American social body in the throes of a
convulsive psychosexual dance. "Sexual Fantasies" was gamely
researched and reported; there were examples of sexual innuendo in advertisements, scenes from the movie *10*, shots of

Times Square sleaze shows, bunny king Hugh Hefner with pneumatic playmates, and interviews with Gay Talese, author of the big sex book of 1980, *Thy Neighbor's Wife.* There was also an interview with Nancy Friday, author of *Men in Love,* the book that preceded Talese's on the bestseller charts. "This is a very erotic nation," Talese assured ABC. "We're caught between the way we were raised and new sexual ideas," Friday said.

By trying to cover so much in less than fifteen minutes, *20/20* covered little in detail. The newsmagazine show, it seems, wasn't quite ready in prime time and on its own to face the topic of human sexuality. If ABC had actively taken up the subject of contemporary sexuality, rather than teasing it and using surrogates to do the heavy breathing, it might have achieved more substantial results. Certainly the nature of the subject challenges all the news-gathering resources of a network. To study sexual fantasy is to study U.S. society in its cultural and commercial aspects as well as in its private relations. Human sexuality, according to a definition supplied by the American Medical Association, "is not confined to the bedroom, the nighttime, or to any single area of the body. It is involved in what we do, but it is also what we are. It is an identification, an activity, a biological and emotional process, an outlook and expression of the self. It is an important factor in every personal relationship and in every human endeavor from business to politics." That is an awesome assignment for television.

ABC might have begun by narrowing its focus, as journalists often have to do, to the topic of sexuality on television. By turning the camera around and lingering, unteasingly, on the human and societal images presented by television, *20/20* might have offered us some surprising news.

But hold it, you might say; is it really possible to say something new about sex on television, or anywhere for that matter, in the swinging 1980s? Who needs more banalities? In fact, there are a lot of things that need saying. We don't need banalities, but we could use some hard information on the topic. The first surprise—shocker, actually—is that no comprehensive analysis of television's sexual content exists. My authority for this is Elizabeth Roberts of the Project on Human Sexual Development at Harvard University.[1] Roberts has been looking into television's role in the sexual education of children as part of the updating of the U.S. Surgeon General's 1971 report on television and social behavior. The visual changes alone in the American sexual landscape in the past decade, or so, have been breathtaking. Author Talese himself got interested when he noticed that a massage parlor was advertising its services in the upper-middle class, East Side New York neighborhood where he lived. Looking only at television, we don't need the observational powers of a Talese to note the differences between, say, the 1960s *I Love Lucy* or the *Donna Reed Show* and today's *Three's Company* or *Love Boat*.

Still the vastness of the subject—that AMA definition—is as fearsome as the worry about being unable to say anything fresh, and that may be why there exists no single study. Roberts, however, has been doing a survey of television studies on topics touching on sexuality. For example, the feminist movement has produced information on how women have been portrayed on television, and this research has given Roberts some sense of television gender roles, the messages all of us receive about appropriate masculine or feminine atributes and roles. As a result of such existing research, and her own work, Roberts has been able to construct five content areas of use in studying sex on television. In addition to gender roles, her categories are body image, affection, love and intimacy, marriage and family life, and erotic content.

As for gender roles, there are no major surprises. In general television men are pictured as problem-solvers, aggressive and dominant, while television women are emotional, dependent, sensitive (cool cat crime fighters like Charlie's Angels or capable single parents like Alice are exceptions that prove the rule). The body image findings also confirm our common sense expectations and conform to the images presented by other popular arts. Most television women are presented as young, attractive, slim, fashionable; but the television demographics are still staggering—no fewer than 85 percent of all television women are under forty; any woman over forty is likely to be shown as asexual and as a failure and/or a victim of some sort (when she isn't just plain silly or eccentric). American society may be youth-oriented and male-fantasy-oriented, but television accents still more these obsessions.

Roberts' categories affection, love and intimacy, and marriage and family are embarrassingly negligible on television. There is little, if any, tenderness or nurturant behavior shown on television; men seldom exchange personal emotions with other men or even with women or children. It is hard to believe in the medium that gave us *Leave It to Beaver* and *Eight Is Enough*, but Roberts reports that nine out of ten television characters don't have children at all.

Though Roberts doesn't deal with specific programs, these particular findings square with our intuitions. When public television presented Ingmar Bergmann's *Scenes from a Marriage*, and when NBC gave us Larry Gelbart's *United States*, the series were treated as ground breaking and revolutionary, precisely because they showed television couples doing what we all do in real life— arguing, reconciling, drifting apart, loving, and hating—or for that matter, doing what couples do in motion pictures, the theater, books. The *Phil Donahue Show* also breaks from the usual talk show mold of show biz people promoting their new Vegas acts or latest films. Donahue, all choirboy charm, manages to get middle-American women to discuss such topics as single parenting and foster care.

The general air of unreality on television doesn't mean that marriage is necessarily idealized. The stereotypical husband/father in the situation comedies is frequently characterized as an inept bumbler in contrast to the strong, resourceful—and un-married—heroes of the action-adventure programs. But then divorce isn't idealized either. The emerging new woman of late 1970s and early 1980s television—a working woman or single parent—often pays a price for her deviation from the traditional married role, according to Roberts, by having problems in her personal relations with lover, husband, or child. Television's happiest men and women tend to fulfill neat sexist roles: the strong, unattached action-adventure male, the economically dependent, family-oriented married woman.

When someone says "sex on television," of course, the person usually has in mind Roberts' fifth category—erotic conduct—sexy or seductive behavior, innuendo, double entendre, intercourse. The depiction of erotic conduct is the area where television offends what I think of as the two major social groupings in the television audience: the sexual fundamentalists who are always after station managers to censor UnGodly, UnAmerican programming, and the sexual sophisticates who object to slick, voyeuristic sexual innuendo. If the cry of the former is "Clean Up the Filth," then the slogan of the latter is "Show and Tell It Like It Is."

Both the fundamentalists and the sophisticates have a point. Among her surprises, Roberts shows that much of television's erotic activity is linked with violence. For example, most verbal references to sex on the action-adventure or dramatic programs usually result from the discussion of rape or other sex crimes. Also Roberts says,

> Most references to intercourse on television (both verbally insinuated or contextually implied) occur between unmarried partners (five times as often as between married couples); references to intercourse with prostitutes comes in second. Together, these account for almost 70 percent of all allusion to intercourse on prime time television programs. When not prostitutes or victims of sex crimes, women characters use their eroticism to entrap men. Prostitute or police woman, sex is a major vehicle for women in achieving their goals. Erotic relationships are seldom seen (or discussed) between people in the context of warm, loving, stable relationships.

Alternatively, in situation comedies and on variety shows, television sex is viewed as an aspect of life to be treated with nervous laughter: "Characters touch, kiss, embrace and through seductive innuendo and flirtation, suggest sexual intimacy; these suggestive messages are usually accompanied by canned laughter and laugh cards to make it perfectly certain the humor is not missed."

And everywhere on the dial contraceptives just don't exist. Pregnancy or venereal disease are often used as the punishment for sexual activity by the wrong people, people who are too young, too old, too poor, too ugly.

Naturally, these messages are seldom direct or clear cut, and, as Roberts says, we can all think of exceptions to the general findings. But in Roberts's view the long-term general messages are more important than the specific content of any one serious program, especially in the formation of children's attitudes, her area of specific interest. "Television," she concludes, "tells the child viewer over and over that human sexuality equals sexiness and the sexiness is an acceptable subject if it is cloaked in humor or ridicule or viewed as a harsh, hurtful, or criminal part of life. . . . Affection and intimacy are viewed as inappropriate to the 'real world.' Sex is seen as a dirty joke or an exciting (albeit illicit) and dangerous activity that frequently leads to trouble. Hardly an integrated, rewarding, and fulfilling dimension of adult life."

One trouble with surveys is that each of the studies reflects a different point of view or different standards of measurement; another trouble is that the cases may be several years old, or absent altogether. Our News Study Group at MIT decided to use Roberts's sexuality categories in a formal study of one week of network programming. We chose the third week in May, 1980, and looked at the ABC, CBS, and NBC stations in both New York and Boston. We also tried to look for specific differences among program categories (news, soaps, commercials, prime time, late night) and among the networks. We also tried for a measure of the seriousness-smarminess of episodes or characters, in the belief that, as journalists, we perhaps could make more valid objective judgments than either the fundamentalists or the sophisticates, or judgments at least as valid.

The first and most obvious impression is that sexual behavior doesn't make the evening news or the morning shows unless it involves a story that would also make page one of the *New York Times* or the *Washington Post*. Local news programs, however, frequently take up sexual topics, and especially during the sweep weeks, those periods when the ratings are being compiled that will help determine next season's advertising rates. We just happened to be watching during the sweeps, but the bemused citizen can always tell it is a sweep week when the local news on channels 2, 4, 5, or 7 offer special reports on such subjects as child runaways (they may take up prostitution), the singles scene, battered wives, male models, sex in the office, and pornography. All this was part of our May fare. Consequently, a day and a night with television can be an exhausting sexual encounter. Here, for example, are some excerpts from one day's monitoring log, prepared by Steven Frann of the News Study Group during our mid-May monitoring project:

8:23 A.M.	Eclipse Sunscreen Lotion	Woman in bikini
8:35	Citicorp Traveler's Cheques	Nude couple in Japanese bath
9:00	*Good Day Show*	Author Erich Segal promoting new book about a "love child"
11:00	*The Young and the Restless* (known in trade as *The Hot and the Horny*)	Derek hired Judy Wilson, who had been planted by George to prove to Kay that Derek can be seduced by a pretty woman.

11:40	Scope mouthwash	Couple kissing.
11:45	*Family Feud*	Question: What are cold showers good for?
12:00 P.M.	*As the World Turns*	Nick told Kim that his estrangement from Steve is from the time Steve tried to force Sheila into prostitution.
12:30	*Ryan's Hope*	Woman commits suicide because her husband is having an affair.
1:00	*All My Children*	Devon had pregnancy symptoms and told Sean he's the father.
1:50	QT Lotion	Woman lying in sand
2:00	*One Life To Live*	Pal calls O, says she's willing to see him again. Richard and Becky embrace.
3:00	*General Hospital*	Monica kisses Rick, who'll file for divorce.
3:15	TONE Skin Care	Woman on beach
3:48	QT Lotion again	Woman on beach
4:00	*Rhoda*	Man makes pass at Rhoda when she hunts for apartment
4:30	*The Mike Douglas Show*	British actor tells about parts he's played in drag.
5:00	*The Match Game*	Host to woman panelist: "After I just

gave you a kiss and a little tongue!"
Sample game question: I think that mugger used to be a doctor. He just tried to stick me up with a ———.
—stethoscope
—thermometer
—scalpel
—rubber glove

7:30	*The Newlywed Game*	What will your wife say was the most famous thing you said on your wedding night? How many modern inventions are in your bedroom?
8:00	*WKRP in Cincinnati*	One-hour long, one-joke story: voluptuous Jennifer has been photographed in the nude
9:30	*House Calls*	"Do you like sex?" "If something's too easy, men don't appreciate it . . ."
10:00	Calvein Klein jeans	Tight shot of woman's crotch and rear
10:30	*Cheryl Ladd Special*	One-hour long, one-thought show of jigglevision

10:30	Tease for News at 11:00	Special report on prostitutes: "A prostitute talks about being trapped into the profession by the money . . ."
11:00	Local News	Special report on prostitutes

Sexy stories on the news are usually tied to some event to provide a fig leaf of respectability. Because a steady level of eroticism throbs through our society, news pegs aren't hard to find. "Sexual Fantasies," the ABC *20/20* sweeps entry, used the peg of two best-selling books for its report—material from another medium and consequently another fig leaf of protection. Typically, television doesn't act so much as react to events validated and made newsworthy by other pop culture sources. Thus Hugh Downs in his introduction: "What's selling [in bookstores] better than anything else this month? The answer, Sex."

"Sexual Fantasies" treated its experts, authors Talese and Friday, respectfully, in effect as two star witnesses from the serious world of print, and the program strove for objectivity. But in the end there was a characteristic failure of nerve. Television always wants it both ways: *20/20* used a visual tease to sell the sequence (we saw the exotic dancer four times in all), but then ABC ended with a spoken moral reprimand to placate any fundamentalists in the television audience who might have been offended:

Reporter Bob Brown: Psychiatrist Robert Coles, in a review of Talese's book [the authority of print again], expressed the concern of many people that all the public fantasizing and preoccupation with sex may have taken the humanity out of it. Hugh?
Host Hugh Downs: That makes sense. Thank you, Bob. We'll be right back.
[Break for commercial]

The stated explanation for these exposés is that they are relevant, contemporary, and only incidentally good for ratings. Much the same reasoning is put forward by programmers for the various entertainment specials later in the evening, programs with themes strikingly similar to the sweep week news specials.

On the first night of our survey, ABC offered Valerie Harper in *Fun and Games,* a movie about sexual harassment on the job. As Carol Heffernan, Harper works on a factory assembly line. Divorced, with a child to raise, she is eager to land a higher paying job in the quality control department. Her boss, a married man with children, is more than willing to promote her, provided she submit to his advances.

Once again the networks have it both ways. They offer sex for sweep week, but the sexists are defeated: Heffernan doesn't yield, and the EEOC saves her. And the same week Harper was fighting sexual harassment, the television film *Moviola* from the Garson Kanin book showed a succession of Hollywood queens offering sexual favors for the part of Scarlett O'Hara. (Vice went unrewarded in the Scarlett sequence, too.)

The New York *Daily News* reported that after Harper "solves the problem of sexually harassed women, she'll turn (in her next special) to battered wives." Kay Gardella of the *News* quotes Harper: "My intention is to illuminate the battered women syndrome and give hope to women. . . ." The same self-serving public spirit motivated NBC in its drama *Rage,* scheduled in the 1980–81 season. According to Irv Wilson, vice president, motion pictures for television, NBC entertainment, "*Rage* deals with *why* men rape. Unless we have a more enlightened approach to treatment of rapists, these horrible crimes will continue. . . . It is our hope that *Rage* will shed some new light on this subject. If it helps to prevent one rape, we have performed a public service."

There's no such pretense of "public service" in the smarmiest parts of the schedule: the game shows, the commercials, and the regular prime-time series. On the soaps, however, sex often comes in the company of love, marriage, or passion. The soaps may be the only place in 1980s America where people still look for "meaningful relationships." [2] One explanation is that the sheer volume of air time—five episodes a week for the typical soap, sometimes as long as ninety minutes each—permits more of everything: more sex, more divorce, more heartbreak, more emotional trauma. Henry Slesor, head writer of *The Edge of Night,* recently told journalist Michael Musto that "Soaps can treat sex a little more soberly because there's more time. We're dealing with people the audience and I get to know very well. Sheer titillation isn't necessary, because there's much more time to develop the characters, and sex can be integrated into the storyline." Slesor added that the soaps' openness is also helped by the fact that network censors don't watch daytime television as closely as they watch *Charlie's Angels* or *Vegas:* "During the day they assume the kids are in school."

As always in discussion of sex on television, the question is, where will it all end? Because television is the most widely received of the popular arts, it necessarily lags behind and warily follows the lead of other media (like the Talese and Friday interviews on *20/20*). To see where television will be tomorrow, we need only to look at books, movies, magazines, and advertising today. The prospect is not pleasant. In 1976 Martin Scorcese's *Taxi Driver* featured Jody Foster, then playing a kid prostitute (that was life). In 1978 Louis Malle made *Pretty Baby* with Brooke Shields, also twelve, in a bordello (that was old New Orleans). Later that year Shields and her friend Lisanna Falk were appearing—jut-hipped, pouty, eye-shadowed, and in bathing suits—in a *Life* magazine photograph. In 1980 Tatum O'Neal and Kristy McNichol, both playing fifteen-year-olds as *The Little Darlings* made a bet: "Whoever loses her virginity first—wins." Writer Sherryl Connelly calls this trend "The

Eroticization of Young America." Dr. Doris Millman of Downstate Medical Center, Brooklyn, New York, has a stronger term: "pandering to adult perversity and making it legitimate."

In its followership way television often serves as the great legitimizer of popular culture. Just the other day, I caught a television commercial for Jordache jeans showing kids bumping their designer denim behinds in a disco number. "That's not provocative, it's charming," a Jordache executive named Martin Block told Connelly. "Young kids only want what their older brothers and sisters want. . . ." The boys and girls in the Jordache disco look to be about ten years old.

TWO AMERICAS: BLACK AND WHITE ON TELEVISION

CHAPTER 5

Over the weekend of May 17 and 18, 1980, blacks in the Liberty City section of Miami rioted—"the nation's worst outbreak of urban disorder in a single city since the riots in Detroit and Newark in the so-called long hot summer of 1967," or so Dan Rather described it on CBS News.

Network television news, as we've come to expect, was on hand to record the violence and report back to the rest of us the fires burning out of control, the looters darting into wrecked stores, the hospital emergency rooms full of the wounded, the surging crowds, the patrolling police. The camera was there moreover as an objective witness, operating under carefully considered riot coverage guidelines—spelled out at CBS and NBC, left unwritten at ABC in the belief that it's better to rely on "the experience and common sense of professional journalists" as one ABC executive explained to me. ABC, CBS, and NBC performed coolly in Miami.

Yet looking at these codes of behavior, talking to network

news reporters and news supervisors alike, and replaying the videotapes of national television's coverage of Miami, I've become convinced that something was missing from the screen. It was as if the sound had been turned down at critical points. The guidelines for responsible riot coverage of the Miamis of America appear to be necessary but not sufficient for the reporting assignment at hand. Equally important, the concern for guidelines—for the nuts and bolts of covering what is happening in an objective manner—may prevent television from finding the stories beyond the immediate breaking news.

"The relations between the races is the biggest single social story in America," says Shad Northshield, the veteran producer who ran NBC News' nightly coverage during the civil rights 1960s and is now executive producer of CBS News' *Sunday Morning*. "But television in general operates on news, and not on causes." Network television's cool professionalism, its code, works against involvement and hot pursuit. The best-intentioned guidelines can be fetters on our understanding of what we need to know. They can, less charitably, be a wall behind which institutional indifference and timidity operate on stories involving race and class in the United States. As a result network television, the medium that a majority of Americans are supposed to be relying on for national news, is not meeting this need properly.

First, some background. Television's codes of news coverage became topics of public debate back in the 1960s with the rise in urban riots and unrest. As the NBC guidelines explain, "there were suggestions following the 1967 riots that television was causing the very disturbances it was reporting." CBS News' production standards elaborate: "It has been asserted that television, by the presence of its cameras, lights and crews, inspires or intensifies disturbances—an assertion based, in large part, on the further assertion that individuals and groups who seek to publicize their viewpoints will, sometimes, perform for our cameras and microphones."

   While arguing the necessity of full coverage of riots, the codes nevertheless set forth certain conditions camera people and reporters should follow. For example, the CBS production standards state in part:

• Be restrained, neutral, and noncommittal in your comments and behavior despite the verbal and/or physical abuse to which you may be subjected by the participants.

• Cover the disturbance *exactly* as it happens with no staging whatsoever; make no request or suggestion of any kind which will, in *any* way, influence the participants to do or refrain from doing *anything*.

• Report the disturbance soberly, factually, and unemotionally.

• Avoid coverage of (1) self-designated "leaders" if they appear to represent only themselves or (2) any individuals or groups who are clearly "performing."

NBC's guidelines, in similar fashion, offer:

• Do not describe a disturbance as a "riot" unless the police or some other responsible agency or official so designates it. Do not call a disturbance "racial" until it is officially so described.

• Avoid reports about "crowd gathering" following incidents involving police in known trouble areas and avoid pinpointing sites of growing tension and possible trouble in a city. Our duty is to report the story when it develops. We should no more predict violence than we would predict a bank run.

• Regard with suspicion any interviewing of participants during riots. It is questionable whether such interviews serve a valid purpose, and they may incite rather than inform. Trained persons, including police, officials, and articulate onlookers may offer useful facts.

   Such rules seem unexceptionable. They are, as Stan Opotowsky, then the chief assignment editor at ABC's *World News Tonight*, says, "the kinds of things you learn to do after years in the field."

   The 1960s riots brought out another less self-evident issue about media coverage. The President's National Advisory Commission on Civil Disorders worried that the media—print and electronic—might be preoccupied with the drama and visual impact of violence to the exclusion of doing more in-depth treatment and giving the background of disorder. In the decade since the 1960s, network guidelines, and the evidence of network practices, reflect a concern for the commission's criticism. NBC's code, for example, says:

> We cannot properly report the violence and ignore its causes. It is essential to the overall reality of the situation to move as early as possible into perspective and background phases on the city, its racial communities, the history of racial relations, and views of individuals and organizations on what caused the eruption. (The news function is not served unless the violence is related to its backgrounds.)

But media sensitivity to the need for care in the handling of racial stories may have other effects, unforeseen by public commissions, or, for that matter, unanticipated inside news organizations by their own code makers. Says Max Robinson, co-anchor of ABC's *World News Tonight* and probably the most prominent black newsman on television: "I sometimes hear from a producer, 'let's be careful about this story; let's not say it's racial. . . .' And I might say, 'Do we know that? . . .' And the answer is 'Well, no. . . .' "

Instead of following a given story wherever it leads (the hard-headed definition of journalistic objectivity) too often television's supervisors, when covering the explosive story of race in America, follow a more cautious objectivity, asking themselves, in effect, How is our reporting going to affect this situation? When Urban League President Vernon Jordan was shot, Robinson recalls that he saw throughout the media an "excessive amount of concern about keeping things cool . . . let's not excite anyone, or stir up people." Unfortunately, the press guideline values of behaving responsibly may work against the basic task of getting at, and facing, the facts. This is especially so when the facts involve the circumstances of black Americans—a story that many white Americans in the audience may not want to dwell upon too long, out of fear, doubt, guilt, or a combination of largely unexamined emotions. As Robinson says, the black story is too "fraught."

Television's treatment of the violence in Miami in May, and television's handling of subsequent events, illustrate the conflict between values and facts, as well as the necessity-but-not-sufficiency of guidelines. Here is a selected record of the images that the networks broadcast, starting with the first night of violence and ending five nights later:

On May 17, the early evening CBS News with Bob Schieffer leads with the restrained, noncommittal news that a "six man all white jury" has acquitted four former Miami police officers, all white, on charges "in connection with the death of Arthur Mc-Duffie, a black man . . . ." Later that Saturday night, Miami violence is the third news item on the ABC *Weekend Report* with Tom Jarriel, following two foreign policy stories and a commercial. The brief neutral item began: "Serious racial violence broke out tonight in Miami, Florida." It ended: ". . . thus far no fatalities."

Sunday night, May 18, Miami is the first story on the Jarriel report. The video images and narration set the style for what I came to regard as the standard urban violence coverage on all three networks—quick-cut scenes of fires, police, crowds, wounded, official statements, and face-in-the-crowd interviews, including a man who said "I couldn't believe [the verdict] . . . I wanted to believe in the American system. No more. Never again." ABC gave no totals of the dead but did note that half the fatalities were white, half black. Over at NBC's *Nightly News*, weekend anchor Jessica Savitch was reporting Mount St. Helens erupts (with five known dead) and Marine helicopter crashes (seven dead) before getting around to Miami. NBC had the violence story plus two other segments that became part of its standard examination of the causes of violence—the McDuffie verdict and another case involving a popular black school official, Johnny Jones—and Washington reaction (what the Justice Department says it will do).

On Sunday night CBS News has an early evening and late night news. CBS started with Mount St. Helens as its lead story but by 11 P.M. had switched to Miami; not so coincidentally, the Miami death count went up during the night, from ten to fifteen. CBS reported without much elaboration that the majority of the dead were black, a somewhat jarring fact because most of the riot scenes depicted images of blacks rampaging, presumably against whites.

Monday night the three networks faced a situation where immediate news judgment rather than sober, objective guidelines must take over. Two eruptions had to be covered and given weight, the volcano and the violence. While NBC treated the stories separately, ABC and CBS decided to twin up the two disasters as "natural and man-made" (ABC and CBS even agreed on that wording). Once into the Miami coverage, however, all three networks stressed the same elements: violence dying down in the Liberty City area, the toll in damage (typically, white businesses destroyed and black consumers suffering), black leaders' statements, federal officials' vows of investigations. Each network had its causes piece, examining the now familiar roots of the violence in the McDuffie and Jones cases and in the economic competition from the Cuban emigrés. These causes examinations were carefully tied to "community leaders." For example, Marvin Dunn, a university official and sociologist—and a black man—appeared on both CBS and NBC.

By Tuesday night, May 20, an order had been imposed in the news, and in Miami. Mount St. Helens erupts again—the big story—while "Miami calmed down somewhat today . . ." (ABC). On NBC David Brinkley sounds the theme of the calming stories: "Life returns to normal and now the economic problems begin . . . ," as perhaps 3,000 blacks are out of work because of the destruction of the weekend.

Wednesday, May 21, coverage is predictable: President Jimmy Carter declares the State of Washington a disaster area and says he will fly off to the Pacific northwest to look at the destruction. The Carter Administration also declares an emergency at the Love Canal area in Niagara Falls. The environmental package is the networks' lead news. Miami slides toward the middle or end of the newscasts and into the vignette stage of coverage: as calm returns, and people pick up the pieces, here are some little illustrative tales. NBC's Ike Seamans, for example, reports even handedly on Eula McDuffie, mother of Arthur McDuffie, and on Tony and Jacqueline Baretta, parents of Charles Baretta, a white teenager, who was "among the first to die in the riots."

On May 22, the newcasts are full of Carter's inspection trip to the volcano in an eight-helicopter fleet (five for the president and officials, three for the accompanying press). Frank Reynolds on ABC: "Good evening. A horrible looking sight. That's the way President Carter described the area around Mount St. Helens. . . ." The president also said the volcanic area could become a great tourist attraction in time. On CBS Walter Cronkite notes, in thirty seconds, that the schools have reopened in Miami; John Chancellor on NBC takes fifteen seconds to mention the schools, using it as a segue to another feature: "The schools in Miami face another problem: how to educate the young Cuban refugees who have arrived in such great numbers. Ike Seamans has that story. . . ." On ABC there is no mention of Miami at all, though ABC has time for a long, light "closer" on the imminent baseball strike (a man-made disaster that failed to materialize the next day).

What does this record add up to? First, the guidelines for violence coverage worked. Reports were careful, balanced (white losses, black losses). Police were quoted but also community leadership. Heeding the 1960s words of the president's commission, the causes of violence were examined. "Coverage was solid, and not provocative," says Stan Opotowsky. "There were no complaints." If guidelines can be thought of as governing the rules of combat, the three networks won the battle.

Still, it's not meant to deride network coverage to say that shots of Miami buildings aflame are little different from shots of Newark or Detroit buildings aflame; looted areas look the same in the 1980s as they did in the 1960s, with only the names of the streets changed. Burning ghettos make good TV but don't advance the story significantly.

While winning the battle of Miami, the networks lost the war, or more accurately, quickly got caught up in covering another battle, the big volcano story. Mount St. Helens was, as Max Robinson suggests, "a safe disaster": horrible, but still comfortable for whites. President Carter thought so, because he went to Mount St. Helens first. When the president did go to the man-made black disaster, Miami, in early June, bottles were thrown at his motorcade. Consider, for a moment, what would have happened on the news if Jimmy Carter had reversed his priorities and visited Miami first. The networks, trailing after him, would have given Miami one or two extra nights of full coverage, one or two extra opportunities to get at stories unbounded by guidelines. Carter certainly wouldn't have talked about Liberty City as an attraction for tanned, camera-toting tourists.

The networks, with or without Carter's lead, might have confronted some of the underlying unsafe grounds of the disaster. NBC, for example, had quoted Miami Mayor Maurice Ferre: "There's no way that those of us who live in air-conditioned comfort with two cars outside and a $30,000 boat in this community can live side by side with people who live ten to a room . . . infested with rats." There was no follow-up of this story of the two Americas, or any clues to its coverage in 1960s style guidelines. At least one network, let it be said, did dispatch a top correspondent and crew to Miami, but they had little time to develop the story, and then found themselves called back home, to go to Detroit for the Republican National Convention, joining 13,000 other journalists covering certified mainstream news.

Network television, it's said, can't be too sociological. When I asked one network news executive how he thought the running story of blacks and whites in America could be covered, he replied: "Why, we've been covering it for years. We're at the NAACP convention this week." Nose to the news, TV usually needs such pegs to hang stories on. It has less time and space for elaboration. Print does certain stories better. All true. In June it was two newspapers, the *Washington Post* and the *Miami Herald,* and not the national networks, that sponsored a post-riot survey of the blacks in the area. Among the more chilling findings was the evidence that one in every four people in the sample had participated in the Miami riots—almost twice the percentage of people who acknowledged joining in the major riots of the 1960s. The greater popularity of rioting in the 1980s has to be added to the suggestions that some of the Miami episodes of violence had a planned and timed quality. But that story was dug up not by national television or the hometown papers, but by a young woman reporter for the *Chicago Tribune,* who quoted police as saying that black Vietnam veterans—urban guerillas—had organized some of the violence. Police officials acted out of their own self-interest in pushing out that lurid story, but it was certainly worth a follow-up, either as a good lead or a police fiction.

Undeniably, there is little time for in-depth treatments on the evening news. So we're left with guidelines coverage—safe, neutral, responsible. But neutrality can become unneutral. "Guidelines cover the technical details," a black journalist told me, "but in all my years in television, I don't recall ever sitting down at a meeting to discuss the different overall perceptions blacks and whites have of the racial climate in America. . . ." When I asked Max Robinson if the problem was more coverage, he replied: "Cover more of what? Of White America? We need special reports holding up a mirror to White America, but do people want to see that?"[1]

Realistically, there's little chance of that kind of coverage, given time constraints and the corporate jitteriness about appearing to be "activist." In truth. it is hard for television to examine white America's institutions because it is one itself. But the Miami record also shows that there are times on the dial when reality is mirrored rather than (unintentionally) distorted.[2] On CBS's *Sunday Morning* broadcast of May 25, the cover story by

Richard Threlkeld touched all the themes of the nightly coverage but brought them together in an intelligible whole. Among
other things, Mayor Ferre was quoted as saying, "I subscribe to
the premise that it's important to have a balanced budget, but
when cities start to burn . . . I'm not too sure that the majority of
America would change its mind really quick. . . ." It was thoughtful television, the kind not often seen on the evening news.
"We're interested in doing stories that other programs don't
have time for," says *Sunday Morning* Executive Producer Robert
Northshield. "That means complicated stories. . . ." Northshield
believes major stories should run ten or twelve minutes, "to
allow time for viewers to insert themselves into the narrative, to
find their reactions to it." Ten minutes are reserved for titanic
news in the evening programs.

No one institution, of course, can change the realities of race
in America, certainly not an "objective," self-restrictive institution
like television. But with time and care television at its best can
involve a lot of us, black and white, more intellectually and
emotionally in its stories and allow us to find our own reactions
to the major continuing American news event of our time. That
would be the guideline for a beginning before the fire next
time.[3] Journalist Max Robinson, of course, is not a stranger to
Black America. Here is how he covered one aspect of that story,
excerpted from the television transcript of a series he did on
Anacostia, a black ghetto in Washington, D.C.:

Max Robinson (on camera):

For the past two weeks we have been looking at some reflections
on life in two census tracts in mid-Anacostia. For the most part
the people we have seen in this series have two things in common: they are poor, and they are black. For most of their lives
they have been desperately struggling to find some dignity,
some meaning to fill the spiritual emptiness that pervades the
ghetto. When I went to mid-Anacostia I had much the same
attitude that most Americans cling to when thinking about poor
black people. I frankly thought of them as a KIND of people
rather than people much like you and me. It took me some time
to see them as individuals caught in a sociological trap not of

their own making. When I really saw this I began to feel many of the things that my fellow mid-Anacostians felt. Without my shirt and tie and apparent news affiliation, I became a faceless black man to most white Anacostians. And even though I was fully aware that all I had to do was to cross the bridge and return to life as usual, I began to feel the frustration, the rage, the hatred, the impotence, the apathy that permeates the ghetto.

Max Robinson (voice on film):

I remember talking with some of the cats on the corner—guys that I would have never talked with before my visit. We would stand and talk for hours about what they wanted out of life. It seemed to mean a lot to them that someone would take the time to listen to them seriously. They wanted what all of us want out of life, but they were puzzled over how to get it.

I remember the two mothers on welfare with their eighteen children living on less than a hundred dollars a week. And the faces of the children haunted me. Children who, before they can glimpse the meaning of race and poverty, are condemned to future generations of welfare payments, condemned to watch *their* children suffer. I could then see why apathy was so widespread. Apathy was a barrier against insanity.

I can remember the long walks with a few new-found buddies as they talked about their scrapes with the law and their desires for a straight life—a good life, as they put it. And as we walked, we could see the policemen pounding their beats as if in a strange land. Their faces appeared to me to be masks of hostility, hiding a more deeply held fear and alienation.

And there were the teenage girls dreaming long dreams of quick success and wondering what the outside world is all about. Young girls who had all too soon seen the tragedies peculiar to the ghetto.

I can remember the numerous discussions on black power. And I could sense the centuries of frustrations—the desire for dignity denied, a place in the mainstream of American life, a decent home, a bank account, and all of the other things that most Americans take for granted. I could sense that centuries of hope had been dashed against the rocks of the white backlash, the pressure for a balanced budget, and this nation's twentieth-century journey into escapism.

And I asked myself why I hadn't looked at the problem before. Had I been escaping? Of course, I had. It was all too easy to give pat answers to difficult problems and refuse to see my brother when his situation was somewhat different from mine.

I did see some forces for change in mid-Anacostia—through

the efforts of the poverty workers. It appeared that America might be awakening to the necessity of eradicating poverty and racial discrimination from her midst. But before the year was out even that initially meager program has been threatened with a large cutback in funds.

"The Trouble with Anacostia," I thought, is the trouble with America.

As I left mid-Anacostia I could not help but search my brain for some solutions. But the solutions to problems piled up over many years are not easy to come by.

Max Robinson (on camera):

It did, however, seem clear to me that for a start, as one poverty worker put it, "America must suffer some." We must suffer the pain of opening our eyes to the problem that exists in our midst. We must be able to see the forgotten community as a community very much like ours, peopled by real people who lack one thing that we have all had—a real chance to share in this land of plenty. America's rejection of the comfortable easy chair of escapism will be the first real step in ridding this country of its most crippling disease. We as citizens have yet to take that first step.

This is Max Robinson.

That report from Anacostia was done by Robinson in 1965. It might have been filed by him yesterday, so little has changed for blacks. Then again, it probably wouldn't have been filed because television at the network level just doesn't commit that much time and thoughtfulnes to the Anacostias of America.

LOOKING FOR
MR. RIGHT:
THE ISSUES OF ICONS
AND AGEISM

CHAPTER 6

When CBS News in early 1980 chose Dan Rather over Roger Mudd to replace Walter Cronkite as chief anchorman on its evening news, some accounts made the decision sound like the work of computer dating. According to *Time* magazine, the darkly handsome Rather, forty-eight, scored higher than the laconic Mudd, fifty-two, on the market researchers' Q scales— ratings that measure the degree of a viewer's positive response to a television personality. *Newsweek* quoted surveys by "influential" news consultant firms showing Rather "projecting almost as much warmth, compassion, and honesty" as Cronkite, while Mudd was "perceived as somewhat cold."

William Leonard, president of CBS News and one of the human minds that did make the decision in favor of Rather, discredits the notion that the choice was in any way computerized. "It's absolutely not true that we used any such surveys," Leonard insisted in an interview we had back then. "It was a *news* decision." And while most network news people speak contemptuously of decisions made by market research—Reuven Frank, former president of NBC News has called the Q ratings "psychobabble," and Leonard says: "It's what local stations do"— these same executives find it hard to explain in human, non-computer terms just what they do look for in an anchorperson. The network anchors put their stamp on the news that 60 million Americans view nightly, to say nothing of the anchors' influence on network profits and prestige; yet, Leonard claims that there is no clear model for predicting an anchor's success.

"With 20/20 hindsight," he says, "you might conclude that this man appears *avuncular* or that this one is *serious*, but, in fact, an individual just naturally emerges. His performance adds up." In this view the anchorperson's job can't be approached as science but as art, and a magical, mystical art at that.

Still there are some overall patterns in the selecting of anchors, as well as some specific anchor models that have appeared in the 1950s, 1960s, 1970s, and now, with Dan Rather, in the 1980s. The clearest pattern involves the tapping of middle-aged, mid-American, white males for network anchor positions, the men the old *Life* magazine used to refer to as the command generation. (Exceptions, like ABC's Barbara Walters and Max Robinson, the first black to anchor a network newscast, tend to prove the rule.) And beyond these obvious factors, certain anchor styles appear, grow, and fade.

In the days of radio, broadcast journalists tended toward stentorian delivery—"the voice from the well," Reuven Frank remembers. Edward R. Murrow, the best of the radio correspondents, had the requisite voice and also conveyed his deep involvement in stories. "What made Ed Murrow the man we remember," says Fred Friendly, his long-time associate, "was his intensity of conscience. You could feel his emotions when he covered the Battle of Britain."

Many radio veterans looked down on the infant television and did not want to make the transition to the new medium in the late 1940s. As a result the first popular network television evening newscasters of the 1950s, Douglas Edwards on CBS and John Cameron Swayze on NBC, were not the superstars of broadcasting; they were good journeymen readers of the fifteen-minute news roundup.

As television sets grew in number, the evening television newscasts grew in importance. Looking authoritative became as critical as sounding authoritative. Richard Wald, now vice president of ABC News, once suggested the result of this combination: anchorpeople cast in the form of paracletes, messengers of God. New skills were also needed, particularly in the live coverage of events like space shots and political conventions. Ed Murrow crossed over to television and, with Fred Friendly, established a new standard for the making of documentaries; but Murrow appeared ill at ease, even ponderous, broadcasting live from a booth at the 1960 conventions. Live television seemed to short-circuit his intensity. "He could never be a television anchor," Friendly now says flatly.

By contrast, a former wire-service reporter and war correspondent named Walter Cronkite had learned to ad lib and do unobtrusive narration (so-called voice-over) on filmed reports while working the nightly television news at the CBS affiliate in Washington. Cronkite, appropriately, was the first person to be designated "anchorman" when CBS structured its coverage of the 1952 conventions around him. A genre was formed.

Television in the 1960s confirmed and modified the serious, yet-not-too-intrusive, authoritative model. Douglas Edwards was unceremoniously dumped, and Walter Cronkite won out over fellow CBS correspondent Charles Collingwood for the anchor job of the expanded (to thirty minutes) evening news. According to former CBS staff member Gary Paul Gates, author of an insider's history of CBS News (*Air Time,* Harper and Row, 1978), Collingwood lost because his superiors viewed him as "too elegant" and "too handsome" for the post. Collingwood appeared to be soft, good enough for important correspondent assignments but not anchor material.

At NBC, meanwhile, the top brass had tired of Swayze. Back in 1956, according to Reuven Frank, two factions at NBC were fighting over who was to be Swayze's replacement. Frank wanted the veteran David Brinkley, "because he had grown up in Washington and knew not to take some things too seriously." Another faction wanted Chet Huntley, a newcomer from the far west who, it was said somewhat mockingly, "liked to read *The Economist* and interview Conrad Adenauer." The casting of Huntley and Brinkley, like so much else in the television business, was accidental. "We couldn't agree on one man," Frank recalls, "so someone said, 'Let's use both.' We may have been subconsciously aware of the contrast between the two, but no one was thinking magic back then."

The Huntley-Brinkley anchor team became one of the longest-running success stories in television. The paraclete and the skeptic inspired a couplet to the tune of the popular song "Love and Marriage":

Huntley-Brinkley, Huntley-Brinkley,
One is solemn, the other's twinkly.

Their success also caused panic at CBS. After NBC's ratings triumph at the Republican convention in 1964, CBS pulled Walter Cronkite from the anchor booth and replaced him with its own version of a box-office duo: Roger Mudd, then thirty-six, and Robert Trout, fifty-five—youth and experience. "It's all better forgotten," says Leonard, who participated in the decision and can still feel the pain. "We overreacted and thought that Walter was responsible for the bad ratings, when it actually was our total performance."

Cronkite was restored to his anchor position, but it took almost another decade for CBS News to catch and pass Huntley-Brinkley. By the early 1970s, the country had gone through an unpopular war, street riots, assassinations, and civil turmoil—"a slum of a decade" Stephen Spender called the 1960s. In Frank's view, the times required a new role for the television anchor: "He had to be a fixed center in all the chaos around him. The news was changing rapidly, and the audience needed a reference point, something dependable, like the familiar typefont of your favorite newspaper."

Frank admits to having come to this wisdom retrospectively, after making what he calls "the biggest mistake of my career." Chet Huntley had decided to leave NBC, "quitting when he was ahead," Frank says. Frank, planning for the day when NBC News would offer seven early evening newscasts instead of five, named David Brinkley, John Chancellor, and Frank McGee— "my three best guys"—as anchors and put them on a rotating duty roster, which meant that on any given day two would appear. "The audience hated it," Frank says. "People were never sure who would be on." NBC dismissed its duty roster after six months, sending McGee to the *Today* show; as Brinkley moved more and more into a subsidiary role, John Chancellor emerged as the face, the typefont, of NBC News in the 1970s.

By the 1970s, too, Walter Cronkite had managed, in Fred Friendly's words, to combine "the sense of your favorite uncle with a world statesman's demeanor. . . . Perhaps no one will ever win such trust again." Younger than Cronkite and with somewhat less reporting experience, Chancellor could not directly challenge the authority of his rival. Instead, he developed a calm, professorial anchor style that in effect distanced him a bit from all the bad news around him. Chancellor seemed to be saying, "There's the news over there in the background or on film and tape, and here I am at your side. Here's what I could find out about what was going on, given human frailty." But even this low-key anchor stance emerged without design. At best, says Frank, "It was a subconscious approach."

The pattern at ABC was generally to lag behind the other two networks, from the 1950s stentorian approach to the 1970s style of reassurance in television newscasting. Without an authority figure of Cronkite's stature or a steadying hand like Chancellor's, ABC did what television calls counterprogramming—it experimented with dual anchors, male and female anchors, triple and quadruple anchors. ABC's most notable anchor failure was the pairing of Barbara Walters and Harry Reasoner, two excellent broadcast journalists in their own right who happened not to get along with each other. There's always a lot of talk about "on-air chemistry" when television people analyze the appeal of anchors. The atmosphere at ABC was instantly recognizable. "When people turned on the program," ABC News President Roone Arledge told me at the time, "it was like coming into a married couple's home after there had been a big fight."

ABC by 1980 had settled on three geographically separated anchors: Frank Reynolds in Washington, Max Robinson in Chicago, and Peter Jennings abroad, with Barbara Walters as a contributor and the orchestrating hand of the New York producer's desk as an invisible fourth anchor. Arledge's reported efforts to lure Rather from CBS with the offer of the sole anchor job provides one measure of how this structure was regarded within ABC.

These patterns of anchor styles, past and present, suggest why the anchor ideal is so constrained that very, very few people can measure up or, more accurately, fit within the narrow window of opportunity.

First, the ideal anchor must be able to write well and report well—but not too well. CBS's Eric Sevareid, it has been argued, became a commentator rather than an anchorman in part because he wrote and spoke thoughtful, complex sentences.

Second, the ideal anchor must have broad experience, at home and running foreign bureaus, covering politics and wars (this last also effectively serves to screen out women). These days the term broad experience tends to mean television experience in the shooting and editing of tape rather than print apprenticeships.

Third, the ideal anchor can't be too young; that would mean not enough experience. Nor can the ideal be too old. The sixty-ish Mike Wallace, Leonard says, would have been a candidate for the Cronkite job a few years ago but not now.

Fourth, the ideal anchor must have certain cosmetic advantages: voice, presence, good looks but not too good-looking (*vide* Charles Collingwood).

Fifth, the ideal anchor, like any good performer, must be able to project ("just as Stanislavsky teaches," says Frank).

Sixth, the ideal anchor should be a company loyalist, a team player. The ideal ought to reflect the self-images of the people within the news organization. Leonard explains: "The rest of us have to be able to say, 'Yeah, sure, that's us up there. We're proud of him.' "

If all this sounds too much like the Boy Scout oath, then it ought to be added that the ideal model must also be fleshed out with some real emotions, including an unceasing drive to succeed. Both Dan Rather and Roger Mudd, for example, can match each other in experience, talent, and news instinct, but a friend who knows them both told me by way of explanation of Rather's victory: "Dan was quite simply willing to work harder at running for the Cronkite job than was Roger."

The audience, of course, provides the final test of the network's anchor ideal and of the anchorman's personal ambitions. Audience acceptance of Rather won't be measured by vague, and transitory, Q scale responses but by the standard of attentiveness year in and year out, for a decade or more, the way Walter Cronkite and Huntley-Brinkley achieved acceptance. How will Rather measure up? He faces at least two obstacles. Most immediately, all the hype surrounding his job may create unreasonable expectations, for example, when a viewer turns on the set, samples the newscasting and dials out, saying, "He doesn't look like he's worth $3 million to me." Then, over the long run Rather has to find the anchor style suited to him personally and to a changing audience in daunting times. Some political polls, as well as the election of Ronald Reagan, suggest that the American public of the 1980s longs for "decisive" leadership but also for what it sees to be "honesty." Rather is known for a kind of tough integrity. By acting himself, he may be the right anchor for the news of the 1980s.

Right after winning the job as CBS's *Evening News* anchor, Dan Rather dropped from public sight. So did Roger Mudd, who after a decent interval, signed up with NBC News. After a few months in seclusion Rather also reappeared—quite spectacularly, in disguise and with a CBS film crew reporting from among the rebel forces fighting Soviet troops in Afghanistan. A number of critics chided his report, shown on the top-rated news magazine show *60 Minutes*—Gunga Dan, he was called in the *Washington Post* by Tom Shales. In truth the substance of the account of rebel fighters wasn't all that new, but the style, the idea of Rather behind the lines, was an inspired one. At the same time it deflated Rather's untoward public image of superstar—he had, after all, risked his life, the viewer was encouraged to reason, so maybe he was worth $3 million a year—and it also showed that Rather was determined to put his own rugged stamp on CBS News.

After thinking and writing about the qualities of the right anchorperson—much of the material above appeared in the *New York Sunday Times* in April 1980—I still felt a certain disquiet about the pinched, narrow window of opportunity for the job. My unease returned one night when I was watching the CBS *Evening News*. A reporter named Joe Wershba was telling the strange story of Norman Shelley, the man who played Winston Churchill. According to Shelley, a retired English actor, he, and not Churchill, delivered those famous post-Dunkirk words about how Britain will fight on the beaches, in the hills, on the streets, and landing grounds. The Wershba story strained credulity; as Shelley told it, Churchill was too busy to repeat the House of Commons speech in which the stirring words were first uttered, so the BBC asked Shelley to broadcast it, imitating Churchill. But equally astonishing to me was the sight of the CBS storyteller himself.

Joe Wershba is tall, stooped, bagel-bald, with a voice closer to

Brooklyn than the BBC or CBS. What's more, he was fifty-nine years old. In the early fifties he and Walter Cronkite broadcast the nightly news for WTOP, the old CBS station in Washington. Wershba has spent the years since as a producer working off-camera, most recently with *60 Minutes*. While I was able to figure out why CBS had asked Wershba to be the reporter on the Churchill piece—Wershba had helped Edward R. Murrow and Fred Friendly with the preparation of their "I Can Hear It Now . . ." record of the period—I had to think a while about why I was so surprised, actually astounded, to see Wershba on the evening news.

It was his age, of course, and his bald head and his delivery. Joe Wershba looked and sounded like somebody you might meet at a cousin's wedding, a block association meeting, or in the office elevator. He wasn't pretty, he didn't have blow-dry hair or that particular voice that television instructs its people to have, one that squeezes out all traces of region and class. Joe Wershba, in short, wasn't the usual television icon. He was a real person, right down to his name. (Quick, name another newsman named Joe on national television.) And television doesn't favor real people very much these days. Rather television offers models of beauty, dignity, responsibility, warmth, and—that good 1980s quality—credibility. Television wants someone non-old, non-bald, and non-regional. A Walter Cronkite can survive, not just because of his image of incorruptible professionalism but because we have been allowed to grow older with him. Cronkite, as well as John Chancellor, was seen as an older American. He was Uncle Walter, ageless.

Television executives will say that they don't discriminate against the old, the halt, or the plain. It would be against the law if they did. But that is clearly what is going on. Of course, executives will say that they merely want people who can communicate. In television news it helps enormously if the communicator can also read, write, and think seriously about contemporary affairs. Some news organizations place these qualities above considerations of style and appearance, and we should be grateful to them. But even the best news organizations aren't immune to the cult of beauty, narrowly defined. CBS News dropped the estimable Hughes Rudd from its morning news program, in part, according to Rudd, because he was too gruff and surly for audiences so early in the morning. Rudd was pushing fifty-eight and was just short of twenty years of service with CBS. (Rather than wait for his gold watch, Rudd has since taken his surliness, and his wit and intelligence, to ABC.) As unpleasant as this experience may have been for Rudd, at least CBS treated him with more kindness than a Boston station recently showed one of its weathermen, who was told he was "too wrinkled and old-looking" to be on the air.[1]

In their more defensive moments, television executives will also claim that they are only a mirror of society, merely pointing their cameras at reality as it unfolds. This mirror theory is correct, but not in the sense usually intended. Television does not mirror so much as it reflects some of our deepest, largely unexamined fears and prejudices. We value conventional beauty—strong chin line, straight nose, lots of hair—over plainness, success over failure, svelteness over fat, the familiar over the unusual. Television would righteously reject any charges that it is sexist or racist in its hiring practices and would point to the appreciable numbers of women and blacks and Hispanics now appearing on television screens in contrast to the situation ten or fifteen years ago. But the fact that the black women reporters appearing on camera in, say, Detroit, all look like the daughters of Lena Horne—if she had daughters who were stunning, five feet ten, and had gone into television—is an irony that's lost only on television executives.

Naturally, television people deny they are ageist, or narcissistic, and point to the existence of a Walter Cronkite, or to Hugh Downs's *Over Easy* on public television, or to the John Houseman character, Professor Kingsfield, on *The Paper Chase*, or to the occasional grizzled guest on *The Dick Cavett Show* or Bill Moyers's *Journal* to prove that television is not against older people. But these are, again, the noble exceptions that prove the dismal rule. *Over Easy,* a kind of sop to senior citizens, has been tucked away practically out of sight in much the same way that Lawrence Welk's geriatric polkas were banished from prime time—and in much the same way that society has banished older people from its consciousness. That is also part of a mirror relationship between our culture and our popular arts. As for the Houseman character, *The Paper Chase* was reportedly kept alive beyond its ratings-dictated plug-pulling time because CBS board chairman William S. Paley, at seventy-eight an aging lion himself, liked the program's theme of a vigorous old tyrant dominating cowering youth. Even with this life-support system, *The Paper Chase* eventually went under.

Two reasons are usually offered to explain the idealized iconography that television presents to its public through the faces of its performers. First, because television is an entertainment medium, it is said the audience would rather look at a young, pretty face than at an old, homely face. As a station executive once explained to me, "We can't put on people who will scare little children." Worse, such faces might scare adults away. Second, television, as an advertising medium, must design programming to attract certain desirable audiences.

These days the viewers most in demand by advertisers are women between the ages of eighteen and forty-nine, a demographic group considered to combine the maximum disposable income (the woman of the house spends the day-to-day money) with the maximum susceptibility to television commercials. (That's what the research says.) Years ago, before television, David Reisman referred to a class of young Americans as "consumer trainees." Advertisers couldn't have said it better. Again, according to the demographic research, younger women viewers as a group "skew" toward young, good-looking men and

young, good-looking women in their preferences for on-air performers. "So, we hire young bucks," a news director explained
to me.

These conventional explanations are adequate, as far as they
go. But the Wershba appearance on CBS helped my understanding of another factor that shapes the images we see on
television. I asked a television producer who also watched the
Wershba story why television doesn't have more such real people on the air, as hosts, anchor people, or reporters. "It would be
too much reality," she replied. "The audience might link the
newscaster to the news. As things are now, television looks like it
is detached from events. So they can't blame us for what we tell
them, because we don't look real."

Once we begin to look at television from this point of view—a
somewhat patronizing version of John Chancellor's distancing
anchor role—a number of elements come into focus. The well-
dressed, well-spoken people, the brightly lit studio sets, the
disembodied announcers' voices, even the occasional ringing
phone or scurrying aide in the background, all give the news on
television an institutional aura, as in a hospital or in the doctor's
suite. When a medical doctor appears in his white coat to talk to
his patients, his degrees on the wall behind him, we listen,
sometimes resentfully if the news is bad but always politely. So,
too, in the institutional television studio, when the newsman puts
on his expensive jacket, or the newswoman her boardroom
blouse. They are dressing for power. They wish to appear as
authoritative, as objective, and, especially, as distant from the
bad news as the M.D. seems to be. They care about your problems, even though the problems are yours not theirs.

If television can be thought of as white coated and objective,
then it can escape any involvement with the information or
feelings it is conveying. And television, in fact, saves up its own
emotions for the highest civic occasions and uses them only then.
Just recall Walter Cronkite's demeanor on the afternoon of the
assassination of John F. Kennedy, or Cronkite's heartfelt words

when in the days of the NASA Mercury program astronaut Scott Carpenter seemed to overshoot his landing zone. Cronkite displays his emotions sparingly. (Tom Wolfe in his book, *The Right Stuff,* captures this moment marvelously.)

Fortunately, some changes are in the air, of all places in television's entertainment shows. The realities of human emotion and real-world information that television too often avoids in the name of the holy Nielsen numbers may also be pursued in the same quest for numbers. In the *Washington Post* Peter Brown reported that ABC's *Happy Days* has been undergoing a change in themes for the 1980–81 season, moving from the froth of the sock-hop fifties to the substantive issues of the uneasy sixties.[2] Originally, the program celebrated the fun years of the Eisenhower era. But for 1980–81, *Happy Days* was moving into "new territory, into heavy territory," according to executive producer Garry Marshall (who also helped create *Laverne and Shirley, Mork and Mindy,* and *Angie*). In one episode, *Happy Days* dealt with the subject of the handicapped, with a paraplegic played by Jim Knaub, a former Olympic-class pole-vaulter who is paralyzed from the waist down in real life. In another *Happy Days* episode, twenty-year-old Richie falls in love with an older woman; in still another, the Fonz gets involved with a deaf girl. In a third episode, the characters Marion and Howard "need to reaffirm their marriage."

Garry Marshall talked expansively to Brown about his plans to use "the enormous power" *Happy Days* has achieved with its audience, presumably for good causes. His new heavy approach is not all that new—in televisionland, it is sometimes called Learism, after Norman Lear, who occasionally used his situation comedies, like *All in the Family* and *Maude,* to carry serious-sounding messages. But an alternative explanation for the evolution of *Happy Days* is that the program's ratings have plateaued and its viewers, growing older themselves, may require more mature themes to hold their attention. According to a study by Mike Dann, the former CBS programming vice-president and now an independent consultant, "the history of a successful sit-com shows a remarkable program loyalty. The millions that started watching *Happy Days* in 1974 will grow up and want more from their viewing." *Happy Days* has to get with its audience, which is getting older.

Dann's theories and the notions of Learism are another way of stating a truth about our culture and our public lives. The citizenry (viewers/voters) is usually ahead of its supposed leaders (programmers/political elites). Whenever television goes over its audience and makes presumptive demands on it, as opposed to going under and doing least-common-denominator programming, television finds the audience is already there. The risk-taking productions of *Roots* and *Holocaust,* the often outrageous humor of *Saturday Night Live,* the adult situations of *All in the Family,* the lively little news dramas of *60 Minutes*—all have done better, in sheer numbers and in audience attention, than initially expected by the cynical observers of popular culture. You can go broke underestimating the intelligence of the American public.

My strong hunch is that there is an audience willing to look at people on television who are nonpretty, nonauthoritative, even nonobjective—and to look at the bald, the deaf, the fat, the old, the whatever. Television worships its demographic research. Well, some of that same research showing how women skew toward young bucks also shows that women and men skew toward performers in television who do substantive jobs, like consumer reporters or investigative reporters, no matter what their age or looks.

A lot of us out there in the audience liked Joe Wershba and would like to see more of him. But we're ahead of the CBS News bosses. They liked him, too—up to a point. One executive said to Wershba—jokingly, of course—"Get a rug [toupee], and we'll make you an anchorman."

TWELVE DAYS OF TERROR! THE THREE MILE ISLAND STORY

CHAPTER 7

Press coverage of the Three Mile Island nuclear accident began offhandedly Wednesday morning, March 28, 1979, when the managing editor of the *Waynesboro* (Pennsylvania) *Record Herald* passed on to the Associated Press news service a tip that central Pennsylvania state police had been put on alert in the Harrisburg area. By the time the crisis ended, two weeks later, anchorman Walter Cronkite on CBS News would talk of "12 days of terror." The press coverage of that period was anything but casual; rather the manner in which the accident at the nuclear plant at Three Mile Island, Pennsylvania, was reported by all the media, and particularly by television, had become an issue in itself.[1]

In any story different actors have different agendas and different messages to convey. This was true of the events at Three Mile Island, a nuclear power plant licensed by the federal government and operated by the Metropolitan Edison Company of Pennsylvania. There were at least three sources of messages: the press, the electric company, and the government. The press grew progressively dissatisfied with the messages of the other two, and they, in turn, grew critical of the press. By the end of the crisis, the White House was spreading the word around Washington that President Carter thought the news accounts of Three Mile Island were outrageous, exaggerated, irresponsible. One distinguished nuclear scientist told me that the television coverage had been pronuclear; another equally distinguished nuclear scientist told me that it had been antinuclear. Most television viewers—ordinary people and presidents and physicists alike—tend to approve of materials that confirm their own judgments or prejudices and to disapprove of contrary information. The scientist who thought television's coverage was proindustry opposes nuclear power; the scientist who thought television was anti-industry favors it. Enough disagreement existed about what television did, and did not, show and tell viewers that our News Study Group decided to examine precisely what appeared on the three networks, from the first news tip to the final reactor shutdown. We found at Three Mile Island that

1. Television news moved with admirable responsibility initially, to the point of being cautious and slow to report developments.

2. Television news reported carefully both industry and government accounts from within the plant, though with a growing suspicion that the full story was not told.

3. Television news eventually proved to be unprepared, or unwilling, to put together the specialized analysis and detailed explanation needed to clarify the whole story; at times, in fact, it avoided promising, but risky, reporting leads in favor of more conventional, and safer, coverage.

To back up these conclusions with specifics, we found it helpful to organize the Three Mile Island coverage into three phases.

First Alarm

Most news organizations had no trouble recognizing a major story in the making on March 28, and each network quickly dispatched reporters to the Three Mile Island plant, or more accurately, to the plant gates, since the state troopers were barring access to the plant itself. On Wednesday night, March 28, each network devoted a long (by network news standards) lead story to Three Mile Island. The ABC *World News Tonight* in particular was evenhanded, noncommittal. Anchorman Frank Reynolds began:

Good evening. For many years there has been a vigorous debate in this country about the safety of the nation's 72 nuclear-energy power plants. That debate is likely to be intensified because of what happened early this morning at a nuclear-power plant in Pennsylvania.

On the *NBC Nightly News*, John Chancellor was also low-key. The cooling system in the nuclear-power plant had broken down, he said, but went on to stress that there was "no danger to people outside" and that the plant was shut down. Then followed reassuring reports quoting Jack Herbein, vice president for power generation at Metropolitan Edison, as well as some state officials and Met Ed workers. Next NBC's Carole Simpson introduced some material from the Critical Mass Energy Project, a group she described as "opposed to nuclear energy." The Critical Mass spokesperson maintained that the Three Mile Island plant had been plagued with safety problems since its opening a year ago.

The *CBS Evening News* coverage the first night was noteworthy because there was considerable reworking of the opening words of Walter Cronkite at the beginning of the program. This is the lead, the headline, and broadcast journalists take care to strike the right tone. After what one CBS executive remembers as three or four rewrites to get the right tone, America's premiere broadcaster said to 16 million viewers tuned to the top-rated evening newscast:

Good evening. It was the first step in a nuclear nightmare; as far as we know this hour, no worse than that. But a government official said that a breakdown in an atomic-power plant in Pennsylvania today is probably the worst nuclear accident to date. There was no apparent serious contamination of workers. But a nuclear-safety group said that radiation inside the plant is at eight times the deadly level; so strong that after passing through a three-foot-thick concrete wall, it can be measured a mile away."

Cronkite later in his report brought up the motion picture, *The China Syndrome*, mentioning "the current movie about a near-catastrophic nuclear meltdown" and assuring viewers that plant officials had assured the public that wasn't the situation.

The network reporters on the scene then offered cautious, factual accounts, but at the same time distanced themselves— sensibly, it turned out—from the story by carefully attributing the statements to officials of one sort or another. Thus Bettina Gregory on ABC said:

. . . The NRC (Nuclear Regulatory Commission) said, "There's a hell of a lot of radiation in the reactor building . . . and [some] was detected as far as one mile away." Officials of Metropolitan Edison conceded that some workers may have been contaminated, but they insisted this was not a serious accident. They said only one-tenth the amount of radiation needed for a general alarm escaped.

And with equal care, Gary Shepard of CBS News reported:

Officials from Metropolitan Edison Company, which operates the plant, attempted to minimize the seriousness of the accident, saying the public was never in danger.

Then followed a tape of Met Ed's Herbein, who said:

We may have some minor fuel damage, but we don't believe at this point that it's extensive. . . . We're monitoring for—for airborne contamination. The amount that we found is minimal. Very small traces of radioactivity have been released from the plant.

The impression the television viewer got was clear: the system had worked. As Max Robinson said on ABC News, "The plant did just what it was supposed to do, shut itself off, but not before some radioactivity escaped." Most viewers, it's fair to conclude, went to bed with little thought about Three Mile Island. When they got up the next morning, March 29, and turned on NBC's *Today Show,* they first heard a soothing reference to the malfunction at Three Mile Island, followed by Walter Creitz of Met Ed talking of the unparalleled safety record of the civilian nuclear-power industry.

That night Three Mile Island again was the lead story on the three network newscasts. The tone on NBC was reassuring: John Chancellor reported that the reactor was hot but normal, the system was operating. On ABC the nuclear malfunction had been moved up on the scale of seriousness to a nuclear accident. Still, ABC reported, the situation was serious but not dangerous. There was a general feeling of postmortem in the newscasts; what remained was for Met Ed to accomplish the complete cold shutdown of the reactor, to begin its extensive cleanup effort and—the thrust of the story now—the long inevitable investigations to find out what had happened. Walter Cronkite seemed to put Three Mile Island in the past tense, and as a mishap at that:

Good evening. The questions still pour in about the nuclear accident. . . . More than 24 hours after the mishap, there is more heat than light in the confusion surrounding the incident. Critics charge "cover-up" . . . even as an industry spokesman says, "The system worked. . . ."

On the other networks, people stories replaced the reactor as the focus. Reporters interviewed area residents concerned about radiation as well as members of Congress who had heard from people concerned about the causes of the accident. NBC's David Brinkley described members of Congress as agitated. ABC was the most people oriented of the network news organizations; its reporters went across the road from the plant to a neat row of suburban homes for comment from a resident. By Friday morning, March 30, the *Today Show* was reporting that the danger was minimal.

Less than two hours later, the calm was broken. An NBC *News*

Update—one of its thirty-second newsbreaks between pro-grams—informed viewers that more radiation had been re-leased into the atmosphere around the plant. Four hours after that, another NBC *News Update* carried word that Pennsylvania Governor Richard Thornburgh had asked for the evacuation of all pregnant women and preschool children within five miles of the plant. The story was building from low-key to high voltage.

The network news that Friday night jolted viewers. Each net-work devoted well over half of its broadcast to Three Mile Island. Frank Reynolds opened on ABC with these words:

Good evening. The news from the Harrisburg, Pa., nuclear-energy plant is much more serious tonight. For the first time today an official of the Nuclear Regulatory Commission said there is the possibility, though not yet the probability, of what is called a meltdown of the reactor core. That would be, in plain language, a catastrophe.

Walter Cronkite was even more chilling:

We are faced with the remote but very real possibility of a nuclear meltdown at the Three Mile Island atomic-power plant. The danger faced by man for tampering with natural forces, a theme familiar from the myths of Prometheus to the story of Frankenstein, moved closer to fact from fancy through the day.

A young journalist I know, a New York City resident, would vividly remember the effect of Cronkite's words on her. Upset by the ominous bulletins and updates during the day, she recalls, she had hurried home to tune into CBS. After all, she thought, the calming voice of Walter Cronkite had helped us all through earlier national traumas—riots, assassinations, astronauts in tricky orbital maneuvers. He would get events in perspective. But Cronkite, she recalled, scared her more than the earlier bul-letins had.

Trouble at the Source

With hindsight, we can see that Cronkite and CBS, along with other news organizations, were mainly reacting to the informa-tion presented by state, federal, and company officials. As these officials lost their self-assurance, television reflected this. When these officials began contradicting one another, the news began to sound contradictory. That led to confusion among the media audience. Deplorable as this might be for the formation of public opinion, it was minor compared to another area of confusion—the events taking place inside the Three Mile Island plant. Underexperienced technicians had misread valves and contributed to the original reactor troubles, and further errors were hampering the search for corrective measures, or so we all were to learn later.

For example, a key clue to the damage that occurred early on Wednesday (day one) inside the reactor core was handed to operators early that afternoon. A pressure spike was clearly traced on a recorder sheet. But no one looked at the sheet until Friday, after two full days of consistent underreporting of the amount of core damage. The oversight, an NRC official later explained, may have been due to what he called the hassle factor in the control room—noise, flashing lights, people getting in one another's way.

In most catastrophes there is a dominant element of what might be called honest confusion. Because of it, no one needs to erect elaborate conspiracy theories to account for what is reported. In the case of Three Mile Island, we saw twin delusions develop: the initial underestimation of the mishap and the subsequent overestimation of the possibilities (what games theory people call worst-case analysis). On Friday, the day of the specter of meltdown, Joseph Hendrie, the NRC chairman, complained that he and Pennsylvania Governor Thornburgh didn't know what was going on. The governor's information, Hendrie said, was ambiguous, and Hendrie admitted that his own information was nonexistent. These two officials, responsible for the safety of millions of Pennsylvanians, Hendrie concluded, were "like a couple of blind men staggering around making decisions." It was an apt image. Looking at the coverage, we can see

that the press was dragged along as the third blind and staggering man.

The Unfilled Picture

Television news has the power to convey feelings, impressions,
auras. In the case of Three Mile Island television first gave the
feeling of nothing more than alert; next came the sense of
reassurance, and then the evocation of dangr. In this respect
television did approximately reflect the reality of the Three Mile
Island events. That is why different people saw different things.
There was something to please, or displease, everybody. Television at its best should do more than hold a mirror to events. The
record of the coverage of Three Mile Island shows that there
were efforts to do more than repeat the official line of the
moment. There were attempts by television journalists to speak
in their own voices. Unfortunately, television news begins to
falter when it tries analysis. Explanations, at least in the case of
Three Mile Island, went by too fast, graphics were too care-
less, scripts radiated tabloid-think, with words too urgent—
lethal, massive, dreaded, nightmarish; or too bland—mishap,
malfunction.

Later that Friday night each network had the opportunity in
special reports to give the necessary time and thought to the
possibility of meltdown. How each responded reveals something
about network news organizations and about television news in
general. CBS News chose to do a one-hour report, immediately
setting itself apart from the thirty-minute reports of ABC and
NBC. On almost all counts, the CBS special report was better
than the other two. Walter Cronkite and correspondent Steve
Young had time to explain clearly the situation inside the reactor as of Friday. Mitchell Krauss had time to look at past nuclear-
power plant accidents. Robert Schakne, who emerged as
perhaps the most informed correspondent during the week, had
time to raise the key question of acceptable risk-taking in the
development of nuclear power.

The shorter ABC and NBC reports suffered by contrast. ABC's was wide but not very deep, a report touching on Three Mile Island, other reactors, the White House, Congress. On NBC John Chancellor was a model of judiciousness: he refused to scare anyone. Calmly, professorially, he showed a drawing of the plant. Chancellor achieved the best tone for television, noting the contradictions and misstatements and saying, "In terms of information, this thing is a mess. . . ." It was a good insight, and could have been used as a lead-in to an analysis of the efforts to control information at Three Mile Island. Instead it was Chancellor's sign-off. NBC opened the door but did not walk in.

Detailed explanations of any kind, whether about nuclear reactors or nuclear politics, appear to tax television's resources. So it was with Three Mile Island. Just as Met Ed's technicians seemed ill-prepared for their trip into the unknowns of an exposed reactor, so too did television's generalists seem over their heads in this particular assignment. This leads to a question often put to news organizations: why not hire specialists who are at ease with scientific disciplines? The usual answer is that television can't employ full-time chemist-correspondents or physicist-correspondents or geneticist-correspondents. Where would it end? But the coverage of Three Mile Island showed the advantages of arranging for expert consultants to help out the television producers and writers. CBS News, for example, arranged for George Rathjens, one of the nation's most knowledgeable nuclear specialists, to be available for telephone consultations. Because he had no special hard line to push—he's prosafety *and* pronuclear—he helped sort out some of the confusion for CBS.

Three Mile Island also raised questions that had nothing to do with technical matters. The story had political and economic meanings that required analysis and explanation. For example, the push for nuclear power largely comes from the manufacturers of the equipment rather than from the utilities operators like Met Ed. An explanation of this in terms of jobs, investments, and political influence would have helped. Yet in these nontechnical, politically sophisticated areas, where the networks are supposed to be at ease, they proved to be relatively sluggish in their coverage.

Television was also much too diffident about looking into the causes of the accident. It didn't put authority's feet to the fire. Were there financial incentives involved in getting Three Mile Island's unit two on line before the end of calendar year 1978? Did safety get shortchanged as a result? According to a passing reference in *Time* magazine, Met Ed qualified for tax investment credits and deductions of around $40 million by meeting the year-end deadline. That aspect of the story needed development. But even when CBS News took an unhurried look back at the story in May ("Fallout from Three Mile Island"), it was remarkably gentle on the plant operators and remarkably reluctant to recreate what went on inside the plant.

The accident at Three Mile Island, when the record is reviewed, proved to be a triple test of competence. It tested the ability of industry to build and operate safe, efficient nuclear plants; it tested the ability of government agencies to regulate these plants in the public interest, and it tested the ability of the press to cover complex stories in a clear, coherent, nonpanicky voice. With the benefit of critic's hindsight it is possible to see that industry, government, and press didn't quite measure up. The three institutions that should be helping the public—and the public's elected representatives—determine the future of nuclear power in the United States needed help themselves. All the bad habits the news institution has built up—overreliance on authority, grabbers, lack of memory, preoccupation with style at the expense of content—came into play at Three Mile Island. Because we've seen them so often in our other case studies, we know the Three Mile Island coverage was no accident.

IS TELEVISION UNFAIR TO LABOR?

CHAPTER 8

In the first episode of *Skag,* an NBC dramatic series offered with a great flourish of trumpets and drum rolls in early 1980, the chief character, fifty-six-year-old Peter Skagska, suffers a stroke, has sexual problems with his wife, and watches as a younger man moves in on his job as a foreman at the steel plant. And that's only the beginning of Skag's problems. Skag has a selfish son he's helping to put through medical school, another son with laid-back ways, and a fifteen-year-old daughter who is her high school's premiere Miss Roundheels. Yet Skag never loses his dignity. He does, once, feel a bit put upon. "What about some kind of liberation for guys like me," agonizes Skag.

The complaint is supposed to reflect an undercurrent of public feeling that American society, and by extension American television, has belatedly taken heed of the interests of women, blacks, hispanics, and gays, but in the process has neglected the ordinary guys, white, middle-aged, hardworking, bluecollar, the People Who Built America.[1]

This new interest in the workingman involved some major talents: the writer Abby Mann, executive producer Lee Rich, and Karl Malden (who plays Skag). Moreover NBC made a serious investment in the series. *Skag* premiered as a three-hour Sunday night special followed by a one-hour Thursday night episode. All this talent and time may strike you as either admirable and artistically honest or gimlet-eyed and cynical. Last fall a University of Pennsylvania study, done in collaboration with the Screen Actors Guild, concluded that television programs rarely show blue-collar people on the job. Is television at last recognizing the contributions of the Skags of our society, the men who pay their taxes, keep their houses tidy, and do a full day's work? Or is television less nobly consulting its own self-interests and the audience demographics, which show that a lot of Skagska families watch a lot of television and have long felt ignored by the media? After all, it wasn't long ago that Richard Nixon and Spiro Agnew elevated to national political strategy the feelings of resentment of a short-haired, supposedly square silent majority.

The cynic's view may be understandable. Television's labor relations have never been very good. From the low-budget *Life of Riley* of the 1950s and 1960s to the well-financed *Skag* of the 1980s, television has always uneasily coexisted with the American workingman. The television image consistently lags behind the reality of the work place. Consider William Bendix's Riley and Jackie Gleason's Ralph Kramden of *The Honeymooners* (also the 1950s and 1960s), Carroll O'Connor's Archie Bunker of *All in the Family* (1970), and Karl Malden's Skag (1980)—three generations of prime time television workingmen.

Riley worked in an aircraft plant, Kramden drove a bus, and his friend Ed Norton (Art Carney) worked in the sewers. When they talked, they were semiliterates: dese and dose and demmers. Maybe they finished high school, probably not. In fact, these "contemporary" workingmen were already anachronisms, throwbacks to a departed (if not dear) era. From 1945 on,

America began changing rapidly, and the character of work in America changed fundamentally. By 1960, census figures reflected the shift from blue-collar to white-collar work. While it is possible to quarrel with some of the census categories, it was nevertheless true that by the late fifties fewer people had manual or production jobs and more had managerial or service jobs. Television workingmen Riley and Kramden were not the typical workers of the postwar era; they were figures from the thirties and early forties.

For viewers to demand realism, or characters reflecting the census, would be obviously foolish. Riley and Kramden were primarily vaudeville or cartoon strip figures, stereotypes, designed for laughs. Television aimed for entertainment; it had no intention of treating working people realistically, or of upholding the dignity of work. The humor was skit humor, often turning on blockheadedness or plain ignorance. In 1971 Norman Lear supposedly brought television up to date, introducing a lacing shot of reality into television comedy. Archie Bunker was a laboring man, working at the loading docks in the construction trades; occasionally he drove a cab. He had a house in Queens—Kramden and Norton rented apartments—but he was, like them, unable to master the language or the world outside his door. Mainly, he was intended to be archetypical: Archie shocked the world by speaking on television the thoughts that workingmen most surely had. He referred, in prime time, to spiks and hunkies, said that Jews were sharp with money, patronized his wife, Edith, and otherwise made plain his blue-collar feelings about women, blacks, and politicians. The point was, his mind was closed.

Actually, Archie Bunker was also a caricature of a near-extinct breed. Norman Lear has told interviewers that he drew Archie Bunker in part from memories of his own father, a salesman in Hartford, Connecticut, forty years before. (Another part of the character came from a popular British series that provided the original Archie Bunker model.) By the late sixties and early seventies, years after Lear had gone west to open-collar Hollywood, the blue-collar bigot of the popular imagination was a diminishing figure in the real world. A number of studies documented evidence that contradicted the common television view of the workingman. For example, Richard Hamilton's *Class and Politics in the United States* showed that on questions related to desegregation and equal opportunity for blacks in jobs, housing, and even schools there was simply no difference between social classes. Another study showed that on eight open-housing and antiwar referendums during the late sixties workers were often marginally more progressive than their presumed social superiors, the businessmen and professionals. Finally, although many blue-collar workers did defect to Nixon, his strongest support came from the putative higher stratum of society. Fifty-four percent of union families voted for Nixon in 1972, according to a Gallup poll, but the professional and business group gave him 69 percent. A more accurate television character would portray a well-dressed, well-spoken white-collar employee with Archie Bunker's views—but that wouldn't be funny.

Norman Lear at least tried. He belatedly played catchup to the reality of the seventies by spotlighting more contemporary characters in *All in the Family*. Eventually, new series were created for these characters: *The Jeffersons* (rising black middle class), *Maude* (women striking out into the world), and, mostly recently, *Archie Bunker's Place*, where ex-laborer Archie Bunker has become co-owner of a bar. The eighties casting at best matches sixties social reality: Archie is now white-collar managerial, though still stuck with his Bunker mentality. Even this may be too much realism. A conservative group called the Media Institute, now established in Reagan's Washington, has recently objected to the Bunker portrait as antibusiness.[2]

Abby Mann's Skag is a more sympathetic character, at the same time up-to-date and anachronistic. Skag treats his wife with respect (no dingbat she), honors his father from the old country, and attends church without believing in religion. Skag deplores the passing of the old values, the morality he was raised to believe in. Skag, in short, suffers from the generation gap, as a character and as a television series: these are the shocks of the sixties being treated tardily by television in the eighties.

Skag is a remembrance of things past. According to Lee Rich of Lorimar, Abby Mann grew up in Pittsburgh. "The stroke was about Abby's family," Rich explained to me, "although Mann's father wasn't in steel, he was in some other business. Abby and I wanted to do something for television for Karl Malden, and Karl's dad was a Pennsylvania steelworker and a man of Serbian descent." More memories of the past.

Listening to the character Skag, we can hear echoes of Nixon era complaints without the Nixonism. But the dialogue of the work place has changed since then. How fresh is Skag's observation that "life is different today from when we were growing up"? Can we, in the 1980s, treat as news Skag's discovery, in the episode called "The Wildcatters," that management and unions often enter into sweetheart deals at the expense of the workers? The real news about labor in the same week that *Skag* premiered included newspaper stories—and this is just a sampling—abut (1) the closing of steel plants in the industrial northeast, (2) the migration of jobs to the sun belt and to other nonunion states, as well as to overseas locations, (3) the continued rise of computer-based technologies, (4) the changing face of labor in the United States as workingwomen and Hispanic workers grow in numbers.[3]

Given the talents involved in *Skag*, I had hoped that the program would explore these eighties concerns in subsequent hours. But early in the series the basic story lines were being injected with heavy doses of hype. In one show Skag makes a trip to an Atlantic City casino, where he meets call girls and singer Tony Bennett in a guest-starring role. Skag's trip to Atlantic City was not a good sign; it was as if the packagers had to find glitz in gambling casinos because Pittsburgh didn't make for production values. When hype appears, cancellation cannot be very far behind, and *Skag* was dumped at the end of its short 1980 season.

Despite the *Skag* disaster, television has been trying to be more relevant. In the CBS series *Alice* Linda Lavin plays a waitress in a Phoenix diner. She's slinging hash and bringing up a teenage son at the same time, and doing it realistically. The program won a pink-collar citation from the National Commission on Working Women for the best portrayal of a workingwoman on television. But the competition wasn't all that keen. Alice looks good largely in contrast to the two clichéd waitresses who flank her—one, the dumb, wide-eyed kid on her way to spinsterhood; the other, the bottle-blonde veteran always keeping sexual score.

On the other hand, CBS did present a believable workingwoman in its television movie *The $5.20 an Hour Dream,* also featuring Lavin. A good part of the film was shot on location in an engine factory in the City of Industry, east of Los Angeles. The overhead cranes and girders, the rows of metal lathes and grinders, and the stacked engine blocks provided a gritty realism. Lavin herself took instruction from two factory women, learning to do several assembly line jobs. The actress came away with a sense of the meaning of blue-collar work: "The difficulty is not so much the physical labor . . . but the sheer monotony," she was reported as saying.

The $5.20 an Hour Dream did begin to break down some of the conventions of prime time television. Usually, television finds it hard to recreate the reality of work—pink-, white-, or blue-collar—because television plays it safe. I don't necessarily mean safe politically or even economically, but safe creatively. The safe way is to write and present characters within the accepted limits of the stereotype, of what everyone knows about workers, women, waitresses, or Serbs.

Walter Lippmann sixty years ago referred to the pictures in our heads, largely false, of the outside world. One of the writers of CBS's popular series *Dallas* has confessed that he never spent a day in the city of Dallas before the series began. But the Dallas he envisioned—wheeler-dealers, the oil crowd, cheating wives, a Peyton Place South—looked right. It matched the stereotypes, the pictures in our heads. As the ratings show, a lot of people seem willing to take the CBS *Dallas* as a substitute for the real Dallas, just as a lot of people may take Skag's world for a real-life steel town. In the case of *Dallas* it doesn't make much difference. The audience knows, or should know, that it is getting high-class trash, a soap opera in prime time. *Skag* purported to be true, telling it like it is (a sixties expression that could have popped up anytime on *Skag*). It was not a bad show by any means, and the critical reception was favorable; even the hometown *Pittsburgh Press* found the series had "an integrity and depth missing from the typical television image of blue-collar America."

But television, like any art, has to be judged absolutely as well as relatively. Shots that open and close episodes with location scenes cannot substitute for the texture of a society or a neighborhood. In Martin Ritt's *Norma Rae* we were made to feel the mind-rattling noise of a textile plant. In Robert Benton's *The Late Show* we sweated as Art Carney, playing the broken-down, private eye Ira Wells (blessedly, a long way from sewerman Ed Norton) took a crosstown bus and dragged his gimpy leg up a steep Los Angeles street. Norma Rae and Ira Wells tell us more about working people in America than Alice and Skag, not because Ritt or Benton are smarter, not because films are better than television, but simply because these moviemakers have worked harder at their jobs. That lesson seems to elude television too often: the work ethic still lives, and pays.

Skag was a presentation of NBC, the third-ranking network in the ratings as the 1980s arrived. One theory of television holds that the number three network should be more experimentation minded, which should mean quality in programming. Free of the pressures of the don't-rock-the-boat psychology of number-one-ship and of the wait-we're-almost-there feeling of number two, the trailing network, it is said, can be exciting, innovative, imaginative. It can go after the premium audiences, younger, professional, better educated, that the advertisers for automobiles and air travel say they want to reach. But there is a contrary theory that holds that the number three network tends to go under rather than over in its level of programming, aiming its appeal at the thirteen-year-olds of all ages in the mass audience. "The advertisers *say* they want quality," a station manager once told me, "but give them numbers, raw numbers, and they're happy." To get numbers, there's no secret where to aim—between the neck and the knees, with car chases, blondes in cutoff jeans, call girls at Atlantic City casinos.

When Fred Silverman was president of number three ABC, his network took the under approach. When Silverman joined number three NBC, he gave interviews suggesting he was going to go over rather than under. There is a widespread impression that NBC has, in fact, used its trailing position for quality programming aimed at "upscale" audiences; for example, *Skag, Shogun, Centennial, NBC Magazine* with David Brinkley.

What actually has happened, however, is a bit more complicated. There was *Shogun,* recommended by the National Educational Association, but there was also the *Adventures of Sheriff Lobo* and *CHiPs.* NBC had gone over and under at the same time, had publicized its quality efforts while standing clear of the schlock, much like the real estate agent who points to the bay view while keeping you away from the waste disposal plant on the other side of the property. And why go under? Well, because television programmers have an under view of blue-collar America, the masses out there.

I talked to a number of people about how under-decisions are made rather than over-decisions. It turns out that the television bureaucracy doesn't behave much differently from any other bureaucracy. The open shirts and the gold chains, the Malibu beach houses and the Mercedes convertibles, the sense of the creative process (words, music, sets, acting), all give off a glow that tends to dazzle the casual observer. But organizationally television is not much different from General Motors or the State Department.

At the bottom are the troops, working under great pressure of budget and cost-effectiveness. "They've got all that time to fill on the schedule. That maw never closes," one writer says. To the workers, it's just a job; they are assembly line grunts turning nuts and bolts. And in any case, there are limits to what can be done to tell a story in the 25- and 50-minute format of the network series.

Next, at the middle level, are the managers. They are trying to figure out what their bosses want. In any given season, there are a limited number of buys that can be made, a half dozen new programs at most. "The successful gets imitated," a film studio executive explains. You can't gamble with the unusual." Near the top are the programming chiefs and production specialists. One woman who has been at this level says: "You have to be a pro with experience, you have to speak the language, you have to have some talent to break through to this level. But by the time you learn the system and make it, you've lost your soul. You've become opportunistic . . . you begin to patronize the audience." Finally, there is the man at the top, who has arrived there by learning the system better than anyone else. One of my informants says of the boss, "he didn't get there by being innovative but by figuring out what *his* boss wanted."

Quality programs are expensive; they are hard to do and take more time to do. Audience responses are not predictable. NBC attempted quality of a kind with *Skag*. When the show wasn't an immediate ratings success, it was cancelled. The last lesson to be learned is the need for a degree of patience and confidence. But that's not one of the lessons the system teaches.

ARABS AND ISRAELIS: THE SHIFTING MIDDLE EAST IMAGES

CHAPTER 9

If a spaceship from Venus had landed in the United States during the last few months of 1978, it might well have reported back to home base that two of the most prominent politicians in the American election campaign were named Anwar Sadat and Menachem Begin. Through the fall weeks, the Egyptian president and the Israeli prime minister dominated American television news programs and newspaper front pages as much as the certified candidates, appearing at news conferences, dinner meetings, and the usual high-visibility media events that characterize our electoral politics.

Yet the Venusian scouts would not be completely talking through their antennas. Begin and Sadat were courting the American media and the American voter, and for reasons not too dissimilar from the motives of the United States politicians. The Egyptian and Israeli leaders both campaigned as if television coverage was the best way to win American public support for their positions—and to undermine support for their opponents. Both Egypt and Israel sought American votes because these votes, in turn, often help shape American foreign policy. Their competition was very determined.

Because the Middle East stakes were, and are, so high, the competition between Arabs and Israelis puts enormous pressure on the American media, particularly television news where, the surveys say, so many millions of Americans get their primary information about foreign events. A degree of public diplomacy has always accompanied the private negotiations of modern nations. With the parties in the Middle Eastern dispute vying so openly for American support, however, the 1979 Egyptian–Israeli–American negotiations represented a significant case of television diplomacy, one worth studying.

Until the 1970s the American television networks have been able to handle the Middle East without too many political dilemmas. The story seemed clear-cut. For thirty years American policy tilted toward the Israelis in their dealings with the Arab nations. There were many reasons for this American tilt, including self-interest, sympathy toward a democratic (non-Communist) friend, and the pivotal role of American Jewish voters in American presidential politics. Beginning in the mid-1970s, however, recognition of America's growing dependence on Middle East oil has exerted pressure in another direction. The consensus of pro-Israeli support was bent, if not shattered. Both policy makers and the press began to feel a need to "understand the Arab position." Divergent interest groups began thinking they saw unfair or even slanted reporting of Middle East news. Some Jews claimed to see blatantly anti-Israel coverage; worried critics thought they saw that the press was ready to "abandon Israel," as one American-Jewish commentator put it. Complicating the story in the period 1976–79 still more, the Carter Administration itself became both a mediator and a party to the negotiation. American news organizations were faced with two or three versions of the same event—Israeli, Arab, Carter Administration's.

To find out how American television news organizations have responded to the new television diplomacy, our News Study Group examined the Middle East coverage offered by ABC, CBS, and NBC over a period of several months. We began by focusing on the handling of the Camp David summit in September 1978 but soon found that we had to go back to the period before Carter, Begin, and Sadat went to the Maryland mountaintop—and also had to continue the story beyond Camp David. Even then we realized that we were dealing with a continuum of events rather than any sharply defined shifts. With this caution in mind, we nevertheless found some general patterns.

Peace Maneuvers

Anwar Sadat visited Jerusalem on November 19, 1977. The Egyptian leader took initiatives that were almost literally breath taking. Ezer Weizman, the former Israeli minister of defense, in his memoir *The Battle for Peace* traces the whole peace process to that moment, which caught the Israelis off guard and never allowed them to recover fully.[1]

About this time the Carter Administration began the shift in foreign policy away from the effort to achieve a comprehensive solution to the Middle East by assembling all parties, including the Palestine Liberation forces and the Russians. The new U.S. plan sought to bring together the Egyptians and Israelis only for negotiations. A new peace process was underway, and the American media, normally sensitive to major Middle East developments, stepped up its level of attention.

The first highly visible event was Sadat's dramatic visit to Jerusalem. This created a genuine spectacle that American television mobilized all its resources to record. No concrete results came out of the visit. As Weizman observed, less attention was paid to what Sadat said than to where and how he said it. But the media images of Sadat were unforgettable.

Until that trip the dominant Middle East images had been, on the Israeli side, the indomitable Golda Meir and the courageous, khaki-shirted Israeli citizen-soldier. On the Arab side the popular images that registered most strongly among Americans were of Yasir Arafat, unshaven and adamant, and the bearded oil potentates, remote and secretive in their flowing tribal robes. Journalist D'jellout Marbrook offered these images of what the word "Arab" connotes: terrorist, hijack, cruelty, oil embargo, sand, boycott, greed, torture, feuds, slavery.[2]

The figures of Sadat and Begin beamed from Jerusalem represented a reversal of symbolic images. Sadat appeared to be urbane, pipe-smoking, English-speaking; he not only looked western but sounded statesmanlike when he talked of peace. Begin, on the other hand, appeared as a remote, even fanatical, figure. He seemed intransigent on the question of Israel's territorial control of the West Bank and Gaza regions. The shift in the presentation of appearances paralleled certain political developments. On several issues the Carter Administration's position was closer to the Egyptians' position than to the Israelis'. From the point of view of official American policy, Sadat was the peace figure. Consciously, but probably not with complete calculation, American television tended to reflect the new "even-handed" Carter Administration line with an evenhanded style of its own. Television was only being fair, by its lights, when it depicted Begin and Sadat as it did. Nor was it far from the truth. If there is one heroic figure in Weizman's own memoirs, Theodore Draper noted in his review in the *New York Times*, it is Sadat; he knew his own mind and refused to budge.

The Framework for Peace

The summit meeting of Sadat, Begin, and Carter at the presidential retreat known as Camp David was not so much an exercise of secret diplomacy as private diplomacy. Carter's press secretary Jody Powell briefed the press daily, controlling the pace of the news as White House people always do. The White House press regulars had good sources, on the president's staff and at the State Department, who steered them in the right factual direction, and the correspondents, in turn, passed on this information to their editors and viewers. The right direction, quite naturally, also pointed toward administration policy, and the atmospherics that the administration wished to create.

For example, when the summit opened, television newscasters stressed, again quite naturally, the importance of the event but avoided talking about the chances for success or failure. "We wanted to avoid setting high expectations," Les Crystal of NBC News explained to us. As it happened, the cautious approach of television news fit the Carter Administration press strategy toward Camp David, a strategy of news control and unhopeful press briefings. When someone sets initial low expectations, it tends to make the final successful results look even more spectacular. It is a tactic Prince Hal boasted of in Shakespeare's *Henry IV,* and a trick familiar to high-wire artists and jugglers (who always miss a beat or bobble a club before the grand finale).

In point of fact, when the Camp David process began, there were more forces working for success than for failure. Begin and Sadat each feared failure if the blame could be pinned on him in the eyes of the American audience. Carter feared failure because he was fighting against his public image of the decent, but inept, chief executive. (He never won the battle.) A few correspondents, for instance, Bob Schieffer on CBS, were to suggest to viewers the notion of failure as a spur to success, but no one carried the idea forward sufficiently to clue viewers to the not-so-subtle game being played.

The administration's tight news control also meant that television—or any other news organization—couldn't dig out the dramatic private moments of the summit. At one point Sadat packed his bags and was ready (so he said) to leave, but Carter talked him out of it. At another point, Moshe Dyan had packed and was ready (so he said) to leave. Through the entire stay, the Egyptians and Israelis were so estranged that they could only communicate with each other through Americans. None of this became news for the simple reason that the stories were not included on the official press briefings.

While this hidden drama was going on, the networks had to rely on other resources to fill out the summit story they had proclaimed as important. NBC News had Henry Kissinger on its payroll to do analysis. He served as a knowledgeable commentator, though he was hardly disinterested; official lines still dominate the news even when the officials in question are no longer in official positions. Marvin Kalb on CBS was a far tougher analyst, as might be expected. At ABC Barbara Walters obtained exclusive interviews with the Shah of Iran and with Jordan's King Hussein (more official news). The Shah interview came over as highly favorable—no surprise—to the Shah.

The televised ceremony making formal the summit's success took place live from the White House East Room, Sunday, September 17, 1978, at 10:28 P.M., when some 100 million Americans were around their sets watching the new fall offerings, a timing that led some critics to reach predictable conclusions. Did *Battlestar Galactica* (ABC's premiere), *King Kong* (the NBC movie), and the Emmy Awards from Hollywood (CBS special) serve as a crowd collector for a White House public-relations triumph, engineering by Carter's media advisor Gerald Rafshoon? Clever as Rafshoon may be, he could not arrange for the Egyptians and Israelis to agree to settle thirty years of conflict in time for a Sunday prime-time television show. However, once an agreement had been reached reasonably close to Sunday prime time, Rafshoon's chance to get maximum exposure for Jimmy Carter was too good an opportunity to pass up. News executives at all three networks readily concede that (1) they did not hesitate a millisecond about deploying their cameras once the White House had announced the ceremonies, (2) they probably were used to boost Jimmy Carter and his achievement, and (3) they would do it all over again the same way.

Down from the Heights

The euphoria of Sunday night carried over into Monday and Carter's appearance before a joint session of the Congress, again live and in prime time. But television news was also out looking into the follow-up stories, particularly from the interests not present at Camp David—Jordan, Syria, the PLO, the Saudis, and the Russians.

The follow-ups also produced the usual little-people-react stories. This is one step removed, if that, from the man-in-the-street interviews that newspapers used to do by sending a reporter outside the building to ask ten unrepresentative passersby their opinions (some papers still do this). The trouble with such individual samplings is that they are just that—one voice that may represent the opinion of one voice. When an Israeli settler declared to the American television camera, "I didn't come from Miami Beach to be an Arab," this hardly explained the complicated issue of Israeli security that was behind the settlements dispute.

In this follow-up phase, too, Barbara Walters, John Chancellor, and Walter Cronkite produced lively interviews with Sadat and Begin. After Carter's speech to Congress, Frank Reynolds ended the ABC News special with the firm observation that, "Problems remain, but there is no reason to downgrade the Camp David results." ABC found reasons the very next night. On the ABC *World News Tonight* Frank Reynolds reported soberly that the "two-day-old framework for peace was already showing signs of strain."

This study of the record of Middle East coverage by television during the Camp David period yielded several lessons. First of all, the conventional charge of media bias conventionally defined is easiest to dismiss. When Egypt joined Israel as a force for peace, in American eyes the news reports about Sadat that followed were less likely to appear biased. But this doesn't mean that the news is neutral. The so-called objectivity of the news is inevitably shaped by perceived national interests. Egypt may be receiving fairer treatment, but it's the Syrians or the PLO who now cry bias. At Camp David ABC, NBC, and CBS carefully meted out equal, straight-down-the-middle news treatment to the Egyptians and the Israelis (though the news analysts necessarily sounded more subjective).

Balance, however, is not the sole test of journalistic performance. In these days of television diplomacy, there is a serious challenge for the television networks—how to avoid being used by the newsmakers. This challenge centers on the need to avoid being *too* responsible to the whole process of dramatic news, getting carried away by events because they deliver exciting images and good television. The highly visual values of good television can make for poor information unless accompanied by drab explanation. The newsmakers and officials, both foreign and domestic, know how to present good television events and thus use the media for the official purposes of public diplomacy.

I'm somewhat diffident about cuffing television on its rabbit ears for not being something else. Television newspeople may be excused for perhaps feeling put upon. If they stay close to government sources, they stand accused by the carpers of echoing the carefully plotted official lines of top-down news. If they pursue the little people's story, bottom-up news, they may produce only emotional posturings. If they set standards for official success, they will be open to the charge of creating news. If they don't set expectations, it seems as if they are abdicating on the analysis and explanation of the news. If they aggressively seek interviews with world leaders, they may provide only uncritical slogans aimed at influencing American public opinion. If they don't get these exclusive interviews, they appear noncompetitive. They are damned if they do and damned if they don't.

What do critics want anyway? One needed step is in the direction of more interpretation and background reporting. Lately, television news has been doing more in-depth reports, longer news, and sometimes three- and four-part series. ABC has a good corrective in its Seven Day Rule. According to Av

Westin, vice president and executive producer of ABC's *World News Tonight,* he and his fellow executives critically watch each story when it is telecast and will redo the story within seven days if they are not happy with the coverage. "Sometimes when the words and pictures are brought together in a breaking story, the results are less than fair," Westin says. Perhaps the most important step would involve redirecting the aim of the camera and rechanneling some of the energy of the news-gathering process. All three networks can turn their cameras around and examine their own roles in the new television diplomacy. If television news has become a stage upon which international maneuvers take place, then television should tell that story as openly and unself-consciously as possible. The risk, of course, is that the public would be let in on how the process really works. Viewers would understand how much of the news is made for them. The Sadat image, for example, did not just happen. He may have been what he seemed to be, decent, intelligent, moderate, but it also happens that he engaged American public relations specialists, including a former Nixon White House press official, to help out in the presentation of the Egyptian case in the American media. (The image builders were successful, so much so that, when Sadat was assassinated in the fall of 1981, he was seemingly mourned more in the United States than in Egypt.) The dissection of this process by the media would contribute, no doubt, to an increased skepticism on the part of the viewers. Such an attitude would be in no one's interest—not the Israelis', not the Arabs', not the Carter or Reagan Administrations'; nobody's except the national interest.

TAKING HOSTAGES: THE AYATOLLAH KHOMEINI AND THE AYATOLLAH CRONKITE

CHAPTER 10

Journalism is a calling that in some part lives off other people's misfortunes. While there have been many breaking crises for journalists to cover in recent years—the economy and energy, the Miami race riots, the Cambodian famine, the Cuban boat people, among others—one especially painful episode challenged American journalists. The seizing of the hostages at the American Embassy in Teheran in November 1979 was, to put the most even face on it, an opportunity for journalists, a chance for scoops, for prestige, for public service, but also a chance for sensationalism and public *dis*service. The margins for success or failure were especially wide for television journalism, both because surveys show that a majority of Americans now get their foreign news from television and because the revolutionary forces in Iran tried to use American television for their own political advantage. The Iranians can read the Neilsens as carefully as anyone else.

The hostage story, then, put ABC, CBS, and NBC News under

the gun, literally in Teheran, and metaphorically in Washington, where the network news coverage was watched as an important factor in foreign policy calculations. Some columnists, in fact, suggested that the Carter Administration was pushed to try the abortive helicopter rescue mission in part because of the constant high visibility given the hostages on the evening news (all those sign-ons and sign-offs about America held hostage . . . Day 230 of captivity for the Americans in Teheran). Jimmy Carter's actions, James Reston wrote in the New York Times, came as much in response to the "Ayatollah" Cronkite as to the Ayatollah Khomeini.

Were ABC, CBS, and NBC News playing the Iranian revolutionary game this past year? At the very least, have the networks been playing their own rating game? We know that the ratings did not suffer from the crisis atmosphere. Audience figures show that some seven million new viewers joined the fifty million or so regular watchers of the network evening news in the first months of the hostage story, seemingly direct evidence of profiting from other people's misery. The example usually cited to "prove" what American television will do for ratings was the interview of Marine Corporal William Gallegos. Hostage Gallegos was made available to U.S. television in December 1979 by his captors, who set certain preconditions about the kinds of questions that could be asked, the amount of editing allowed, and the timing of the interview. They wanted it aired in prime time. Judged by their sophisticated bargaining positions, the student militants apparently majored in American mass media studies at Teheran University. Gallegos was offered to all three networks, but only NBC News—the network with the poorest ratings—agreed to the terms of the interview.

NBC News defended its action by arguing that legitimate news interests were served in the broadcast—that American citizens, and administration officials, could hear and see for themselves some of the conditions of captivity.[1] ABC and CBS adopted a rather Olympian posture. "We would not surrender our editorial control, and that's what the Iranians wanted us to give them—control through unedited access to an American audience," Roone Arledge, President of ABC News, explained to me at the time. Yet a month before, correspondents from ABC and CBS—along with NBC and the Public Broadcasting Service—got in line in Teheran to interview the Ayatollah Khomeini himself. Questions had to be submitted in advance, though editing control remained with the television people. All the correspondents went ahead with those restrictions, except public broadcasting's Robert MacNeil, who objected more on grounds of pecking order than principle. MacNeil had been promised an exclusive interview but was relegated to fourth in line by the ratings-conscious Iranians.

A television interview with the leader of the fundamentalist religious sect responsible for the revolution in Iran—the country, these same television networks had been assuring us for decades, that was America's strongest ally in the Islamic world—is genuine news, even with restrictions. So, too, are the controlled interviews with hostages, as long as viewers are told of the preconditions of control. Perhaps more to the point, however, was the night-after-night attention to Iran that seemed to put television in the position of making news, not just reporting news.

The news-making charge has a familiar old chestnut sound to it, and the networks' defense has a certain cliché sound as well. As Roone Arledge said, "The hostages are a big story, and it's television's responsibility to cover it. The story occupied the President every day, it occupied the newspapers every day, it occupied the public every day."

Still, the hostage story received much more nightly television attention than, say, the capture in 1968 of the U.S. Navy vessel Pueblo and its crew by the North Koreans. In part this was because television had access to Teheran, while it did not have access to North Korea. To that extent, Arledge agreed, "Television has kept the hostage story going." It is precisely this access that the press had in Teheran which helps explain what made the hostage story unprecedented and removes it from the level of cliché discussions. The Iranians committed an act of war against the United States—and then invited the American media, print and electronic, to cover the story, to have access live and in color behind enemy lines. The invitation was extended so that the revolutionary forces could get their own access, via the American media, to American public opinion (as well as providing television and circuses for Iranian domestic consumption). When the American media ceased to be useful to the Iranians, as they saw it, the revolutionary government ordered the cameras capped and the U.S. reporters out.

Given this record of manipulation, another scenario was possible for American television coverage. One network correspondent suggested to me, privately, that ABC, CBS, and NBC should have noted the taking of the hostages the first night and then carefully modulated their coverage subsequent nights. That way, the Iranian militants would not have been able to play up to the television cameras and newspaper photographers day after day, trucking in demonstrators to shake fists and chant "Death to Carter" and otherwise staging media events and arranging photo opportunities. "We've been excessive," the correspondent declared.

The response of network news executives to the charge that they were used is threefold. First, they make a distinction between the initial crisis coverage and the subsequent vigil coverage. "At the beginning," Arledge said, "the question was: 'Are the hostages alive or dead?' 'Will there be war or peace?' We put on what we could get, and there was lots of U.S. flag burnings and mobs shouting. That's what was happening." But when the life-or-death phase seemed over, coverage settled down into more informational programming, such as ABC's late-night specials. These tried to fill in our thirty-year gap in understanding about Iran, about the Shah's record, about the operations of SAVAK, his secret police.

Next, as far as modulation is concerned, the networks maintain that they did downplay certain aspects of the story. Specifically, videotapes of American demonstrations against Iranian students in California were edited to avoid creating broadcast images that might further inflame the Teheran marchers. Network coverage of possible U.S. military options were self-censored for similar reasons. "We didn't report all we heard," one executive told me.

Finally, there is the question of being a propaganda conduit. Around Day 100 of the hostage story, CBS News' President William Leonard received a letter from a U.S. senator. "I wonder what would happen," the senator wrote, "if American networks stopped paying so much attention to the Ayatollah and his gangs? What would happen if you simply stopped beaming Iranian demonstrations night after night into our living rooms? The purpose of television is to bring us the news—not propaganda. I believe that without the encouragement of television cameras, the demonstrations in Iran would slow down and stop." Leonard's answer is that "removing our cameras and reporters wouldn't bring the hostages home one day earlier, and would end our role as the freest press in the world." He adds: "What our critics fail to realize is that the American people deserve to know the full extent of the Iranian problem, not the watered-down, self-censored view of that crisis. To pretend that the violent feelings of many in Iran toward the Shah—whether they are right or wrong—would not exist without our cameras being present is simply to avoid reality."[2]

The networks' reply to the charge of manipulation, then, is that the public responsibility of the press is to report as much of the story as it can to its audience. There is even an argument in favor of what I think of as the broken bones approach to press performance. For a moment, take the extreme case and say that U.S. cameras didn't show up at the embassy gates; then also say that, as a result of this all-networks decision, the crisis in some way is resolved and all the hostages released. Still, that resolution isn't the role of the press. Or, as Roone Arledge says, "the precedent for the press laying off a story in the interests of 'national security' or the 'national interest' are, to my mind, all bad." In other words a few broken bones—the continued misery, and perhaps death, of hostages—is part of the price of a free press.

Perhaps more people would be more willing to pay that price if journalists in general, and broadcast journalists in particular, owned up to the extent that they are being used routinely by news sources. When Jimmy Carter summons the cameras to a 7 A.M. announcement on the day of the Wisconsin primary, an eminently forgettable news story (quick, class, who can remember what it was about?) but an important voting date, official manipulation of the press became part of the story. When the TV news camera is being used by sources—governmental, private, American, Iranian—the viewer should be let in on the game as a matter of course. It's admirable that television told viewers how events in Iran have been staged for the benefit of American television audiences. Now we need more continuing examinations of news making, some sort of truth-in-news labeling, whoever the source of the manipulation.

The best demonstration of the powers of official manipulation, and of the press' relative impotence in those political and policy matters that count, came in mid-May, 1980, when the hostage story appeared to shrink visibly before our eyes. After the aborted rescue attempt of April 24th, the Iranians ordered out remaining U.S. journalists. This cut down the outward flow of stories somewhat. There were still other western journalists in Iran, but in Washington at the same time something equally important to the flow of information happened. The Carter Administration cut down its own flow of information—its briefings, its political statements, its air of crisis management. In effect, the administration declared the situation no longer news.

John Herbers in the *New York Times* was among the few journalists who correctly caught the shift when he wrote: "The subject of the American hostages in Iran has receded both as a leading item in the news and as an issue in the political campaign, at least in part, some officials say, because of the Carter Administration's decision to stop treating it as a major crisis." *The New Yorker* magazine also commented on the "news about the absence of news" in its Talk of the Town section:

> The moment of change came when the president made his incomprehensible statement that world affairs had become more "manageable" after the failed mission, thus freeing him from his vow to stick to business in the White House and refrain from campaigning for re-election as long as the hostages were being held in Iran. The news organizations, which so often follow the president's lead, fell in step with him this time, too, and inaugurated their policy of ignoring the hostages.
>
> Since the disastrous mission to release the American hostages in Iran, coverage of the hostages, which once blanketed the news columns and the airwaves almost to the exclusion of any other news, has evaporated. In an instant, the frantic urgency about their release dissipated, and they seemed to disappear from the face of the earth. Gone were the interviews with their friends and relatives, gone the impromptu delegations of clerical would-be peacemakers, and gone the whole sideshow of eccentric free-lance meddlers, including the congressman who went to Iran to conduct his own negotiations and the American Indian who wanted to mix up his cause with the highly publicized hostage question. Gone, too, were reports of the "rising impatience" of the American people, which was thought to have so much to do with the decision to launch the rescue mission, and which was supposed to play such an important role in the fluctuating popularity of the various presidential candidates, according to the polls. Now the time that was said to be "running out" politically for the Carter Administration if the issue was not resolved has lengthened again, and appears to stretch out into the indefinite future.

In short the crisis was declared over—the late Senator George Aiken's solution to Vietnam: call it victory and bring the troops home for a parade. The Iranian coverage, for all its ambiguities, did leave one definite legacy for broadcast journalism. ABC News, under Arledge, moved vigorously into the 11:30 P.M. time slot, first with nightly updates on the hostages and then, in March 1980, with a regularly scheduled newscast called

Nightline. Arledge's background had been in television sports before he took over at ABC News, and some critics feared he would bring a "Wide Wide World of News" insensitivity to his new assignment. But by the simple stroke of initiating *Nightline,* ABC effectively doubled the amount of international and national news available nightly on the network. On that ground alone, ABC deserved two cheers, if not three. Some rivals, and critics, at first dismissed *Nightline* as neonews or non-news, a rehash from the early evening newscasts. But these criticisms overlooked two factors; first, many people, particularly younger professionals, are not at home to see the 7 P.M. newscasts; second, *Nightline's* willingness to spend six or eight minutes on a single story must be counted an improvement over the headline service of the early evening. Sometimes more, later, is better.[3]

Looking back at the early hostage coverage, the familiar pattern of the blockbuster story emerges. We journalists get onto the big event—Pope in Town! Mount St. Helens Erupts! John Lennon Shot Dead!—and ride the news furiously, until the story and the audience appear exhausted. Then we want change, any change; there's been too much coverage. Enough overkill. But there are certain big events, like the Iranian revolution, that don't go away. *The New Yorker's* Talk of the Town writer suggested that the hostage story was overplayed at first and then underplayed, that the interests of the nation and the audience were better served with more modest coverage.

This raises public policy questions about journalistic processes—a fancy way of saying that our daily news dramas often have serious real-world consequences. Journalists try to avoid such discussions about their work; we are in the business of truth, not consequences, or so we say.

But even granting, for a moment, this view of press freedom, does the same argument apply to news dramas that swing all the way to drama? Consider another Middle East story that appeared on television, the PBS-distributed program, *Death of a Princess.* This British-made film purported to be the story of a beautiful young member of the ruling family of Saudi Arabia who was beheaded for her adulterous affair with a commoner. While it wasn't a grabber like the hostage story, it had some sex appeal, TV-wise. Normally, the programs offered by PBS engage a small audience (by commercial standards). But *Princess* was preceded by an official "letter of deep concern" about the alleged inaccuracies, distortions, and falsehoods in the program. The letter was sent by the Saudis to the U.S. State Department and forwarded on to PBS by the Acting Secretary of State Warren M. Christopher, who added his own worries about the "sensitive issues" involved (we get our oil from these people). This, in turn, was accompanied by newspaper advertisements from the Mobil Oil Company urging PBS to review its decision to broadcast the program in light of the best interests of the United States (that is, Mobil does business with these people). As a result of all this posturing, a furious debate was joined on the future of America's oil supply, the meaning of the national interest, and the sanctity of the First Amendment. In response to all the excitement, the show had to go on—if for no other reason than to prove PBS' freedom and insulation from government and corporate pressure. (Mobil, along with Exxon, Texaco, and the U.S. Congress, is among the biggest contributors to public TV.) Predictably, too, the program achieved the highest ratings in public television's history, besting the competing programs on the commercial channels. Although the Republic still stood after the telecast, the price of Saudi oil did go up for American consumers, as it has been regularly for a decade.

Death of a Princess was a documentary drama. Docu-drama quite simply is a bastard television form that, on the evidence of the past few seasons, deserves beheading itself—with fifty lashes reserved for *Princess'* creator, a Britisher named Anthony Thomas, and *Princess'* American sponsor David Fanning of WGBH-TV in Boston. In the docu-drama form, the episodes and the characters are dramatized depictions "based on" real-life events and people, rather than journalistic representations of reality. A documentarian setting out, say, to portray the covert activities of the U.S. Central Intelligence Agency over the last thirty years—the subject of another major, though largely unremarked, documentary called *On Company Business* shown on PBS around the time of *Princess*—has a basic assignment. He or she must find the principal players in the story, persuade them to sit still for the camera, then ask reasonably intelligent questions designed to get out the facts, or versions of the facts, and finally relate these individual parts to some general idea or pattern. This diligent approach does not exclude drama in the sense of enticing viewers, holding their interest and building up to confrontations and/or conclusions and enlightenment. All that is supposed to happen in documentaries happened in *On Company Business*. Its producers, Howard Dratch and Allen Francovich, did their work over a four-year period. Hard work, in fact, is the mark of documentary investigation.

But Thomas and Fanning chose another route. By his own account, film-maker Thomas could not penetrate the reclusive Saudi establishment (in the same way that Dratch and Francovich managed to get the CIA subjects on camera). The closed Saudi society, with its feudal ways, frustrated Thomas. It happens all the time in journalism—reporters coming up short, finding dry holes after months of digging. Usually, journalists have to take their lumps ("Boss, I've wasted three months of my time, and $15,000 of your money. . . ." "Well, don't let it happen again." Or, less charitably: "You're through here.").

Thomas and Fanning went ahead anyway. They hired actors, leased Egyptian settings, combined characters and created a dramatic story line with stops along the way for sexual byplay, blood and guts (one tangential scene is recreated in war-torn Lebanon to add melodramatic effects) and a lot of jaw clenching and unclenching by the Thomas journalist-character as he pursues his Roshomon-like story, with different characters providing different versions of the truth.

The purpose, of course, is to provide production values in

conventional television terms. The Thomas character doesn't just interview a source sitting in a chair—first the camera pans along a beach stocked with bikinied women, and then it comes in to the cafe where the interview occurs over coffee and melon. But Thomas and Fanning want us to know that they are telling their sex-and-violence saga of the poor little princess not just as prime time entertainment but to reveal the bigger political story of traditional Islamic society beset by the intrusive effects of petrodollars, western secularism, and hedonistic consumerist values.

The appropriate reply to this pretension is, Camel dung! The Islamic revolution, Arab attitudes toward women, the inequities of a feudal society, the American economic and political stake in the Saudis' rule are all important real-life stories, too important to be brushed by on the docu-drama track of the beautiful princess. For too long, American television documentary makers have ignored the rest of the world. Few of us know very much about Islam; the region cries out for careful investigation and documentation (if for no other reason than because of our oil dependence). But that course requires persistence and hard work.

An American documentary maker pronounced a proper epitaph for *Death of a Princess* when he told the *New York Times:* "In a way, I was filled with envy—every interview was superbly paced, every person seemed perfectly cast, and there was never any problem with language. When I do a show, I have to deal with real people, not with actors. It's a lot harder. . . ."

And a lot more honest, too, he might have added.

RETURN/RENEWAL: THE DAY THE HOSTAGES CAME HOME

CHAPTER 11

In the remarkable twenty-four-hour period from 8 A.M., January 20, to 8 A.M., January 21, 1981, the release of the hostages from Iran and the inauguration of Ronald Reagan—events separated by 6,000 miles but related in the political fortunes of the United States—moved along a parallel course toward resolution, meeting on television, the medium preeminently capable of creating a split-screen reality. While some news events are covered best by print journalism (only a long reading, for example, could do justice to Nixon's White House tapes during Watergate), January 20th and the days that followed belonged to television, with the networks acting as the producers, the prompters and—in a new and disturbing role—the reshapers of reality. We witnessed not one narrative event, but two entwined—return/renewal; transit home for the hostages, the transfer of authority from the Jimmy Carter to the Ronald Reagan presidency.

CBS's Walter Cronkite told viewers they had seen "one of the great dramatic days in American history." Jeff Gralnick, the executive producer of ABC's *World News Tonight,* also had superlatives for the day: "It was the most fragile, complex technological operation ever put together in the history of television." Les Crystal, NBC's senior executive producer for the coverage, recalls that on Tuesday night, when the hostage plane landed in Algiers, 60 million Americans—the three networks' total—"shared in a common experience, mass communications in its true sense."

Three of us at the News Study Group at MIT, after sharing these same experiences as viewers and then replaying the three networks' videotapes and reading the transcripts, were drawn to another, less lofty, perspective about the return/renewal day.[1] We found that with the split-screen reality, we got a double vision. Was it a great victory we were celebrating? Or, was it a wound we were covering over?

The television images were confused and ambiguous—the hostages running a gauntlet of jeering Iranians at the Teheran airport; the dogged Jimmy Carter leaving the White House for the last time without achieving final security for the hostages, defeated again by the Iranian clerics who may have cost him his presidency; the new president, relaxed, telling a Capitol Hill luncheon that the hostages had left Iranian air space; the flood-lit Algerian runway as the fifty-two Americans clambered from their aircraft, each an individual in dress and demeanor. And with these onrushing messages, we viewers felt our own personal split-screen of tumultuous emotion; pride/anger, joy/guilt, confidence/doubt, patriotism unabashed/patriotism tempered.

Television, indeed, could give us the highest of highs and then gratuitously dismay us with the most banal idiocy. By most accounts, the purest moments of return/renewal came at 4:45 P.M., when the last float of the inaugural parade, carrying the Mormon Tabernacle Choir, stopped before President and Mrs. Reagan at the reviewing stand. The women in the choir were dressed in blue; the men in blue suits, white shirts, and red ties. The blue-and-white float carried the lettering AMERICA: A

GREAT NEW BEGINNING (from a line in Ronald Reagan's speeches). The hostages were en route home. The choir sang "The Battle Hymn of the Republic." President Reagan brushed away a tear and then walked with his wife to the White House.

Then, on NBC, the cameras cut to Tom Brokaw, co-anchoring NBC's parade coverage. He commented on the fact that Ronald Reagan and his brother Neil were teary-eyed, and observed that they were probably thinking of their childhood in small-town Illinois and of their father, "an affable sort, a shoe salesman, though, who had more fondness for liquor than he might have—might have been better for his family if he had not been so fond of it. But anyway they've come a long way. Today, President of the United States. A grand day for him, obviously. The hostages have been freed. . . ."

NBC was not alone in the gaffe department; each network had its share. But each, too, had its triumphs. To make a personal but, I hope, fair evaluation of the performance of the three networks' hostage coverage, I broke the story down into three phases:

1. The captivity. On one criterion alone, I commend NBC News: It did not get into the day-counting gimmickry of CBS and ABC (America Held Hostage . . . Day 255, etc., etc.). Thus NBC did not pour superheated hype on a political situation already volatile.

2. The return. CBS was the winner for its technical excellence, for Dan Rather's sharp commentary, and for the skilled use of former hostage Richard Queen.

3. The aftermath. ABC deserves all the praise it has received for Pierre Salinger's story of the secret negotiations, broadcast as a three-hour edition of *20/20*. This show was nothing less than a quantum leap for television news. The investigative reconstruction of a complex event has traditionally been the exclusive province of our quality newspapers and news magazines. These reconstructions—called ticktocks in the trade—are

usually presented a week or two afterward. ABC News was on the air within forty-eight hours with its clear beat, and a valuable story.

Looking back at the networks' coverage, it became clear to us at MIT how television reshaped the day and our reality. Three characteristics of television, it seems, made the day greater than the sum of its parts and masked the longer-term meaning of events. In the end, television's hardest news did what critics accuse television's entertainment of doing: giving the public what it wants.[2]

The first quality, as Gralnick says, is television's technological prowess, its ability to make all the world a stage. The networks are proud of the logistics of return/renewal day: Washington wired for sight and sound at a dozen different vantage points; land lines bringing images of families from twenty states into New York studios; satellite transmissions emanating from Germany and from Algeria. "Live from Algeria," proclaimed a CBS superimposition picture—a thrill in itself to viewers, even if they didn't know that the satellite feed blacked out as the plane approached Algiers and didn't come on again until just fifteen minutes before the plane landed.

At ABC Gralnick recalls that his crews had been preparing in earnest for the hostage release since October 1980: by early November an ABC studio was built in Frankfurt near the Air Force base where the decompression hospital had been set up. People were also posted to Zurich, Geneva, and the Azores—"in case of need." All told, ABC had about 450 people at work on the two stories, evenly divided. About the same number were deployed at CBS and NBC.

The capabilities of the new technologies were determining the magnitude of the event before it occurred. "I had my hands on a series of keys," says Gralnick, "which allowed me to talk to Peter Jennings (in Frankfurt), Ted Koppel (in Washington), Algiers, and the rest of the world. It was a machine ready for the biggest story ever."

The networks had wired the world so well that reporters covering the swearing-in ceremony at the capitol, sitting in the best seats in the house, only had to turn to little TV monitors to find out what was going on half a globe away at the Teheran airport and half a mile away in the motorcade of the outgoing president and the president-elect. Even state secrets became public over television. Right before noon, President Carter, riding to the swearing-in ceremony in the limousine, received a telephone call from his aides that the hostages' departure would take place within 15 minutes. House Speaker Thomas P. "Tip" O'Neill, who was in the car, told NBC's Tom Pettit and ABC's Brit Hume, who in turn broadcast the word.

At times television itself brought the latest news to officials. Mrs. Theresa Lodeski, mother of hostage Bruce German, was interviewed as she celebrated in the bar she runs in Edwardsville, Pa. Moments later, former (by a few hours) Secretary of State Edmund Muskie telephoned her: "I just saw you on NBC, and you looked terrific. I'm so happy for you."

Technology and planning awarded each of the networks the scoops that helped drive the TV machine. CBS had a phone arrangement with Tony Allaway, of the *London Times,* at the Teheran airport. "As soon as the plane left, Tony drove to a secluded spot ten minutes away and phoned us," says Joan Richman. ABC's Jennings, in Frankfurt, managed two calls to the Teheran airport control tower and to the VIP lounge and then advised New York. And each network had former hostage consultants, earlier returnees—Richard Queen at CBS, Lloyd Rollins at NBC, and William Quarles at ABC. They acted as spotters when the planes landed and offered now-it-can-be-told interviews when final freedom was assured.

These interviews were among the most gripping and substantive narratives, particularly Richard Queen's with CBS's Dan Rather and later with Richard Wagner. Rather scored one of the sharpest beats when he held up to viewers and to Queen two still photos of the hostages running the gauntlet in Teheran, flanked by their guards:

Rather: Do you recognize any of the militants?
Queen: Yes. I'm pretty sure that one was about the slimiest of the militants. I called him Weasel, and my roommate called him Rat Face.

But often the technical machine produced trivia. Even with two stories as big as the inauguration and the hostages, the networks could not maintain a consistent level of newsworthiness in their reports for live coverage stretching to twelve and thirteen hours. The inauguration coverage was slowed by fillers like the price of stand tickets, the parade horses and how they get used to bagpipe music, and reruns of the fireworks. This need to fill was also evident at the inaugural balls, where celebrants were mindlessly interviewed. In general all three networks appeared uncomfortable at the balls, with Barbara Walters in pink and lavender admitting that she felt guilty at the celebrations while the hostage story was unfolding. But the networks were trying to have it both ways, looking in at the parties while suggesting that it was somehow inappropriate to celebrate.

Though the networks were always on top of the hostage story, they could not be omniscient. The demand that correspondents produce something fresh and newsworthy every half hour or so could not be met. This was particularly so late Monday night. Judy Woodruff, in an NBC *Special Report*: "We don't yet know, frankly, what is going on. We only know that we are told to stand by and wait." Lloyd Dobyns, also of NBC: "We are all becoming very good at standing by and waiting. This is what we know so far: almost nothing, except there has been some sort of hinting at financial arrangements."

Also, the dependence on foreign or non-network news sources in Teheran and even in Algiers meant that nearly all the news was qualified as "unconfirmed report." "We have it from two sources that . . ." "According to a UPI report . . ." "Information about what we are seeing is sketchy." As Roger Mudd put it, "We are really flying by the seat of our pants. . . ."

The second characteristic of television, again displayed clearly during the coverage, is its unparalleled ability to convey feelings. Television is an emotion-rich, information-poor medium. Ideological critics of television faulted the January 20th coverage for empty chatter, rushes of emotion, lack of reflection (Are they all really heroes?). To some, it looked like a national soap opera. But those critics (on the left) who wanted the day given over to an examination of the misdeeds of the "corrupt, false" Shah, who provoked the Islamic revolution, and those critics (on the right) who wanted an airing of Jimmy Carter's presumed culpabilities in "allowing" the hostages to be seized and then to languish in captivity were all looking in the wrong direction. Television fulfilled a different role that day.

In truth, the nation wanted, needed, a psychic lift, not cool analysis, and television obliged, knowingly. "The country is very, very frustrated right now," said Les Crystal. "We had been humiliated for 444 days, and we had a need for heroes, for success; we wanted to bury our feelings of impotence, and the hostage release gave the public a chance to express its yearnings for old values, for standards, for old feelings about the country's prestige." ABC's Gralnick used almost the same words: "The nation needed purging from 444 days of embarrassment." A third world country—non-Christian, small and weak except for its access to oil—had defied a nation accustomed to being number one. "We managed to rub the nose of the biggest superpower in the world in the dust," television quoted an Iranian negotiator as saying.

Television judged that people wanted to express feeling. Walter Cronkite, respected, attended to, can delineate as well as reflect mood. Tuesday morning around 10:30, when it seemed clear that the Iranians were holding the hostages until Carter was out of office, Cronkite said: "I try to remain the cool correspondent, impartial and unaffected by events, but it seems like the most uncivilized final touch to an uncivilized performance that I can imagine."

Journalists, hostages, families became as one in their feelings. CBS's Joan Richman remembers most of all the scene in the CBS studio as the hostages deplaned in Algiers: "Richard Queen and Barbara Rosen, hostage Barry Rosen's wife, were with us. As the doors of the plane opened, Barbara and Richard moved closer together until their shoulders were touching. Finally they were holding hands. As the first hostage came out they were shaky and teary. Then they broke out in smiles from ear to ear. We cut to them and put them on the air at that moment." Another CBS staffer, looking around the studio tearfully, saw she was not alone: "There wasn't a dry eye in the house."

With the hostages' freedom, it was time for anger to be replaced by joy. The inauguration's rhetorical New Beginning, in fact, became a real-life new beginning for the 52 and for 225 million other Americans. Pent-up emotions could be freed, including the long-unfashionable feelings of patriotism. The inauguration parade, with its images that resonated from our childhood, and the nation's, became the vehicle for celebration. Television that afternoon brought viewers a sea of familiar and reassuring symbols: an opening pan shot of the American flag at full mast over the White House, the new president on the reviewing platform, the flow of high-school bands and riders on horseback, smart-stepping Marines and Coast Guard. These were comforting sights and powerful images of American power and stability, of a nation newly rejoicing and meeting the affirmation of its dreams; they were the validation of the basic soundness of our institutions.

But if the hostage story had only collective or national meanings, it would not have become the extended dramatic experience it did. The hostages also carried private weights. They were sons or daughters, fathers, sisters, brothers, and husbands. Each of us could identify with one of them. We view the networks' tapes and transcripts and see that the most visceral, personal

words are repeated: family, home, freedom, separation, re-
union. Who among us has not waited for a plane—or train or
bus—carrying a loved one? Who hasn't prepared to receive
someone long absent? When NBC's cameras showed, in a few
masterful cuts, the young children of one of the hostages preparing to go to meet their father—modest frame house . . .
helping neighbors . . . carefully folded new clothes . . . ap-
prehensive ride to the airport, stuffed animals clutched protec-
tively—a universe of personal feelings was engaged.

Television helped make their story our story. Not surprisingly, the medium collectively and correspondents individually lost
the journalistic distance that is supposed to separate news events
from news reports. It was appropriate, then, that CBS News
should buy lunch and send it up to the men and women of the
Iran Working Group at the State Department building—and
then allow a prideful Robert Pierpoint to announce the gesture
to viewers.

The fact that the networks brought us, in small and large
ways, the January 20th banquet of emotions comes as a consequence of television's third characteristic—its increasingly com-
manding presence at all our national feast days. Television on
January 20th not only became stage and prompter—the consequences of its technological and emotive powers—but partici-
pant as well. The passive patriotism of the networks during the
inaugural parade became a positively expressed stance later in
the day. Walter Cronkite ended CBS's parade coverage by noting, "We have witnessed a peaceful and ceremonious transfer of
power." And Marvin Kalb, opening an *NBC Special Report* that
night, declared, "It has been a very, very special . . . extraordinary, historic, fantastic day. . . ." America changed presidents,
doing so "without a hitch, and without a coup, and given the
general, revolutionary state of the world these days, that was quite
a political achievement." Thus the two events were finally and
emotionally tied together: The hostage story represented the

results of foreign revolution and anarchy; the inauguration stood for American peace and order.

The seizure of the U.S. Embassy and the hostage story were events that began as insult and injury, legally an act of war. They ended by being heralded implicitly as straight-out victory. Some day Congressional hearings on Iran, as well as the Reagan Administration's stewardship of the nation, will help determine the accuracy of that optimistic judgment. Network television seldom steps out to stage front and declaims its underlying attitude. On January 20th, ABC's, CBS's, and NBC's openness was understandable: the Iranian clerics had jerked them around professionally, too.

Patriotic stances are exceptional. More typically, broadcast journalists get caught up in their magic machines and may not even seen the results of their work. Jeff Gralnick very humanly explains how the process itself takes over: "It will be months," he reflects, "before I can disengage from the technological success and talk about the hostages' release as a human experience. . . ." Maybe years from now the hostages crisis will be remembered as much as an occasion that doubled the amount of network evening news as for a sad episode in the chaotic wake of a militant religious revolution half a world away.

In any case television on return/renewal day moved forward to stage center, playing its own split-screen role of actor and watcher. ABC News achieved the biggest coup of the entire coverage when it offered, later in inauguration week, its three-hour account of the secret negotiations involving the United States, the Iranians, and various Arab and European intermediaries. And how did ABC get onto its great scoop? Two French lawyers, acting as intermediaries, sought out Pierre Salinger, ABC's Paris bureau chief. They thought that Salinger, the former press secretary to John F. Kennedy, would still have some Washington connections to help start the snagged negotiations again. They were right. Salinger aided in restoring the

official lines of communication—while simultaneously beginning to cover those negotiations. He became intermediary/
reporter, two roles in one, a dangerous game for any journalist
or news organization to play. With that development the phrase
"television diplomacy" has taken on a disquieting new meaning.

FULL DISCLOSURE: JACK AND JUDITH AND NELSON AND MEGAN AND TEDDY AND . . .

CHAPTER 12

Like almost every other insider who worked in Washington editorial offices in the early 1960s, Tom Wicker had heard stories of John F. Kennedy's swinging life in the White House. Also, like almost everyone else Wicker, then the *New York Times* White House correspondent and now its best columnist, had remained silent and did not publish those stories. Almost two decades later he is still wondering why, this time out loud.[1] Had he possessed some good evidence—say some statement or documentation supplied by one of John Kennedy's supposed woman friends—Wicker declares that he most certainly would have broken his neck to get a story into print, especially the one involving Judith Exner. It would read something like this:

Washington—President Kennedy has been having intimate meetings in the White House, apparently with the connivance of the secret service, with a young woman known to be personally involved with two Chicago leaders of organized crime.

Reporter Wicker, as well as the other up-and-coming journalists covering the White House, would have written this story even though most of them liked Kennedy's wit, charm, youth, and style and felt a generational kinship with him, probably admiring his politics, too, after the staid and elderly Eisenhower years. The reporters' normal distrust of politicians and the muckraking instincts of the trade would have triumphed over their good wishes for Kennedy's success, Wicker concludes.

I, too, personally felt, in the early 1960s, both of these strong magnetic fields—the pull of Kennedy's charm and the attraction of the big scoop. So I can savor Wicker's argument that "everything a president does speaks to his character and integrity and therefore is the public's business." And I can agree with the journalistic Law of Full Disclosure that Wicker derives from his thoughtful analyses of the Kennedy, Johnson, Nixon, Ford, and Carter years. The law states: Reporters should write, and their newspapers publish, what they know.

Wicker's law is not one of those subjects involving what reporters call inside baseball discussions about the techniques of journalism, details of facts and statistics, the nuts and bolts of the news. Wicker's law instead raises important issues about the way presidents try to control the news, brashly like Lyndon Johnson or ineptly like the all-thumbs Nixon; about the all-purpose use of the fog-gray curtain of national security, usually the first refuge of the government scoundrel seeking to keep secret anything embarrassing, inconvenient, duplicitous, or scandalous; and finally about the issue raised by John Kennedy's alleged sexual athletics: where and how to draw the line between the individual's right to privacy and the public's right to knowledge.

In the last few years the audience for news had two good opportunities to watch journalists struggling to draw the line, in theory balancing competing rights. One story involves Nelson A. Rockefeller; the other Senator Edward M. Kennedy, John Kennedy's youngest brother. It's instructive to look at these two cases side by side and see how much the bookish theory is at variance with the practice of journalists.

Nelson Aldrich Rockefeller, the four-time Republican governor of New York State and vice president of the United States during the Gerald Ford caretaker presidency, died in January 1979. I heard the news on a radio bulletin as I drove through ski country in New England. THE CREATOR OF THE NORTH MALL IS DEAD, the Albany, N.Y., station announced. It took me a minute to realize that the bulletin referred to Nelson Rockefeller. He was responsible for the multibillion-dollar complex of office buildings at the state capitol in Albany. Up in the north country, the mall legacy rated higher than Rockefeller's vice presidency. But everywhere a common theme of the obituaries and editorial appreciations was an awed expression of marvel that a billionaire's son like Rockefeller, who didn't have to lift a finger on this earthly journey, nevertheless spent so much time working so hard in the public's interest. The *New York Tmes*'s James Reston offered this theme when he wrote about how Nelson Rockefeller had died as he lived, at his desk, working, planning, full of enthusiasm for life.

Reston, as he and everyone else now knows, had been caught in that particular nightmare of journalists: the verdict locked into type back on the editorial pages of the paper, even as the case was coming apart with late-breaking news on the front pages. Rockefeller, it seems, had not died in the manner his press spokesman had said he had. The spokesman, a long-time Rockefeller retainer named Hugh Morrow, had, in fact, attempted what looked like a cover-up.

Morrow gave out two or three versions of the governor's final moments. Morrow's first version had the time and place of death wrong—off by one hour and one mile. The apparent heart attack had occurred at Rockefeller's townhouse at East 54th Street in New York and not at his office at Rockefeller Center, as Morrow had first said. There were also questions about how Rockefeller died, what he was wearing when he died, and who was present when he died. A mysterious young woman was belatedly acknowledged to be at his side. Her name was given as Megan Marshack: she was called a research aide and editor for an art book project that Rockefeller was working on. On the fatal Friday night, she was dressed for work in the office in an unusual way; according to press reports she was wearing a long black evening gown. Also Rockefeller was described as wearing shoes but no socks. The two sartorial descriptions just sat there in the first news stories unadorned, unexplained, as big as one of Rockefeller's famous winks. Two weeks later the mystery of the final hours deepened: the *New York Times* after diligent effort uncovered the fact that a second woman had been present, for a time, and had played a part in the attempts to revive Rockefeller. The second woman turned out to be Ponchitta Pierce, the hostess of a weekend show on NBC television. Pierce was a friend of Megan Marshack, and a neighbor in the co-op apartment building where Marshack lived a few doors down from Rockefeller's town house.

Journalistically, then, the story of the last hours of Nelson Rockefeller had everything—famous public figure, mystery women, confusion, and apparent high-level cover-up. There was even the possibility of criminal negligence. Why had Morrow given out false or misleading information? Why had Marshack waited more than thirty minutes to call anyone for emergency medical or police help? Why did she call Pierce, who then came over from her apartment, and finally made the 911 emergency call? Why was Rockefeller cremated less than two days after his death, without an autopsy? (Morrow said cremation was a Rockefeller family tradition, but another brother, John Rockefeller, was killed the year before in an automobile accident, and was not cremated.) And, for that matter, what did twenty-five-year-old Megan Marshack do precisely for Nelson Rockefeller to earn her $60,000 a year salary, plus the $45,000 loan he gave her to buy her co-op apartment? (Under the terms of his will the loan was forgiven.)

One explanation apparent to anyone over the age of thirteen neatly ties up all the loose ends. If Megan Marshack had been Nelson Rockefeller's mistress, and if they had been engaged in some kind of sexual activity or were preparing for such activity that Friday night, then a logical scenario suggests itself: a rendezvous, privacy, excitement, a coronary occlusion *in medias res;* then panic and attempts to revive the stricken man, hasty efforts at dressing or rearranging the scene, the hope that a friend could help or that the circumstances could be kept private or that the press could be diverted

This scenario makes sense in the abstract, and nine out of ten journalists would subscribe to it—privately. Nelson Rockefeller, they told each other, had a long track record with younger women. Just about every reporter who covered him had a story about his personal habits to tell—privately, around the office water cooler or at the bar after work. As long ago as 1964, Rockefeller suddenly divorced his wife and married a campaign volunteer under conditions, as the columnist Joseph Kraft observed, "virtually advertising adultery. . . ."

But the stories of Rockefeller's philandering ways were secrets that the reporters shared with one another and with their editors, and not with their audience (somewhat like the rumors of Jack Kennedy and his "girls"). The only news organization that did any real reporting on Rockefeller's last hours was the *New York Times.* The New York *Daily News,* for whom such a story would seem made—given the *News'* good police sources and its reputation for irreverence—handled Rockefeller's end with the respect that *L'Osservatore Romano* accords to papal affairs. The *New York Post,* after a slow start, gave the story the kind of sleazy attention New Yorkers have come to expect from Rupert Murdoch's Australian hired guns. Mostly, the *Post* rewrote the facts dug out by the *Times,* tricking them out with big pictures, heavy innuendo and come-on headlines aimed to win a few extra street sales. When one of Nelson Rockefeller's grandsons, eighteen-year-old Steven Rockefeller, went on an ABC TV program to talk about his grandfather's death, the *Post*'s page one headline, in 72-point type, read:

I HOPE
MEGAN
MADE HIM
HAPPY.

But generally network television and the other national news outlets were as respectful as the *Daily News,* doffing their caps as peasants do when the master's carriage rolls by for the last time. The *Washington Post,* normally so competitive with the *Times,* confined itself to routine coverage by its own New York reporter. As if unable to find anything to say itself, the *Washington Post* contented itself with reprinting a short elliptical piece from the *Village Voice,* in which Alex Cockburn suggested that Nelson Rockefeller had forever spoiled the devious husband's line, "Dear, I'm working late at the office."

Later, Myra McPherson and Jeffrey Kaye advanced the *Post*'s coverage a bit with a profile of Megan Marshack: "The Woman Who Was There." The story reported that in the summer of 1975, Marshack, then twenty-two and a reporter for Associated Press Radio in Washington, had learned that Nelson Rockefeller liked Oreo cookies. So she bought a box of Oreos, opened it, rewrapped each cookie individually and presented them as a gift to the vice president. According to McPherson and Kaye, a few weeks later Marshack was hired by Rockefeller. At *Newsday* on Long Island, editors were so starved for Marshack nuggets—as long as they didn't have to find the stuff themselves—that they splashed the McPherson-Kaye Oreo story over three full pages.

The more I heard and read tidbits about Megan Marshack, her cookies, her black dress, and her co-op apartment, the more I became convinced that, perversely, a cover-up of a certain kind had worked after all. Yes, Megan Marshack was the topic of jokes on television by Mark Russell, Johnny Carson, and *Satur-*

day Night Live, and yes, I and all the other insiders were convinced that we knew the real story. But when we got away from the office or the corner hangout, and talked to people out there, our readers and listeners, many of them were not in on the story. Without the context of Rockefeller's sexual character—familiar to the insiders but never sufficiently aired for outsiders —the general consumers were out in the cold. They didn't know what they were supposed to be reading between the lines. They didn't know what all the hints and winks were supposed to be about. At least a dozen nonjournalists, average readers, asked me, "What is all this about this girl anyway."

It does no good to dismiss these people as naive. At election time, they are asked to vote and make decisions about public policy. That's why, in theory, the public is supposed to have a right to know. It's not a specific constitutional right, but an evolutionary idea that information is good. And that is why the Law of Full Disclosure should have been applied in Rockefeller's case. It makes no sense to dismiss—as some editors have apparently done—the entire discussion as an unwarranted invasion of privacy. What difference does Rockefeller's behavior make anyway? To say that is to miss the point about public knowledge.

Some of those who understood Nelson Rockefeller in life—and who could reconstruct the situation, the more sophisticated media consumers—have voiced objections to any coverage. As the eulogies put it, Nelson Rockefeller was a great American, a public servant, a man of honesty, devotion, piety, decency, etc. . . . So he went out on a banana peel. . . . His public life and works are there for all to admire.

True enough. But what do we know about the lives of our public figures? The answer is, Mostly what their publicity apparatus wants us to know. Definitions of greatness and service may differ and may or may not be affected by whether the great man in question kept one or ten women. The coverage of Rockefeller's last hours was circumspect in the most fundamental ways. Isn't it just possible that Nelson Rockefeller's death was consistent with his life? Isn't it possible that both were largely fictions? The critic and writer John Hess put it succinctly in a commentary on New York's public television station:

He began his career trying to drive Americans underground, into air-raid shelters, and he remained a hawk to the end. He nearly bankrupted New York with grandiose and foolish building projects, using a ploy by John Mitchell to avoid a vote on those moral obligation bond issues. He was ultimately responsible for the nursing-home scandals and for the Attica massacre and passed the buck to his appointees. He filled the prisons with a savage drug law and dumped mental patients. As vice president, he played the buffoon at the last GOP convention, then retired to peddle overpriced art reproductions. Through it all, he enjoyed a reverent press.

That press, of course, remained reverent to the end, with the *Times* alone deserving credit for at least surfacing the facts and presenting them in a cool, objective manner. But its finely tuned stories make me wonder if it is possible to be "too responsible." The press can't have it both ways. It can't be tough and follow the facts wherever they lead and then suddenly grow coy. With Megan Marshack and Nelson Rockefeller the press had to Go All the Way.

If there is some hard information available that would serve the public interest, then it should be shared openly with the public. An accounting of Nelson Rockefeller's character is one such story. Every day, the power brokers and power seekers of our society—men like Rockefeller, Kissinger (his clone), and others—come before us with their public-policy solutions and ask us for their support. We ought to know them better; a man's public life and his private habits emanate from the same animus. Journalism can't be arranged like some Victorian novel where the writer discreetly pulls the curtain over the climactic scene after allowing the rustle of a long black evening gown. Rockefeller's death illuminated his life, once the puzzle could be put together, a good validation of the Law of Full Disclosure.

The Rockefeller case also shows why full disclosure seldom works in textbook fashion. It runs up against two unwritten rules of journalism. The first is that journalists usually tell their best stories to each other but not necessarily to their publics. The second is that, while all souls may present themselves as equals on judgment day, the rich and the powerful in our society are given unusually good letters of introduction by a complaisant press.

The coverage of Senator Edward M. Kennedy's presidential bid a year after the Rockefeller-Marshack episode would seem to be a case of full disclosure running wild. Here was a candidate who wanted to talk about serious issues and instead the press was fixed on the shrill theme of "Chappaquiddick," sounding like a stuck whistle.

When Roger Mudd of CBS interviewed Senator Kennedy on the eve of his presidential announcement, roughly one-fourth of the program centered on the events at the Dike Bridge some ten years before. A few weeks later, the *Washington Star* weighed in with a three-part series complete with the now-obligatory questions. How much drinking took place at the cookout? Was there really a coverup? Along with this came a wheezy organ obligato, featuring heavy-footed reporter Martin Schram at the keyboard: "Chappaquiddick. The word tumbles out with a cadence all its own, like a cantata that carries an undercurrent of timpani. The sound is at once familiar, yet somehow foreboding; precise, yet somehow undefined."

Even the news stories about Kennedy and the baggage of his past made news themselves. The *Washington Post*'s Haynes Johnson and Richard Cohen, also at the organ but with a somewhat lighter tread, each wrote columns on the relationship of private morality to public behavior, and on the press' treatment of Kennedy. And when the *New Republic* decided not to run an article by Suzannah Lessard about Senator Kennedy's womanizing, that became a running story. (The piece eventually appeared in the *Washington Monthly*.)[2]

Skeptics of the press might ask, Where was the special section on Kennedy's oil decontrol position or why the networks didn't devote as much attention to Kennedy's proposals to revise the U.S. Criminal Code as they did to his personal life? Where, in sum, were the press's discussions of the "serious issues" of the campaign, as opposed to its fascination with sex and scandal?

This time the skeptics were wrong. While there most certainly were substantial issues facing the voters in 1980, the "character issue" just as certainly deserved to be one of them. Call it sensation, or soap opera, or Camelot, or hyping the ratings—the press may have had its wrong reasons, but it did the right things. With Rockefeller, full disclosure helped sharpen the public record retrospectively. With Kennedy, the Chappaquiddick theme made a prospective contribution to the record and to informed opinion.

Here is the reasoning. In 1980 the men who would be president said, in effect, *we can do better than Carter: we're leaders, he's not*. Differences in ideology separated the candidates, as well as their views on the specifics of, say, the SALT agreements. But in the early stages of the race, Kennedy, Connally, Bush, Reagan, and the other candidates had offered, along with their philosophy and position on issues, their experiences and their temperaments, their personal qualifications as presidential material. This, of course, is true in any year, and in any election, for offices above the level of town dog catcher. As voters, we are entitled to know these personal traits, to know what kind of person this is, what fires his spirit, what dampens it.

The issue of character affected candidate Kennedy the most. We wanted to know about the private man behind the public Kennedy, and not just for prurient reasons. A great deal of such journalism can be a case of more being less: Teddy Journalism, not serious adult analysis. The *Post*'s Richard Cohen pointed out: "No one has had his life more scrutinized than any of the Kennedys. Something like 134 books have been written on the general subject of the Kennedys. . . . At least four books have been written about Chappaquiddick alone, not to mention reams of newspaper copy. Ted Kennedy, after all, is maybe the only senator whose office had to issue a press release denying that he was having an extramarital affair."

For all the tonnage of copy, Cohen can't see what has been proved about Kennedy. The same lack of conclusion amid the plenitude of information bothered Lewis Lapham, then the editor of *Harper's*. Lapham offered two images of the man Kennedy, one based on the New York gossip and the other on the Washington gossip:

The New York sources prefer to speak of Mr. Kennedy as a dullwitted rich kid, well-meaning and fond of women, forced against his will into the campaign by the ambition of political mercenaries, among them the worthy gentlemen who helped him frame the television statement excusing the incident at Chappaquiddick. The Washington sources portray Senator Kennedy as a man of keen intelligence, industrious and concerned, a paragon among senators, who attends committee meetings, memorizes briefing papers, feels compassion for the constituency of the poor.

Lapham concluded that because so much has been written and said about Kennedy, and because the reports are so contradictory, the result is that Kennedy remains invisible.

It is true that the sheer weight of thrice-told tales can entomb our understanding, just as an avalanche can bury a skier. But that doesn't mean the true shape of the character of Senator Kennedy, or of any other candidate must remain invisible. Nor does it mean that the links between private and public behavior—whatever they may be—must also remain out of sight, or unfathomable. Nor, finally, does the fact that so much of the Teddy Journalism falls on its face mean that we can't hope to do better. Models also exist for nonfatuous journalistic performance.

Such models are based on three assumptions: that character is knowable, that private behavior and public behavior spring from the same sources of character, and that we journalists can steer ourselves down this particular trail of character analysis, provided we prepare intelligently and exercise caution. The best journalism can link politics and personality. That's why, when it comes to our national leaders, the line of disclosure has to be drawn to favor the public.

During the last months of the Nixon presidency, it became fashionable among some journalists to engage in a kind of analysis-at-a-distance, of Richard Nixon. He was variously described as being suspicious, depressed, anxious, remote, brooding, and in any number of other such clinical terms. We know now that Nixon had much to be suspicious, depressed, anxious, etc., about. At the time it seemed inexcusable for journalists to practice psychology without a license. Their psychojournalism gave both psychology and journalism a bad name. A couple of years later, as it happened, I joined up with a professional historian to do an interpretive biography of Jimmy Carter. Interpretive biography, or psychohistory, when done with care and thoughtfulness, seeks to apply the insights of psychology, from Sigmund Freud to Erik Erikson, to public figures. It attempts to relate character to policy, while avoiding name calling and case-book labeling. Our Carter study will have to speak for itself, but from it I learned some of the obstacles interpretive writers face in dealing with the character issue.[3]

First, people don't like psychohistory. There is a widespread apprehension that the interpretive writer plans to reduce a complex public figure to some overly simple, psychological category (oral, Oedipal, or whatever). Second, there exists the widespread conviction that interpretive writers believe they can achieve scientific knowledge of their subjects. Neither fear is justified. Character analysis, done with care, steers clear of the mark of the sexual reductionist, and the inventive novelist. The best character analysis depends on access, interviewing, reporting, research, and interpretation as well as upon intuitions. Doris Kearns used all these skills in her character study of Lyndon Johnson, with excellent results.

Second, there are private and public connections. Richard Cohen, arguing the case for the differences between private and public morality, rather faintly endorses character analyses and the Chappaquiddick investigations. He does not, however, expect too much of them: "You may not know any more about how Kennedy would act as president than you knew before," he writes. Cohen also quotes, approvingly, James McGregor Burns, biographer of Edward Kennedy as well as Franklin D. Roosevelt, who holds that a man's private morality may not have anything to do with his public morality. Richard Nixon, for example, was a good family man, exemplary in his private life, but a corruptor of the presidency. Finally, Cohen offers the example of Franklin Roosevelt, who had a long-term secret relationship with Lucy Rutherford Mercer ("While FDR," Cohen writes, "may not have been very nice to his wife . . . this does not change the fact that he instituted social security—that he was a great president.")

Variations of this private-public argument have been applied to Edward Kennedy. Feminist writers, or more properly women who write about contemporary male-female themes from a woman's perspective, have wondered aloud about how to reconcile the good *Senator* Kennedy from the bad *bedroom* Kennedy. Senator Kennedy's stands on women's issues—such as ERA and abortion—win him praise; but his alleged sexual habits—one-nighters, quickie affairs, "lunch and a dalliance, over and out, on with the pressing schedule," was how Suzannah Lessard characterized it—suggests an unsettling attitude about women. Lessard sought to capture some of that attitude, and women's reaction to it, in her article title: "Kennedy's Women Problem, Women's Kennedy Problem." Many women (and many men) remain convinced that Kennedy was off on a reckless (considering his position) sexual adventure the night that Mary Jo Kopechne died. What bothers them is that over ten years later, approaching his fiftieth year, apparently he is still an undaunted adventurer. Charles Peters, editor of the *Washington Monthly*, offers a rather matter-of-fact explanation. Kennedy, he says, happens to belong to that generation of males who believe that "anyone who passes up a chance to get laid is a fool."

But men's deepest attitudes toward women, love, and sex, we know, aren't picked up in the locker room at college or in other hangouts where "the boys" gather. We absorb these basic lessons much earlier, literally at our parents' knees. The family books about the Kennedys reminds us of the consistency of male Kennedy behavior, from the patriarch through the older brothers to baby Teddy, the last of nine children. *Newsweek* offered an anecdote about a Kennedy aide who advised the senator not to make a run for the presidency. According to *Newsweek*, Kennedy replied, "My father always said, 'If it's on the table, eat it. . . .' "

The *Wall Street Journal,* in a long piece on candidate Kennedy, assured its readers that the senator was a pragmatist politically. But if pragmatism describes the Kennedy political style, how different is that from his opportunistic personal style? They are just different words, one more polite than the other, for the same attitude of winning, scoring, triumphing in a power relationship. Edward Kennedy, far from being invisible, may be a not-unfamiliar character type: someone who believes he has some special dispensation not to be judged as other men are judged. The rules don't apply to Me.

James Fallows, Jimmy Carter's former speech writer, recently complained that journalists on the whole have very little sense of history. "A long time ago," by the journalists' reckoning, might be something that happened three years before. Al Smith put it more generally: "America is a ten-day country." We laugh at the banality of the bumper sticker wisdom: Tomorrow Is the First Day of the Rest of Your Life. Yet most of us really behave as if our yesterdays don't count. Perhaps this is one of the characteristics of an optimistic people. But also journalists have certain characteristics and certain notions about the value of looking for the roots of behavior in early life experiences (an assignment which, for male journalists, seems somehow "unmanly").

It is no surprise then that, when a press watcher looks at the initial treatment of the 1980 presidential race, a disproportionate amount of the most thoughtful coverage of the character issue was the handiwork of women writers, like Susannah Lessard. Among other things they helped put the abstract idea of full disclosure in a real-world context. As women, and minorities who are not "one of the boys," play greater parts in the collection and certification of events as news, the notions of what is news will, we can be thankful, expand.

TELLING IT LIKE IT ISN'T: *LOU GRANT* AND DAVID HALBERSTAM

CHAPTER 13

Newspaper men and women see themselves as hard-bitten, jaded, cynical folk: "Cut the chatter, sweetheart, and gimme rewrite. . . ." But when Edward Asner, a.k.a. Lou Grant, gruff city editor of the fictional *Los Angeles Tribune* on CBS television, visited the newsroom of the real-life *New York Post* in the spring of 1980, supposedly adult reporters and editors acted like teeny-boppers greeting the Beatles. "I've never seen anything like it," reports John Van Doorn, at the time the *Post*'s managing editor. "They really liked the guy. I guess Lou Grant is what all journalists want their editors to be like . . . he has this good working relationship with his reporters and his bosses alike."

Ed Asner, for his part, requites the journalists' love. "I might have been a journalist if I hadn't become an actor," he informed me, not at all gruffly and with obvious sincerity, during an interview. Some of Asner's best friends, he says, are journalists and he visits newspaper offices whenever he gets the chance. A day after his trip to the *Post,* he dropped in on the newsroom of the New York *Daily News,* the last of the hard-bitten, but really good-hearted, big-town dailies. A cynic might observe that the Asner/Grant visits were related to Asner's featured role in the motion picture *Fort Apache: The Bronx,* then being filmed in New York, as well as to the *Lou Grant* show's strong run for ratings' prestige as the 1979–80 television season wound down (for a couple of years now it has finished regularly in the top ten or top fifteen TV programs, watched by upward of 30 or 40 million viewers).

But much the better news story revolves around the deeper matter of both the press' and the public's ready acceptance of *Lou Grant* not only as an intelligent television show but also as reliable model of American newspapering today. Traveling around the country and talking to journalists, I find them admiring the little touches of the program, the VDT equipment, the office politicking, and other real-life details. Seth Freeman, producer of *Lou Grant,* reports that working journalists tell him, "Lou Grant is the way I *wish* my editor was." Some editors report that they sometimes say to themselves, on the job, "Now, how would Lou Grant handle this? . . ." In short, Lou Grant's art looks like nature, and more, nature imitating art.

If that should turn out to be true, it would be only just. The creators and developers of the *Lou Grant* show, James Brooks, Allan Burns, and Gene Reynolds at MTM Enterprises, did a great deal of reportorial digging and research when they spun off Lou Grant, a Minneapolis TV news director on the *Mary Tyler Moore Show,* and made him Lou Grant, Los Angeles newspaper city editor. "We went around to a lot of newspapers, the *Los Angeles Times,* the *San Francisco Chronicle,* the *San Jose Mercury,* the *Washington Post,* and we talked to a lot of newspaper people," reports Freeman. "I read all those transcripts," says Ed Asner. "There was a five-foot stack of research, and then we did a lot of pulling, pushing, and thinking. Gradually a new Lou Grant emerged."

According to Asner, *Lou Grant* reversed the old *Mary Tyler*

Moore ratio of comedy to drama to achieve a more serious, quieter, deeper character. Basically, Lou is the same, a newsman of tough integrity, decency, and honor. If any given script situation offers the possibility of trimming versus an honest course of action, we can be sure which way Lou Grant will go.

In fact, Lou Grant is an archetype, a mythical character. His values are genuine; they are the familiar shibboleths professed by the journalistic establishment, the American Society of Newspaper Editors and the American Newspaper Publishers Association. They make up what Herbert Gans, in this excellent study *Deciding What's News* (Pantheon Books, 1979), calls the hidden values of the news: moderation as opposed to extremism, individualism as opposed to collectivism, reform as opposed to tearing down the system, independence, the dignity of work, enlightened democracy, responsible capitalism. The hidden values of the news help explain why lone transoceanic sailors, Florida sharecroppers fighting foreclosure, and mountain people resisting federal park preserve plans become good copy. They touch our hearts; they embody the Spirit That Made America Great.

On *Lou Grant,* the progressive moderation of the man and the progressive moderation of his newspaper are in step. But real life isn't like that; a lot of editors and publishers offer only lip service to the values they put in the papers from time to time. For example, at the Spring 1980 annual meeting of the ANPA—held, in the honored tax-deductible tradition of corporate America, in Hawaii—a featured speaker was President Ferdinand Marcos of the Philippines. The Marcos regime, as it happens, stands accused of a long list of civil rights violations, including the shutting down of newspapers and the jailing of editors and publishers. As one publisher explained to me, "Maybe many of us didn't know much about Marcos's record" —a telling fact in itself—"but we certainly learned about it from the anti-Marcos pickets outside our luxury hotel." That knowledge didn't stop the publishers, my friend said, from giving Marcos a standing ovation.

Lou Grant's values are more Ed Asner's values than those of most real-life city editors, whose aspirations aren't that much different from their fatcat publishers'. Regular *Lou Grant* watchers would have no trouble passing this test: Where did Lou stand on the presidential candidates, Iran, federal funding of abortions, and the ERA? Now, check your answers against Ed Asner's own stands. He told me when we talked in the early summer of 1980 that he was planning to support John Anderson for president. He also thought that the United States should apologize to Iran if it would help get the hostages back ("What the hell, we've lost face already"), and he said he contributes to the National Abortion Rights Action League, to Oxfam, and to the emergency committee for the National Organization for Women. Although I did not ask Reynolds, Freeman, or the other *Lou Grant* writers and producers about their politics, I'd be surprised if any of them were working against these causes, just as I'd be surprised at finding many editors and publishers working for them.

According to newspaper industry surveys, about 65 to 70 percent of the U.S. dailies endorsed the Republican presidential candidate in 1980, not much down from the 80 percent GOP endorsement records during the Roosevelt years. The really arresting newspaper trend among American newspapers in recent years, however, is the decision not to endorse anyone for political office. More and more inoffensiveness is deemed to be next to godliness. Lou Grant is mythical because he takes stands in the first place, and his stands are those of a Westwood liberal rather than a newspaper editor at, say, the *Los Angeles Times*.

But *Lou Grant* is also mythical because it perpetuates the image of a serious American press; the program takes one or two outstanding newspaper exceptions, like the *New York Times*, for the journalistic whole, and mistakes the lip service values for the actual performance. On *Lou Grant* reporters investigate such institutions as big business, the churches, and the police, whereas on many papers press releases from these institutions are often merely rewritten and printed.

Of course, *Lou Grant's* investigators go only so far. In the show called "Inheritance," beautiful, bright reporter Billie Newman (Linda Kelsey) writes a story about DES, a drug that may cause vaginal cancer in the daughters of pregnant women who took it. As with many *Lou Grant* episodes, "Inheritance" was based on a recent news story, in this case a *Ms* magazine article by Jan Worthington. When Newman finds out that her own mother had taken DES, she is angry with her. Patrician Mrs. Pynchon (Nancy Marchand), the *Tribune* publisher, meets the reporter and defends the mother. "You have to try to think what it was like when your mother was young. It was the age of discovery. There were wonder drugs. My younger sister had pneumonia, and her life was saved because of penicillin."

Stewart Weiner, writing about *Lou Grant* for *Los Angeles* magazine, telephoned Worthington and asked her about the DES script. She told him, "It's OK, but very tame stuff. Mrs. Pynchon could have been shaking her fists at the drug companies and the sheepish doctors, not apologizing for them. The message might have been that women are responsible for their own bodies."[1] That message, however, is unlikely to be heard anywhere on CBS, except perhaps on *60 Minutes*.

Still, *Lou Grant* is often ahead of the times, and the *Times*. In another episode, "Cop," hard-charging investigative reporter Joe Rossi (Robert Walden), the Carl Bernstein look-alike, checks out a homosexual murder. One of the cops on the case is revealed as a gay, but throughout the program the treatment of homosexuality is sympathetic. "This is the flip side of the motion picture *Cruising*," a CBS official told me with pride. "It's nonsensational and nonexploitive." The script is also upbeat. The gay cop "proves" himself by saving the life of his patrol car partner, a heterosexual who disdains homosexuals but is won over at the end. Rossi pronounces the verdict: "He's a good cop."

In a related plot line, Billie Newman looks into a fire that killed several patrons in a homosexual bar. A timely journalistic issue is joined: Should the *Tribune,* in Newman's story, print the names of the homosexual dead, a list including a lawyer, an army major, and some husbands and fathers? Should the *Tribune,* in Rossi's story, print the fact that the cop who caught the gay killer is himself gay? First, the gay fire episode:

Pynchon: What are we going to do?
Grant: If we print the names, we'd just be printing facts. We aren't telling people what to think.
Pynchon: No, but we know exactly what they will think. Everyone is going to assume those men were gay.
Grant: That's a fair assumption. If there's a fire at a basketball game, everyone would assume the victims were basketball fans.
Pynchon: There's not exactly a social stigma attached to liking basketball.

Now, the gay killer story:

Rossi: There's something I didn't put in the piece because I'm not sure it's part of the story. It's a human angle about [the cop's] personal life. What do you think?
Grant: I think you were right. I don't think it belongs in the story. We'll run it like this.
Rossi: Right.

The standard television production values of a police car chase and a shoot-out in this script cloud but do not completely obscure its connection to the real world. In Washington, D.C., a few years ago, an early afternoon fire trapped several men in a theater featuring homosexual movies. One Washington newspaper printed the names of the dead, including respectable family men, while the other paper did not. ("This intrigued us," Freeman said. "There is no unanimity on these topics.") On *Lou Grant,* however, Lou's journalistic standards define the line separating the permissible from the nonpermissible. His art improves on nature. If only real editors performed so well.

To the credit of the *Lou Grant* show, not all episodes are wrapped up neatly. Toward the end of the season, there was an admirable willingness to leave some of the major issues of our time unresolved. In one program the *Tribune* exposes a fringe church that tithes its members as high as one-quarter of their meager earnings and encourages them to borrow money to keep the church's overseas missions going, and to keep the reverend in $500 suits and Caribbean trips. It was a scam operation based on any number of recent news stories, on both the east and west coasts. The *Tribune* gets the goods on the smoothy minister, but the faith of the flock that has been shorn remains undisturbed. The episode even lets the chief sheepshearer have the last word: In exchange for their money, the minister declares, "I give them hope, God, myself."

In most *Lou Grant* episodes, one or another of the systems usually works. The good guys of the press usually win, for *Lou Grant* romanticizes the system of journalism, and distorts it. The program revels in detailed realities; it gets the little things about journalists right but misses the big issues about journalism.

In this respect, again, it is in crowded company. Last year, in *The View from Sunset Boulevard,* the conservative writer Ben Stein undertook an exposé of liberal values in Hollywood's prime-time programs. Stein had it wrong. The real dirty little secret of the real Sunset Boulevard is that prime-time television plays it safe rather than ultraliberal.

On *Lou Grant* the geography makes this possible. Lou moved to a city editor's job in Los Angeles rather than in, say, Washington, Boston, or Chicago. It was more cost-effective and convenient to make programs near home (MTM's, Asner's) than on the road. But sunny Los Angeles also happens to be a journalistic climate that is removed from a whole range of news: foreign policy stories, state and federal legislatures, the White House, lobbies, the federal courts, the regulatory agencies, the Pentagon, commodities trading, the bond market, Wall Street—in short most of politics, economics, and government. Even the portraits of daily newspaper life are selective. The real-life *Los Angeles Times* has recently invested $215 million in new plants to try to smother its competition. The real-life *Herald-Examiner,* the other Los Angeles paper, is currently trying to stay alive under the ownership of the Hearst family, historically one of the most incompetently managed private fortunes in the country. The *Times* is also trying to move into cable television operations, a hedge against the day when cable television seriously challenges the broadcast networks for a large market share of viewers.

All of this may be too inside an approach for a *Lou Grant* script. It would be asking too much of prime-time television, even serious television like *Lou Grant,* to take on these issues. But even on the anecdotal level, there is room for more journalistic discussion. For all its little touches, *Lou Grant* misses out on the issue raised more than fifty years ago by Ben Hecht and Charles MacArthur in their play *The Front Page.* Back then, Hildy Johnson, the Rossi of his day, sounded off:

> Journalists! Peeking through keyholes. Running after fire engines like a lot of coach dogs. Waking people up in the middle of the night to ask what they think of Mussolini. Stealing pictures off old ladies, of their daughters who get raped in Oak Park. A lot of lousy, daffy buttinskies, swelling around with holes in their pants, borrowing nickels from office boys. And for what? So a million hired girls and motormen's wives'll know what's going on.

Lou Grant must have an answer to Johnson. Tom Stoppard, in his play *Night and Day,* raises some of the same questions about the nature and responsibilities of journalism and does it with wit. Shouldn't there be equal time for this nonromantic view of the press as clown and entertainer? In Stoppard's play the press, for all its snooping after trivia and sensationalism, still gets the third-act accolade: Information is light. Journalism is worthwhile.

But why not just enjoy the *Lou Grant* characters as journalistic types—Rossi's Carl Bernstein imitation, Mrs. Pynchon playing Katharine Graham/Dolly Schiff/Helen Copley, Lou as the good-hearted Jewish uncle figure. Viewed as entertainment, *Lou Grant* fits comfortably in the idealized traditions of popular culture.

Frank Van Riper of the New York *Daily News* recently examined
the myth in an article published in the *Nieman Reports* at Harvard.[2] As Van Riper pointed out, newspaper reporters have
usually been treated in pop culture as something special and
idealized: Joel McCrea as the patriotic soldier of the press fighting against fascism (*Foreign Correspondent*); Humphrey Bogart
defending the public against organized crime (*Deadline U.S.A.*);
the exploits of real newspaper people on television's *Big Story* in
the fifties; *All the President's Men*, Alan J. Pakula's *High Noon*
version of Watergate.

Along with Van Riper, I prefer several motion pictures that
present less-than-ideal portraits of journalism. One is *The Great
Man* in which a beloved television personality is revealed to be
corrupt. (Some real-life examples come to mind.) The other is
the science fiction classic *The Day the Earth Caught Fire*, an utterly
believable account of an ordinary reporter's discomfort, but
perseverance, in covering the big story of nuclear disaster. I'd
like to make Lou Grant's city room staff sit down and take notes
on that movie story.

Next to *Lou Grant*, probably the major popular source of
current information about contemporary newspapers has come
from David Halberstam's book *The Powers That Be*. A best seller
during much of 1979, *The Powers That Be* is an account of four
powerful media institutions—CBS, Time Inc, the *Washington
Post*, and the *Los Angeles Times*. Halberstam, once a serious,
effective newspaper journalist, has been bitten by the big-score
bug. His book is supposed to be nonfiction but for all its prodigious research, it is actually in the romantic tradition of *Foreign
Correspondent* and *Lou Grant*; Ed Asner plays a lovable, unreal
city editor. Halberstam, who knows better, inflates the whole
press process into a similar mythology. Halberstam holds up a
mirror to the media men and women who, he assures us, exercise an immediate power far greater than that possessed by the
President, the Congress, the courts or any other institution in

our society. In Halberstam's book a CBS camera crew in Vietnam overnight could "become as important as 10 or 15 or 20 senators."

Such claims of press power are so totally wrong headed that the pages of *The Powers That Be* turn into fun-house mirrors: Everything about the media becomes larger than life. Everything about life becomes much smaller than the media. Thus, in August 1965, when CBS News' reporter Morley Safer files a story showing U.S. Marines setting fire to Vietnamese thatched huts, it's not just a vivid narrative by a first-rate correspondent. In Halberstam's vision, the Safer film is awesome. This one incident, on one day in the war, carried one night by television, was "shattering to an entire generation of Americans, perhaps to an entire country." But if that televised scene was so important in turning all of Walter Cronkite's viewers against the war, then Halberstam ought to explain why the war continued to grind on for Americans for seven years and how Cronkite himself was able to remain hawkish, along with Middle America, for at least three more years.

In much the same pop-eyed reworking of history, Halberstam tells us segregation existed in Washington in the pre-civil rights era because the *Washington Star* wanted it that way, and not the House District Committee or the courts or a succession of ten U.S. presidents. In Halberstam's fun house, television elected John F. Kennedy in 1960 (presumably Richard J. Daley and his precinct captains were at home on election night, watching the Cook County ballots being counted on television). And, Halberstam says, television undid Lyndon Johnson in 1968, not the flag-draped coffins coming home to each congressional district or the demonstrations or even the Vietnamese, North and South. The enormities of the Vietnam War, and of the Watergate scandals, become, in Halberstam's refractory world that enshrines media power, a media story. The essential combatants in the crises of Vietnam and Watergate, Halberstam writes, were the press and the presidency, thereby reducing everyone else,

Senate, House, Supreme Court, Judge Sirica, Movement people, doves, and Democrats and Republicans of conscience, to supernumeraries. Even a dumb piece of fluff like CBS comedy series *Hogan's Heroes* turns, in the Halberstam house of mirrors, into "the most informative and perhaps most memorable portrait of Nazi Germany" for the millions of supposedly stupified, ahistorical American kids who watch it—and naturally believe everything they see on the television.

But the most distended shapes in *The Powers That Be* belong to the media men and women that Halberstam admires. Robert Donovan, a journeyman Washington bureau chief in the 1950s, turns into "a glistening journalistic figure." An able, Saigon-based reporter, and friend of Halberstam's, becomes "the beloved [Frank] McCulloch." The *Washington Post*'s executive editor Ben Bradlee, one of the heroes of Watergate, is endowed by Halberstam with "an abnormally powerful chest and shoulders." (The real-life Bradlee is a trim figure with the build of Fred Astaire—the actor Bradlee though should have played him in *All the President's Men*.) This is the same dramaturgy of *Lou Grant*.

Most of the reviewers of *The Powers That Be* have not only politely refrained from throwing stones at this crazy house of mirrors. They have constructed media fun houses of their own, writing admiringly about Halberstam as a journalist superstar, in the same way he wrote about the journalist superstars he admires. The Johnsons get to review what their Boswells have written about them in this tight mutual admiration society. Former *Washington Post* man Ben Bagdikian is one of Halberstam's many sources. "Well-respected" and "hero" are two of Halberstam's lesser descriptive terms used for him. In his review in the *Chicago Sun-Times*, Bagdikian returns the compliments, calling *The Powers That Be* "the most important book so far on contemporary news media." News magazine interviewers solemnly examine Halberstam's power that is. *People* magazine pictures Halberstam and his bride-to-be on the beach. The advance for his book was $300,000 but, after all, he did put seven years into the effort, and, if he makes a million or so, well, what does that average out to be? Not much more than any star makes in the media.

There have been a few dissents. James David Barber in the *Washington Post* said he wasn't sure what point Halberstam was trying to make. Nicholas Lemann in the *New Republic* had a devastating time with the portentous Halberstam style. The *Business Week* reviewer found Halberstam antiprofit and a political liberal appealing to a coterie of his politically liberal friends.

The fact is, Halberstam put a great deal of time and effort into his study. The weight of the anecdotes does overwhelm the thin thread of his argument. But that may be a plus. Readers may remember what Truman Capote told Kay Graham when she asked him who was more beautiful, Babe Paley or Marella Agnelli, or what Mamie Eisenhower cattily said to Mollie Parnis about Pat Nixon, long after they have forgotten the overwrought theories about media power. In Halberstam's world, fighting reporters, like Halberstam, and editors and publishers who back up fighting reporters, are godlike (and passive reporters and editors and bottomline publishers are bad). But that doesn't make Halberstam an ideologue. If anything, he's a romanticist of the journalism profession (his word) and the chronicler of a new elite that includes himself. *The Powers That Be* gives *Times* man Halberstam a chance to write his own memoirs, slipping in, among his four nominal subjects, a big slice of the *New York Times* adventure.

If there is one thing that journalism really doesn't need right now, it is to be told how great journalists are. To the extent that we preen ourselves in our own mirrors and behave like a new elite, we have become, in that tired phrase of the 1960s, part of the problem rather than part of the solution.

One of the problems of journalism today is that the media don't have real power compared to the true rulers in this country. If Halberstam thinks that the press is omnipotent, then he hasn't spent time at a real-life power center such as Exxon in Houston or Chase Manhattan in New York or in the offices of one of those senators he disdains. A better analysis of power has been done in the other media book of 1979, Herbert Gans' *Deciding What's News*. Gans is a sociologist; his academic style doesn't provide the good summer read that *Newsweek*'s reviewer promised in Halberstam's book. While *Time* magazine airily dismissed *Deciding What's News* as plodding in the same issue that it praised *The Powers That Be*, I suspect that Gans will be read and studied long after the hammocks of summer have been stored away.

Gans is an explainer rather than a story teller in the *Lou Grant* or David Halberstam mode. One of his best points concerns the hierarchical nature of the news. Gans shows that the news in America comes primarily from elites. Names just don't make news; official names make news. Most news, Gans demonstrates, come from those he calls the knowns—the president, senators, mayors, police officers, corporation executives, celebrities. Gans cites one analysis of 2,850 stories in the *New York Times* and the *Washington Post* (Halberstam's putative powerhouses). Almost eight in every ten of these stories come from public officials. The unknowns—the poor, the black, the unemployed, the enlisted men in Vietnam—tend to make the news only when they appear to threaten or to confound the knowns. "Perhaps the place of ordinary people in the news," Gans writes, "is most dramatically illustrated by the day in 1974 when Congress approved a change in the pension law that affected millions of workers, and all the news media, daily and weekly, gave far more space and time, as well as headlines, to the appointment of Nelson Rockefeller to the second-highest office in the land."

There is another problem with the Halberstam approach. Some journalists have begun to believe their press notices. The media's overfascination with official elites is now mirrored by its own epic concentration on the media elite. Halberstam's is the wrong story in the wrong place at the wrong time. The undeniable energy of his narrative and the density of his reporting give a false color to the whole story. For Halberstam to treat Vietnam and Watergate as press–president confrontations (Walter Cronkite vs. Lyndon Johnson, Katharine Graham vs. Richard Nixon) is to offer top-down news of the most errant kind. Gans' analysis shows us a better place to look for (1) an understanding of the journalist's work and (2) better ways to do that work. Gans does this without ringing in knowns like Truman Capote and Mollie Parnis. It may not sell but it's serious.

Powerful, glistening, brilliant, aggressive, beloved superstars loitering to catch a glimpse of themselves in the looking glass aren't using the powers they do have for any useful purpose. They are, in the end, reduced to entertainment figures, not much different than the actors on the *Lou Grant* show, and no more credible.

ILLUSIONS OF POWER

PART III

CREATING THE
"PERCEPTUAL
ENVIRONMENT"

CHAPTER 14

By the early fall of 1979, just about every political journalist in the land was prepared to swear on his holy copy of Theodore White's *The Making of the President* that:

1. The press's quadrennial attention to the New Hampshire presidential primaries amounts to excessive overkill, making less (26,000 votes) sound like more (crucial evidence of next November's outcome).

2. The press's newly found interest in the straw polls at the Florida state party conventions in October 1979 represents an empty, overblown media event because, after all, the actual Florida primary choosing delegates to the national conventions won't be held until March.

3. The press's premature rush to judgment in New Hampshire and Florida has the effect of creating media-certified front runners and signifies obsessive psychology that ignores the results of later, substantive primary results, such as the eight primaries

held in early June (when fully one-fifth of all delegates to both the Democractic and Republican conventions are chosen).

4. As a consequence of all of the above, today's presidential primaries have become mass media campaigns, with political power slipping away from traditional institutions, pre-eminently the two political parties, and toward other institutions. In the old days, a party boss like Colonel Jack Arvey of Illinois could make an Adlai Stevenson or a Paul Douglas. Now a Barbara Walters interview on ABC or a *New York Times Sunday Magazine* article can certify a candidate. The press is the new power broken, or so it's said.

This litany of home truths is usually offered up by journalists somewhat self-deprecatingly, as in the attitude, isn't it a shame unaccountable people like us have such power. Alternatively, other journalists may rail against press power with near-religious fervor, like prohibitionists denouncing the devil's brew whiskey. And yet both groups, the self-deprecators of press over-kill and the thunderers about the intoxication with media events, could have been found, two hundred strong, in Nashua, New Hampshire, at a Democratic picnic on a Sunday afternoon in early September 1979. The occasion, held just a few days after Labor Day, marked—ready?—the official start of Campaign '80. The presidential nominating process, which used to begin in the snows of New Hampshire in past Januarys, now is getting underway the year before on the day the children go back to school. Worse, the '80 campaign itself, the primaries, nominations and election, appeared to be wrapped up before the 1979 baseball pennants were decided: Like a motion picture track run at fast forward, Campaign '80 was settled in September 1979, with the press's election of Senator Edward Kennedy. If anyone needed added confirmation of the power of the press, the Kennedy victory was evidence enough. As Richard Reeves wrote about Kennedy's early September inclination to run: "We did it! The press drafted Teddy Kennedy."[1]

Reeves is one of the best and most attended political correspondents around. His ideas are worth listening to; we nod when he argues that the new political bosses are the press (national political reporters to be more specific) and that we had the power to make Senator Kennedy into Candidate Kennedy. But he was wrong in his reading of what had been going on throughout the summer and fall of 1979, and he was not alone in the error of his ways.

The same misreading of the political process can be found in the major academic study of the 1976 campaign, the three-year effort conducted by a team of political scientists and funded by the Ford and Markle Foundations and eventually published as *Race for the Presidency: The Media and the Nominating Process.*[2] An alarm is sounded in the study over the potentials for media manipulation of an unwitting citizenry in the electoral process. Adds Professor F. Christopher Arterton of Yale: "The fact that these fears have proved largely undocumented cannot be taken as a conclusive demonstration that the media exert little influence upon our politics." When the double negatives and the passive voice constructions are combed out of Arterton's words, the message is like Reeves's: "You did it! And isn't it a shame for the political process!"

Perhaps it is already too late to clear away all the false apprehensions about the press in campaigns. Still it's worth the attempt to sort through the images and the realities of, first, the making of Jimmy Carter by the press and, then, its canonization of Edward Kennedy.

The Ford-Markle study of press-candidate interactions was headed by the distinguished political scientist James David Barber of Duke University. As Barber argues in his introduction, "the old worry was that politicians dominate reporters, brandishing the sword of state; the new worry is that reporters dominate politicians, ruling the rulers with their pens. The worst of worries is the haunting fear that something has gone wrong with the way these characters dominate one another—

and maybe the rest of us—as we puzzle over who ought to be president." Professor Arterton, one of the Barber team, attempted to find out what had gone wrong, principally in the 1976 Democratic primaries. His method was admirably straightforward: he and his associates interviewed campaign reporters and the press secretaries and television advisors to the major candidates. He reports that these media managers all were convinced that what the newspapers, radio, television, and the news magazines had to say about their candidates affects votes on election day.

This is a fairly safe attitude, and hardly astounding; media managers are no more likely to downgrade the efficacy of their work on behalf of the candidate than opticians are likely to recommend against reading glasses for their customers. If Arterton had interviewed the campaign treasurers and accountants, then he surely would have heard about the decisive importance of fund raising and bookkeeping, for dollars are what make the campaign wheels turn, including the wheels of the media.

But Arterton's chief evidence for press power lies in what he calls the perceptual environment of the campaign. Strictly speaking, primary victories only have meaning as they contribute to delegate counts; a Florida straw poll, from this point of view, is meaningless. Even a New Hampshire win only involves nineteen delegates. Consequently, a given candidate's primary victories have to be understood in relation to the overall race for the magic number of delegates. A candidate who receives, say, in New Hampshire, only a bare majority of the votes may be showing a weakness that will be more evident in later primaries. Conversely, a candidate who loses narrowly in New Hampshire may actually be growing in strength. This, says Arterton, places great importance on the context of victory or defeat, and on the event's analyses and interpretations, both done by political journalists and by practicing politicians. These interpretations, mainly the press's, make up the perceptual environment of a campaign. Writes Arterton: "The interpretation placed on campaign events are frequently more important than the events themselves." Though Arterton takes pains to attribute this view to those who manage presidential campaigns, it's clear that he endorses this view.

In his analysis of the 1976 Democratic primary race, he finds the perceptual environment decidedly pro-Carter. For example, in a front page *New York Times* article appearing on October 27, 1975, correspondent R. W. Apple, Jr., found that Jimmy Carter appeared to be leading in the Iowa state caucuses. This story, Arterton says, "not only put the spotlight for the first time on Carter's growing strength, but it also signaled the fact that the Iowa caucuses would be an important event from the perspective of news-reporting organizations." When Carter won, the press was ready to give him plenty of ink and air time. Then, after the New Hampshire primary, the press's perceptual environment went to work again. NBC's Tom Pettit described Carter as "the man to beat," and *Time* in its March 8, 1976, issue declared that Carter's "is the only campaign that holds real possibilities of breaking far ahead of the pack." *Time* put Carter on its cover that week, as did *Newsweek;* yet, complains Arterton, only five states at this point had selected or apportioned delegates, less than 5 percent of the total needed for real, as opposed to perceptual, victory.

Similarly, while the press was puffing up Jimmy Carter, it was ignoring other candidates, notably Terry Sanford, Fred Harris, and Lloyd Bentsen. For example, Sanford, a former governor of North Carolina and president of Duke University, had an early strategy of running in selected primaries and relying on North Carolina sources for his funds. He would not, initially, try to qualify for matching federal money by raising money in the required twenty states. But, says Arterton, this strategy "ran headlong into a perception [that word again] among journalists that 'qualification' constituted an important test of which candidates should be taken seriously." Sanford didn't qualify by this press-imposed standard; therefore Sanford wasn't a viable candidate. Press power demonstrated once again, and the media's rush to judgment, with its too-early elevation of front runners and its put-down of the losers, its apotheosis of momentum and other fantastical currents, its fixation with its own opinions. In short the perceptual environment at work.

As it happens, the reality of Iowa and New Hampshire doesn't match the perceptual environment theme. It was, in Iowa, Democratic party activists who in the first instance arranged the caucuses. They were not responding to the press but rather were trying to grab some of the attention away from the so-called first-in-the-nation New Hampshire primaries (a lot of people like to see their names in the paper or to be interviewed by Roger Mudd, and in that sense the press is powerful). It was Carter, and not the press, who shrewdly recognized that a good showing by a Baptist, conservative southerner among the generally Catholic, normally liberal-leaning, undeniably midwestern voters in the Iowa caucuses would attract media attention as well as contributors' dollars and volunteers' support. Similarly in New Hampshire, the performance was in the first instance the thing, not its representation in the press. There, Carter not only began to distance himself from the pack, but he also managed to create a middle-ground stance, distinct from the crowded left-of-center position among the candidates.

There are fashions in political reporting. A decade ago everyone was caught in Marshall-McLuhan's notions that *The Medium Is the Message*. Today the believers in press power in campaigns talk of the importance of the perceptual environment. In truth the message is the message, and the environment is the environment. The perception that Carter was the press favorite at the beginning of the primary races just isn't so. Our News Study Group found that Ronald Reagan and George Wallace received more attention than all the other candidates combined (with the natural exception of Gerald Ford, who made daily news simply by performing his White House duties). The *Times*'s Apple did not make Jimmy Carter. Carter himself told the News Study Group interviewers that all Apple did was to be a good reporter. Apple went to Iowa and learned that the Carter forces had grasped the importance of Iowa—which would caucus before New Hampshire—and that the Carter forces had been carefully working the districts. Apple, said Carter, only reported what had already happened. The achievement was Carter's, not the *Times*'s.

As for Terry Sanford, Lloyd Bentsen, and the others—all those presumably condemned to also-ran status by the lords of the press—they were as known or, more properly, as unknown, as Carter when the campaign began. Did the press, then, do them in? The political writer Jack Germond remembers the phone calls from people asking why the press had not given more coverage to Sanford. As Germond explained it, "the reason we didn't pay more attention to Terry Sanford is that the Democratic party wasn't paying very much attention to him, the political community wasn't paying much attention to him, and the voters at large weren't paying much attention to him." Once again the message came first.

During Campaign '80 press-candidate interactions predictably made good copy, particularly on the Democratic side (the Republican candidates—Reagan, Bush, Baker, Ford, Connally— were at first relatively quiet, content to let the Democrats wound each other). The two major developments were the fall of Jimmy Carter, at least in the public opinion polls, and the rise of the noncandidate candidacy of Senator Kennedy. Richard Reeves, in his characteristically brisk fashion, made the case that both were largely press stories: "It looks like there won't be two Carter terms. The press, among others, thought that the Georgian didn't deserve a second chance. Most national correspondents made up their minds about that earlier this year. Since that time we have savaged Carter and built up Kennedy. Reporters and commentators went after Carter because they had become convinced he was a lousy president—and because it is our nature and craft to promote conflict."

Many political commentators may have been convinced that Jimmy Carter was a lousy president, and many more thrived on, though not promoted, conflict. But the press didn't convince the people that Jimmy Carter was a lousy president. Those who believed he had been ineffective—and the public opinion polls and the election results demonstrated that a majority of voters held to this view throughout the summer and fall of 1979 and into 1980—were convinced by Carter's performance, not by the views of the Broders or the Krafts or the Restons. Even a casual student of newspaper op-ed pages knew that political columnists were more understanding of the trials of Carter, a post-Watergate president trying to govern in troubling times, than the public had been. While Carter created some of his own problems, he inherited others.

After the Johnson and Nixon years, Carter correctly understood that large numbers of Americans had become disaffected with the powers and perquisites of the imperial presidency. They wanted, or thought they wanted, an austere, low-key, demystified president, a figure dressed in blue jeans and open-collar shirts rather than a morning suit. The idea of a stripped-down presidency, as it happened, matched Carter's own style, and Carter had no difficulty fitting the part of the nonimperial presidency. But such an appeal can wear thin after a while: it seems contrived. Worse, it runs up against the deep-rooted desire of a good part of the electorate for a strong leader, for a father figure of sorts. Many people also look for a higher level of conduct from the President and his First Family, and his chief aides. The office supposedly elevates the occupants; if they act like regular people, it worries other regular people—an aura of authority seems missing. If they go to Studio 54 or to tacky parties, it angers people.

Carter, then, found himself at the center of contradictory American images of the President: one of us, but in important ways separate from us. One of Carter's familiar campaign themes held that America needed a government as good as the people. But people, as Columnist Carl Rowan observed, "seem to be saying they wanted a president wiser, more frugal, and braver than the people." As public disaffection with Carter grew, press stories reflected this. But of more immediate practical importance, Democratic party activists and office holders began to get restless. Much has been written about the death of the old politics—the passing of the bosses, smoke-filled rooms, and wheels and deals—and the triumph of the telegenic new politics. But the parties aren't over. A group of liberal Democratic congressmen began the Draft Kennedy Movement at a time when the press appeared willing to take him at his word that he was not a candidate. When Democratic congresspeople went home during legislative recesses, they found the expressed dissatisfaction with Carter so strong that they could see their own re-election hopes dimming. At newspaper editorial lunches for congressmen back home, journalists around the country sat back and listened while the politicians told them that Carter had to go.

About the same time, in New Hampshire, two women named Joanne Symons and Dudley W. Dudley began to attract wide press attention for their role in the Draft Kennedy Movement. A lot of the coverage had fun with Dudley's double-barreled name (she was born Dudley Webster and married a man named Thomas Dudley). But the real news was that the two women were veteran Democratic party activists: Dudley had worked in the campaigns of Eugene McCarthy, George McGovern, and Morris Udall. After watching the growing Draft Kennedy Movement during the summer of 1979, the political scientist James McGregor Burns concluded: "This is probably the more authentic, uncontrived, unmanipulated presidential-draft movement in recent American history." Burns may have been a Kennedy sympathizer, but his point rings true. Nobody wrote that story, in part because it didn't have the sex appeal of stories about press power, in part because the reporters who write the obituary of the old politics instinctively look only for jowly pols in back rooms and therefore miss the pleasant new faces of the old politics.

But still, aren't the Florida straw votes, the Iowa caucuses, and the New Hampshire primaries puffed up all out of proportion to their importance by the press? And doesn't that amply demonstrate the press's intrusive role in the campaign process? Narrowly seen, the press, particularly television, is the biggest noisemaker in a campaign. Most likely if New Hampshire and Iowa and Florida didn't exist, then it might be necessary for the press to invent them. Campaign politics are fun and games, as opposed to the onerous task of covering government, with all those contradictory, confusing, seemingly intractable, heavy processes, like monetary policies, the cities, energy and jobs, resource allocations, that grind on in the four years between the highs of election campaigns. Campaigns get journalists out of confining spaces and on the road. The more spirited the contest, the more likely the stories get air time and column space. Sometimes we do sound like sportscasters hyping less-than-heroic figures.

The Washington columnists are as hard up for solutions as the Washington politicians that they berate. The press experts are often stuck for fresh insights. Discussions of inflation, SALT II columns, and energy analyses are deady subjects; it's hard work to cover them and to get readers and viewers to pay attention. It's like being in a seminar room full of stale hot air. But campaign politics and campaign people—that's another matter. There's no heavy lifting there; it can be as enjoyable as a picnic lunch on a sunny September day in New Hampshire in the company of Joanne Symons and Dudley Dudley. The picnics offer no explanation of what's going to be done about the economy, or energy, or food prices, but you can't have everything.

The press didn't invent Florida or New Hampshire or even Dudley W. Dudley. The Draft Kennedy people and the Carter re-election committee conducted the battle of the buses in Dade County, Florida, fighting each other to tie down transportation to take their respective supporters to the caucus votes. The Carter operatives sent Jody Powell, Rosalynn Carter, and Robert Strauss to Florida to speak. In New Hampshire the candidates began working the morning coffees and the shopping centers in the summer of 1979, with Evans, Novak, and the rest trailing after them. True, the press gave the election to Kennedy before one straw ballot was counted, but only after the political experts and party activists had gone public with their messages.

The story of press-candidate interactions that Arterton and others should have told would show that the press is usually reactive, not active. The press is often the last to know what's going on. Political reporters, we understand, are like the generals, always prepared to fight the next war with the weapons of the last war. This helps explain the otherwise puzzling position of the press in the last five elections: always one step behind the story. In 1968, it could be argued the press thought the major story was the new Nixon (and Joe McGuiness wrote the best seller of that campaign *The Selling of the President*). Actually, the 1968 story was the social issues, reduced to the AAA formula of Acid, Abortion, Amnesty, that drove normally Democratic Humphrey votes to Nixon and Wallace. In 1972, the press geared itself to cover the social issues, but the real story was Watergate, money (CREEP's swollen treasury started the whole process, and the dollar was the father of Watergate), and Richard Nixon's ability to divert almost all of the press from following the lead of Woodward and Bernstein. By 1976, as we have seen, everyone had become attuned to press-candidate interactions, and the press vowed it would not be fooled or stonewalled by Rose Garden strategies. In fact, the Ford–Carter race turned on issues of competence and character, and the only direct role the press played was a passive one, covering the televised presidential debates arranged by the League of Women Voters.

As Campaign '80 started, the new catch phrase in the columns was leadership, a version of the 1976 competence and character theme. In the fall of 1979, I wrote the following in the *Washington Journalism Review:* "If I had to guess the actual 1980 campaign themes—now, rather than in 1984—I would strongly urge that we look in the direction of issues and ideology. Whoever runs for the Democrats or Republicans in 1980, I suspect they will run with frank appeals to party and to the old politics. In such a race [people like] Dudley Dudley will be more relevant to the vote count than Barbara Walters."

A fair reading of the 1980 campaign and the victory of Ronald Reagan makes this passage look very good.

THE CANDIDATE IN THIRTY SECONDS

CHAPTER 15

Two decades ago, when television first became instrumental in political campaigns, some commentators worried that presidential candidates would no longer run for office—they would, in Columnist Marquis Childs's phrase, pose for office.

While those early fears may have been overstated—there's little evidence that candidates today are any prettier, or of lower intellectual qualities, than they were in pretelevision days—it's nevertheless true that media is now the largest single budget item in the national campaign. In one sense, in fact, television is becoming the entire public campaign. In 1980 the federal campaign finance law allotted $29.4 million apiece to Ronald Reagan and Jimmy Carter. Each man spent more than half of this allotment on so-called paid media, largely thirty-second and sixty-second television spots but also five-minute telebiographies and thirty-minute campaign night specials. And a good deal of the remaining campaign money went for staff salaries and travel to set up free media—candidate appearances on the evening television newscasts.

Each year, it seems, the candidates increase their attention to media, and stir renewed public worries about the telegenic emptiness of presidential campaigns. Early in the 1980 race, for example, before the Iowa caucuses, Jimmy Carter noted how much he missed not being able to do some campaigning. "It would be good for me to go from one media center to another," he said, thus completing, verbally at least, the transformation of what used to be called cities and towns into sets for television or camera opportunities. With the election of Ronald Reagan, former actor and public relations man, as President, the process that Childs fretted about has been completed. A performer reigns in the White House. The people liked the show, and have spoken. Still if this isn't the time to fight it, then at least we can try to understand the elements of theater. This, then, is a dramatic review of the politics staged for us in 1980.

The playlets of political advertising begin with a guild of specialists. Every candidate now has a media adviser, a Gerald Rafshoon, a Robert Goodman, a John Deardourff, who crafts the overall advertising campaign. There are also film and video specialists who may come out of documentary making, like Charles Guggenheim, the Academy Award winner who made the 1980 spots for Edward M. Kennedy, or out of advertising agencies, like Malcolm MacDougall of Boston (Ford in 1976, the Republican National Committee in 1980). Also the film or tape product—the political spot or polispot—has to be edited and supplied with voiceovers, graphics, sometimes even original music (Deardourff and his partner, Doug Bailey, produced an upbeat jingle for Ford in 1976 and a country-and-western patriotic tune for Howard Baker in 1980). Still another specialist, the time buyer, places the spots on television schedules where they will attract the specific audience voter desired by the candidate. Ruth Jones, the time buyer for the 1980 Ronald Reagan campaign, and one of the few women in the upper echelons of the media image business, often tries to place commercials in news adjacencies—that is, slots within or near the early evening newscasts. Political time buyers also like news magazine programs like *60 Minutes* or the *Today Show,* and intelligent entertainment series like *Family* or *Lou Grant.* "We try to avoid being next to shows with too much sex and violence," says Gerald Greenberg of Allscope Service, which was the time buyer for the George Bush campaign. Finally, or really initially, there is the candidate's market researcher, typically a public-opinion poller who helps determine what voters are thinking about and thus helps shape the themes of the candidate's advertising campaign.

Early in January 1980, for example, a national audience watching ABC television saw a thirty-minute special sponsored by the Carter campaign. Among the White House scenes were ones of a decisive Jimmy Carter meeting with his aides ("I'll make a decision on it today!") and of a loving Jimmy Carter helping daughter Amy with her math assignment. After taping the footage, media adviser Gerald Rafshoon and producer Robert Squier sat Carter down in his private study and asked him to talk about his family. His recorded remarks became a voiceover for the taped footage, itself edited. The Carter voiceover says:

I don't think there's any way you can separate responsibilities for a good husband or a father and a basic human being from that of being a good president. What I do in the White House is to maintain a good family life, which I consider to be crucial to being a good president.

Later during the primary races, the Decisive Scene and Family Scene were recut into thirty-second polispots. In the latter an announcer's voiceover told Massachusetts viewers in early March:

Husband, father, president—he's done these three jobs with distinction.

The whole package, however, was conceived in the fall of 1979 when Patrick Caddell, Carter's public-opinion specialist, reported that many voters regarded Carter's character as his

greatest strength, while there was significant doubt about the
character of his rival, Edward Kennedy. The survey finding
became a Carter theme. Not so incidentally, the guild people
who perform these political specialties are paid extremely well
for their work, with six-figure salaries often supplemented by a
15 percent fee leveled on the total advertising buy.

Political advertising is highly predictable, as patterned as
Kabuki theater. Like any specialized art or craft form, the number of variations are limited. The thirty-second and sixty-second
formats restrict political advertising to certain conventions. Because it is advertising, the candidate's spots usually are well
written, well lit, well shot, well produced. Because it is politics,
the candidate's spots typically say nothing as forcefully as possible. John Deardourff, who was Senator Baker's man, claims he
can make a thirty-second political spot that actually says something but that nobody wants to do that kind of commercial.
(Deardourff offered as a theoretical example a thirty-second
statement for a candidate on the topic of abortion and commented: "I haven't been able to sell that to anyone but my wife.")

Even the longer-form commercials, the five-minute or thirty-
minute programs, follow certain clearly defined rules that would
be expected in a medium that takes great care to avoid straining
viewers' alleged short attention spans. When Ronald Reagan
went on television in the fall of 1979 to announce his candidacy
in a five-minute polispot, the candidate used less than three
minutes to explain why he wanted to be president. Then: quick
cut to another, younger, more vigorous talking head, the actor
Michael Landon, who used the rest of the time asking for campaign contributions and telling viewers where to send their
checks.

At MIT the News Study Group has assembled hundreds of
kinescopes and videotape samples of political advertising going
back to the 1952 Eisenhower–Stevenson race. We can examine
these commercials historically, comparing, say, a 1960 Nixon
with a 1980 Connally, as well as looking at them dynamically, for

example, monitoring the changes within a struggling campaign such as Edward Kennedy's in 1980 as it shifts styles from primary state to primary state in search of the right approach. By study of these tapes, and interviews with the guild specialists, it is possible to make a general typology of the political advertisement.[1]

Political commercials address their audiences in five basic rhetorical modes. The initial commercials in a campaign are in the ID, or biography-personality mode. If the candidate has a low ID, that is, not many voters can identify him, then a biography-personality commercial enables viewers to meet the real man. It is a selected reality, of course, the highlights but never the lowlights of a career. In 1976, for example, Jimmy Carter began with a 3 percent recognition in the polls; Rafshoon offered primary voters Carter's Huck Finn boyhood . . . the Annapolis years . . . the dusty fields of southwest Georgia . . . the new south governor extending a friendly hand to blacks and whites . . . . In 1980 George Bush began with a low ID similar to Carter's and took the same tactical route of fifteen-hour campaign days and ID spots that told the Bush story in fast-paced jump cuts: Yale baseball captain . . . World War II Navy pilot . . . oil wildcatter . . . envoy to China meeting Chairman Mao . . . Congressman . . . CIA director . . . energetic candidate . . . . The Bush candidacy offered a bonus every documentary maker fantasizes: a Navy newsreel cameraman was present when the young flier, shot down on a bombing mission, was fished out of the Pacific waters.

Sometimes high recognition can be worse than low recognition and requires a different approach. Carter by 1980 needed no introduction; instead his media adviser attempted to wrap the man in the office; a Carter campaign spot on the eve of the Iowa caucuses reminded viewers four times of the President but used Carter's name just once. An early John Connally commercial, featuring silver-haired Big John in a dark, pin-striped suit standing in front of an enormous American flag, stirred in many viewers a mixture of bad memories—General Patton, Richard Nixon, Lyndon Johnson. Later Iowa commercials put Connally in a denim jacket sitting before a blazing fire as he talked about acreage yields in Texas compared to Iowa—Folksy John. In the general election campaign Ronald Reagan's media men, led by West Coast ad man Peter Dailey, had no problem with the candidate's high ID. But they wanted him known not as actor-PR man but as leader. Consequently, his experience and years as California governor were stressed in the polispots, where he was also consistently referred to as Governor.

After the ID spots—Act I in the media drama—the advertising campaign moves to either contents or auras spots. Edward Kennedy, who seemingly needed no ID, started in Iowa by talking to voters about how he had consulted with his wife and children before running, attempting to create his own positive image of family. The approach was quickly junked. "It just wasn't believable," says David Sawyer, a media adviser who was called in by the Kennedy campaign but did not stay. "People wanted to know what he would *do* as president." The Kennedy campaign eventually found its voice when the candidate began talking, first in a major speech at Georgetown University, about 18 percent inflation rates and Carter's foreign policy. Kennedy's new polispots also showed the senator speaking out against the draft and opposing nuclear power, in effect re-introducing and IDing Kennedy as a liberal. Ronald Reagan's 1980 commercials from the start were high in content. He ran an ideological campaign about the return to conservative values. "Reagan sells himself," according to his producer, Elliott Curson. Instead of a slick approach, Curson's Reagan met foreign policy head-on. The most dramatic Reagan spot began with newsreel scenes of the Soviet hierarchy reviewing Russian missiles in Red Square. Whereas Bush shook hands with Mao, Reagan set up Brezhnev as his opponent.

Reagan ran on the political right, muting content only toward the end of the campaign when he was safely ahead. The centrist candidate, seeking support from all sides, avoids content as much as possible; his Act II conveys auras like the Carter family spot. In the Republican primaries Baker and Bush clearly offered the best aura campaigns. With Bush, the cumulative aura was that of momentum; Robert Goodman and his associate Ron Wilner photographed Bush on the move, enthusiastically leaping out of the campaign jet, vigorously pounding fist into palm on platforms, besieged by a thicket of microphones in a mass of bodies, and enjoying it all. The idea was to build on Bush's good looks, to contrast his youth and vigor with Ronald Reagan (Bush was fifty-five and Reagan sixty-nine when the campaign began). "I told George to perform, to get emotionally psyched up," Goodman said to an interviewer. "As recognition and interest—momentum—built for Bush, we tried to feed it," Wilner told us. Bush had lost twice in Texas political races, but in Bush's momentum commercials, cheering crowds and the bright badge of victory, a convention balloon drop—boldly, and misleadingly, lifted from an all-candidates' meeting in Ames, Iowa—signified the winner's image.

With Baker the dominant aura was that of character. In the Deardourff and Bailey world the words, music, and image all fit each other. The camera focused on the earnest, serious senator as he attentively listened to a group of voters in a comfortable living room with fireplace and ornamental musket. For the New England campaigns, the commercials were shot in Amherst, New Hampshire, with a group of genuine granite-staters who, commented the *Boston Globe*'s Martin Nolan, "looked as if they had been dreamed up by the William Morris Agency."

After auras and issues the next act of a media campaign—if the voters haven't walked out on the candidate, as they did with Baker—is likely to involve the endorsement commercial. Just before the New York primary the Kennedy camp switched media advisers from Charles Guggenheim to David Sawyer of New York. Sawyer made two commercials featuring actor Carroll O'Connor, better known to television viewers as Archie

Bunker. O'Connor did what all well-known people do in the tiny world of commercials—link his aura and sponsorship to the product. He also combined this praise of Kennedy with sharp criticism of Carter, the rival product. This is the next form of polispot that appears about this time in a campaign—the dramatic attack commercials, also known as negative commercials.

As the name and the timing implies, attack commercials take aim late in the campaign not so much at the candidate's virtues as at his opponent's presumed faults. Perhaps the most notorious attack commercial was the Daisy spot that William Bernbach and Tony Schwartz did for the Lyndon Johnson campaign in 1964. The ad all but said a vote for Barry Goldwater was a vote for nuclear war, though Goldwater's name wasn't mentioned. Instead a child picked at a daisy, counting the petals, her playful chatter gradually supplanted by a deep, disembodied male voice conducting a missile countdown. Then: a nuclear explosion, and the Vote Johnson message.

In 1964 the overkill was Johnson's; his lead was so great he didn't need to play off Goldwater's superhawk stance. In 1980 the backrunners, predictably enough, went on the attack. Maverick John Anderson stood in front of a bank of television monitors showing the other talk-alike Republican candidates and stressed "The Anderson Difference," a telecopy of the commercial for Anacin cold tablets. The slogan was the handiwork of Bob Sann, a New York advertising man. In Massachusetts the Anderson campaign spent $400,000, highest of any candidate, on television and radio polispots aimed at the target audience of moderate Republicans and independents. (State law allows independents to vote in party primaries.)

George Bush, the mid-runner who did well in the January caucuses, initially justified his early aura of momentum. By the Florida primaries, however, the Bush campaign had been shaken by Ronald Reagan's resilience, and Bush did what the script called for: He went on the attack, making radio commercials which claimed that Reagan "has no real understanding of the dangers we face in the decade of the eighties. . . . He didn't even know who the president of France was."

California Governor Jerry Brown, the youngest and most telegenically compelling face in the Democratic field, chose high-content, high-aura, high-attack commercials, an all-purpose mode that combines all the forms (appropriate for a candidate with much less money to spend than his opponents). The camera opened on a head and chest shot of Brown, dressed in a three-piece suit. The candidate looked intently at the viewer—or, as the media managers would say, made good eye-contact. Camera comes in tighter while an unsmiling Brown reads the teleprompter copy written by his campaign manager, Tom Quinn:

The president isn't a magician. He can't snap his fingers and solve all our problems. But the president can give us an intelligent foreign policy, one that protects our future.

Toward the end of a campaign backrunners may have to return to square one and reshoot their dramatic presentations. On the eve of the Massachusetts primary, needing a big victory, Edward Kennedy returned to a variation of the mode he had first tried and abandoned in Iowa:

I have come to ask for your help. I do not ask merely on the basis of fond memories and old friendship. I ask for it on the basis of common principles and concern.
It is you who have inspired me to make this fight.

At the end, he was identifying himself as a Kennedy, and a son of Massachusetts.

These five rhetorical modes of political commercials, we found, were matched by cinematic styles of presentation that are also highly predictable. The styles are those that any one paying attention to television commercials, or film documentaries, would intuitively expect: *cinema verité*, the jostling cameras and quick cuts of the Bush momentum spots; the *news camera*, not so much something that looks like it is real but reality itself, such as the spots made from Kennedy's Georgetown speech or the decisive Carter in the Oval Office; the *omniscient narrator*, a camera looking in on reality as in the unstaged Baker living room conversations; the *one-on-one* sincere sell, such as Kennedy on Massachusetts election eve; and, finally, what for lack of a better name I've come to think of as the unabashedly outright *commercial commercial*. The candidate stands in front of a dark, executive desk, with imposing bookcases and an American flag on a staff in the background, just like the self-assured doctor figure, or engineer or other television authority who recommends Dristan or Uniroyal Tires. Anderson's ad man Sann says it was just incidental that The Anderson Difference slogan resembled the Anacin cold tablet commercial, which also just happened to be his handiwork. Philip Crane, who looks handsome and sincere enough to qualify for commercial work, should he leave the Congress, also relied heavily on the commercial commercial, as did Ronald Reagan who used to do television commercials for General Electric products among other accounts.

Political advertising can be fun to watch and, by the testimony of those who produce the polispots, fun to make. But politics has a more measurable and serious bottom line: Do polispots help candidates win? And, if we can intrude the idea of the public interest, do they contribute at all to voter understanding of candidates and issues?

The prevailing wisdom feeds the pleasurable paranoia most of us harbor about omnipotent media Rasputins who manipulate our minds, or assuredly, the minds of those out there, the masses. The actual evidence is less sensational. The best commercial of the 1980 campaign, by near unanimous agreement, was a Howard Baker spot apparently showing him taking on an Iranian student during a meeting at an Iowa campus. Artful editing transformed the short, mild senator into a tall tiger chewing up a dark, unshaven militant who looked like a stand-in for his cousins in Teheran 10,000 miles away. But all this advertising creativity produced little or nothing for Baker at the polls. In New Hampshire George Bush's campaign manager proclaimed that commercials were 60 percent of the fight, but the Reagan camp put its time and efforts into phone banks and shoe leather to get out Reagan's loyalist vote from 1976.

Back in the 1950s and early 1960s, when the experts started fretting about media manipulation, television was still a fresh experience. It had believability. A CBS series could promise us, *You Are There.* The first time a viewer saw a sincere candidate with good eye-contact, it might have been effective. By the hundred and first time, it has become an artifice.

Still the form has its defenders. "Campaigns are not philosophical discussions, despite what the League of Women Voters thinks," declares the columnist David Broder. "They are not referendums on issues. You are choosing candidates, live human beings. And one of the facilities that you want in a leader is the ability to compress and narrow choices in a way that makes them understandable and accessible to people. Using television to do that is not a distortion of the process, it is very much the essence of leadership. There's nothing wrong with the discipline that's involved in refining your thought to the point that you can express it in three or four declarative sentences." Broder's fellow columnist, Richard Reeves, agrees: "If political commercials are as evil as some think, they are a necessary evil. Candidates for the highest office—and the lowest office—have the right to say what they want to say, the way they want to say it."[2]

In my view political spots serve two public functions. First, they help to remind some voters that something important is taking place. In 1968 Richard Nixon spent $20 million of television and radio advertising in the last weeks of his campaign only to see his fifteen point lead over Hubert Humphrey dwindle to less than one point. According to the Democratic strategist Vic Fingerhut, the Nixon media blitz served mainly to alert poor, less-educated Democratic voters that there was an election going on. Similarly, in Iowa in 1980, the blizzard of statewide television commercials and the media's dazzling presence stirred interest in the caucus meetings: If John Chancellor is here, it must be important. But the weather on caucus night, mild for January, probably helped attendance more.

Second, political spots appear to reinforce the preferences of already committed voters or leaning-toward-favorable voters. It is a familiar advertising mechanism: people who own mileage-saving Datsun cars, or who prefer the conservative policies of a Ronald Reagan, pay more attention to advertising confirming Datsun's MPG value or Reagan's anti-gun control stand. But for the rest of us, who is likely to buy a new car, or cast a vote, solely on the basis of a thirty-second televised message? Most of us go down to the showroom, kick the tires, or at least talk over our choices with friends and family, or check out other sources for information.

In 1968 perhaps it was possible to write, as Joe McGinniss did, about the selling of the president. In 1981, post-Vietnam, post-Watergate, fewer and fewer people were buying advertising messages. "The sixties," says Phillip Friedman of David Garth Associates, "that was the dark ages of television. You can't work in those styles today." John Sears, who masterminded the early Reagan campaign, puts the same idea another way: "By the time something becomes known as particularly useful, it no longer works for you. The voters are much more sophisticated than they ever have been before. These educated voters hear constantly that candidates are sort of trying to sell them toothpaste out there on television all the time. They'll invariably react against it."

Television and the rest of the media have helped school a new generation of viewers/voters in politics-as-media. A commercial can only be as good as a product, or, as Elliott Curson says, "Commercials help those candidates who help themselves." The best media packagers, it seems, can't put over a candidate whose character and stands on the issues fail to engage voters, party loyalists, and likely contributors over the long, arduous campaign.

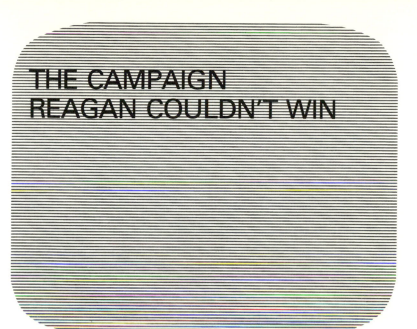

THE CAMPAIGN REAGAN COULDN'T WIN

CHAPTER 16

During the 1980 presidential campaign, Henry Anatole Grunwald, editor in chief of Time Inc., joined Ronald Reagan's traveling press corps for a brief spell. In the news magazine world, this is called Showing the Flag: a home office panjandrum travels with the reporters in the field—the troops—and visits with the candidate (or the prime minister, or third world leader), gets a feeling for the situation, and then heads back to New York, sometimes late in the week, to supervise the closing of the magazine. Normally, there is nothing unusual about the practice—I did it myself, when I was an editor at *Newsweek*. But times change; Grunwald used Time's corporate Lear jet to swoop down on Reagan. The sight of the Time Inc. jet parked on the Tarmac next to Reagan's rented 727, the Friendship '80, struck a proper symbolic note for the 1980 campaign.

While Ronald Reagan and corporate republicanism were winning the biggest conservative victory since the Eisenhower years, Time corporate journalism was back where it historically has

been most comfortable, traveling side by side with a free enterprise president, advising and consenting on the direction of the
country. Henry R. Luce's vision of the American Century now
gets to take one more swing in the batter's box before the
century slips away.

Immediately after the election, in fact, Grunwald announced
an unprecedented plan for the seven magazines of the Time
publishing empire; each one, *Time, Fortune, Money, Life, People,
Sports Illustrated,* and *Discover,* would take on the theme of revitalization of America, to show that the country still had resources and assets to draw upon, that America was not really the
helpless, pitiful giant of the last few years.

The project had overtones of both arrogance and fatuous-
ness—a *Sports Illustrated* essay on the theme of athletic competi-
tiveness is, to put it mildly, quite a reach—but the fact is that
Henry Luce's *Time* over its fifty-eight years of existence has been
much more than a Republican fellow traveler. Luce tried might-
ily to make Thomas J. Dewey president, succeeded with Eisenhower, and didn't live to regret Nixon. By 1976, with Luce dead,
and with the nation in a post-Watergate mood ready to try
something—anything—that seemed different from the Nixon
gang, *Time* gave a very favorable press to an obscure one-term
governor from Georgia named Jimmy Carter. Hedley Donovan,
Luce's successor as Time Inc.'s editor in chief, and a man of
intelligence and decency, liked the intelligent, decent Carter and
particularly the global policy views of Carter's foreign policy
adviser Zbigniew Brzezinski, who spun out upbeat, glossy sce-
narios about the technotronic era, the joys of transnational econ-
omies and, of course, the virtues of trilateralism. On *Time*'s
other hand, Henry Grunwald, Vienna-born and a long-time
admirer of Henry Kissinger—the two are physically so much
alike that they can be mistaken for each other at crowded Manhattan receptions—shared in Kissinger's more gloomy Spengler-
ian fears of an America growing too soft to oppose the militant
march of socialism. In 1976 Donovan won that war in the

editorial pages of *Time* magazine, and Carter and Brzezinski rode into office. By 1980, however, editorial power in the 34th floor suites at the Time-Life building on Sixth Avenue had again shifted. Donovan had retired from Time Inc., taken a White House job as a Carter adviser and retired from that. The decline of the west, the dimming of the American Century under Carter, was proceeding apace. But, yes, the Time was changing too. Grunwald was running Time Inc., Reagan was replacing Carter, and the *Washington Star*—another Time Inc. property—was suggesting to Reagan in its editorial columns that he ought to pick Kissinger for his secretary of state. Although that advice was not taken, Grunwald said he was more optimistic about getting across the Time revitalization message of building up American defenses. In early December, as the special magazine issues were being prepared, Grunwald told interviewer Jane Perlez in the New York *Daily News:* "if any one in the Reagan Administration wants to be inspired by (our) articles, that's fine."

Many otherwise sensible people, I know, get exercised when the normal pro-defense, pro-growth, pro-enterprise, pro-corporate, pro-technotronic impulses of American business—and publishing and broadcasting are capitalist businesses—are consciously expressed in the media. In fact, this happens less than anyone thinks. The revitalization series is newsworthy precisely because each Time Inc. magazine, from *Fortune* to *People* (the gossipy side of the American spirit), is toeing the same line so openly. If these same readers and viewers looked around through 1979, they would have seen the revitalization message plugged all over, in *Newsweek, Time, New York Times, Business Week,* and on ABC, CBS, and NBC. Why? Well, why not?

Spiro Agnew's speech writers conjured up an establishment media cabal, which got together to work things out. That was a right wing scam to distract folks from the Nixon gang's own cabals. More serious critics on the left, like Todd Gitlin at Berkeley, are also mistaken in pointing to big finance, or Wall Street, or other traditional capitalist manipulators as secret orchestrators of the news. The real secret is that nobody has to engage in cabals. The press picks up on the prevailing atmospherics of the dominant social institutions, in part shaping some of the currents and eddies, but mostly being shaped by them, trimming sails here, setting off on a hard-to-starboard course there, watching the telltales for the shifting forces in the larger world.

At MIT our News Study Group has been observing these press tacks and hardabouts since 1972. While we started by studying the Nixon–McGovern campaign, we have since looked into the patterns of press performance on a variety of stories, foreign and domestic, observing, for example, how the press images of Arabs and Israelis began to change after the oil embargo of 1973. Consequently, when we looked at the 1980 presidential race and the campaigns of Jimmy Carter, Ronald Reagan, and John Anderson, it wasn't too hard to pick up the freshening atmospherics of 1980 and to hear the bracing calls for enterprise, revitalization, and getting the canons on deck.

By late 1979 the direction of the American wind was unmistakable. A number of people in the important institutions in our society—in the Congress, in the labor-industrial complex, in the banks—had come to the conclusion that Jimmy Carter could not, and should not, be re-elected. The columnists and commentators most closely wired to these institutions began reporting what their sources were telling them. This widened the circle of talk—to use Walter Lippmann's phrase—about Jimmy Carter's unelectability. By the end of 1979 a kind of ABC outcome—Anybody But Carter—had been agreed upon by the people who are paid to write about or think about or practice political affairs full time. In that sense the 1980 presidential campaign was over before 1980 began. Probably for Carter, the campaign was over in mid-1979. Beginning with the awful period of rising inflation, rising interest rates, and increasing unemployment, Jimmy Carter's conduct of the presidency could not win a majority approval rating in the various public opinion polls. The only excitement left for the actual 1980 campaign, then, was: Given ABC, who would succeed Carter as the next president?

Should journalists have been more resistant to these institutional currents? Campaign reporters are generalists; they are, to take the most obvious example, largely ignorant of economics, one of the reasons the subject has been covered so dismally in past campaigns. As a result the press may report surging interest rates, or declining bond markets, but it has to take the opinions of others—experts—on what these developments mean, not because individual reporters are pro-Capitalist but because they are blissfully ignorant. The press is always reacting to the hot news and the latest trends rather than understanding the underlying phenomenon that makes news and trends.

As a result of this dependence, the press is usually the last to know the new news. Even in its presumed specialty of electoral politics, the campaign press is continually taken by surprise. The political staff of the *Washington Post* could complete a major analysis of the last campaign, published as *The Pursuit of the Presidency* and in its 427 pages fail to grapple with the big unresolved postelection question: To what extent do the election results reflect a genuine turn to the right among the great mass of voters? And this from the brightest people working for, arguably, one of the two or three best newspapers in the country.[1]

The revelation that journalists are smart but not deep is hardly going to startle anyone nowadays, anymore than the recognition that journalists are dependent upon their sources, largely official, for the news. It may, however, be something of a surprise to learn how much like their sources journalists have become, and why it is so easy for a consensus to develop on something like Anybody But Carter. In the mid-1950s, when I first came to Washington as a reporter, and not "journalist," the resident press corps still reflected the patterns found by Leo Rosten in his pioneering 1937 study of the press. The Washington press corps then was predominantly white, male, and midwestern in origin; most in the press corps had gone only to high school, though all dressed in white-shirt respectability. By the late 1950s and early 1960s, the press corps began to change, and by 1980 the writer and Brookings Institute scholar Stephen Hess was able to report that a transformation had occurred in significant respects.

Hess interviewed 1,220 newspeople in Washington for his study, *The Washington Reporters* (Brookings, 1981). Forty years after Rosten, Hess found that the press corps is still overwhelmingly white (96.4 percent) and male (80 percent). But now it is very well educated (30 percent having attended graduate school), middle class and northeastern in origin. Even when newspeople grew up in other parts of the country, they tended to take on an eastern coloring after a while in big-time Washington journalism. Hess also found that the press corps feels itself cut off from mainstream America, and even from its own editors and home offices. Washington journalists talk mainly to their sources, and to each other. They also do a lot of talking. They are, Hess found, highly verbal, articulate, and opinionated; they have a stylistic bias toward a type of elegance and verbal play. This explains, says Hess, why journalists may like a William Buckley and dislike a George McGovern.

Hess did not specifically talk about press corps attitudes toward Jimmy Carter, John Anderson, or Ronald Reagan in his inquiries. But no one had to be around much longer than a brief stay in Washington during the campaign to encounter the enormous personal hostility that many journalists felt toward Jimmy Carter. The politest term for this antipathy would be Hess's stylistic bias; Carter's own partisans thought it outright bias related to Carter's southern, rural, Baptist roots. Those who disliked him countered that it was not for class or regional reasons but because he was mean-spirited, inbred, self-righteous, a loner, comfortable only with his wife and small band of Georgia brothers. Even given his mean, small, distant nature, they say, they could have abided that if he hadn't so mismanaged the economy, U.S. foreign policy, etc., etc., etc. Of course, if journalists had a more knowledgeable grasp of economics and global issues, it's possible that we might have drawn some other conclusions about Carter's performance. But that literally is academic now and doesn't change the reality that, by late 1979, the circles of talk within the Congress, the business community, and the big-league press were saying that Carter had to go. And so ABC played itself out in three phases:

1. On the Democratic side, the premature nomination and election of Senator Edward M. Kennedy as president;

2. On the Republican side, the meteor campaigns of John Connally, Howard Baker, and George Bush, ABC candidates who were similarly nominated and elected;

3. In both the later primary campaign and the general election campaign, the free press pass that an amiable, relaxed media granted amiable, relaxed Ronald Regan.

The Kennedy Nomination

Partisans of the Massachusetts senator are likely to buttonhole the unwary and transfix them with the tale of how the press got their candidate, much like the Ancient Mariner telling his rime to the Wedding Guest. The Kennedyites can point to all the just-one-more-time Chappaquiddick reprises in the late summer of 1979, on the tenth anniversary of that episode; to the stumbling, fumbling image of Kennedy in his interview with Roger Mudd on CBS in the fall of 1979, right before Kennedy announced he was running; to all the news clips on the evening television showing a shouting, fist-waving Kennedy as the network cameras highlighted the most strident fifteen seconds out of the candidate's fifteen-hour day; to the extreme case of publisher Rupert Murdoch's *New York Post,* which endorsed Jimmy Carter in the New York State primary. Senator Kennedy suffered somewhat in the more genteel hands of Roger Mudd and the networks, but he was hardly a victim of press cynicism (Murdoch

excepted). Kennedy did pay the price of the press's bad judgment and its languid habits.

First, there was the press's incredible silliness in awarding the
nomination to the senator in the late summer of 1979, a full year
before the election campaign. What happened then was the
press's failure to remember how quickly events can change political balances—a common occupational disability shared with
those Democratic office holders who were urging Kennedy to
run, in large part or wholly, because of their own concerns for
re-election with the weak Carter at the top of the ticket. Kennedy announced, and then the Iranian hostage crisis and the
Russian invasion of Afghanistan temporarily changed Jimmy
Carter's political standings. The same Democratic congressmen
who were worrying about their own skins now saw a Carter
resurgence (equally temporary).

Second, there was the press's failure to convey the substance
of the policy questions, or issues, at stake on the Democratic side
(also on the Republican and Independent sides). This is a familiar fault, repeated every four years in presidential campaigns
and nightly on television screens and in news pages. It is part of
the arrested adolescence of American journalism. We have short
attention spans, projecting our own surface interests onto the
audience; we are easily diverted from the serious; we run in
packs. The shortcomings of the press would fill a book; in fact,
they have filled several books (see, for example, Herbert Gans's
Deciding What's News, or my own MIT Press studies). Less well
explored is how institutional constraints—time, money, space,
among others—on the news product and on the news people
keep most journalism from being too serious.

In 1980, as before, journalists were alternately bemused and
distracted by the visible, easy-to-cover, fun parts of the campaign—the horse race, the television commercials, the media
events, the Rafshoonery, and the rest of the stylistic ginger-
bread. As usual reporters gave less attention to the weightier
matters of staff organizations, political strategies, campaign

finances, and overall public policy alternatives. Looking the wrong way, the press missed the inherent structural weaknesses of the Kennedy presidential effort, the organizational story that is not on television or in the morning papers. In every political contest, there are two campaigns—the visible photo opportunity activities and the closed door decisions, deals, and commitments. When the media know very little of the latter, it is, in part, because they are kept occupied by the former.

Finally, the Kennedy campaign demonstrated the truism that the press clings to certain political mythologies long after the rest of the citizenry has abandoned such fairy tales. One reason for this is the press's, particularly the Washington press's, isolation from society (as Stephen Hess found). In the 1980 campaign the journalistic circle of talk paid homage to the myth of Camelot. Because so many journalists are still so enamored of the Kennedy family, their early assumption was that the voters were similarly starry-eyed. Another enduring journalistic myth centered on the supposed political savvy of the big city boss. When Chicago Mayor Jane Byrne deserted Carter to endorse Kennedy, many reporters assumed that the heiress of the old Richard J. Daley machine knew what she was doing and could deliver voters the way The Boss used to deliver. With our hindsight, it's possible to see why Kennedy won the big industrial states of New York and Pennsylvania while losing Illinois. In the former Kennedy had the ABC issues working for him; New York Jewish voters were angry about the botched Carter Administration vote in the United Nations on Jewish settlements on the West Bank; Pennsylvania blue-collar voters worried about the economy. In Illinois Kennedy carried the millstone of Jane Byrne around his neck.

The press, then, shortsightedly gave the nomination and election to Kennedy. But it was, as usual, reflecting the political myopia of its sources. Presidential races are not won or lost in the media. The idea that they are is a growing myth in itself, one fed by misconstrued tales of press power. Presidential races are won and lost in the real world, in real-world events. Unscripted developments like the hostage taking in Iran "got" the Kennedy candidacy. The Kennedy campaign's lack of early organization "got" Kennedy. In their defense it should be said that the Kennedy people had initially counted on a 1984 campaign, until they started believing their own campaign clippings in late 1979.

The Meteor Campaigns

At the start of the 1980 presidential campaign, covering the Republican candidates looked to be about as exciting as watching a refrigerator defrost. Ronald Reagan was so clearly the front runner—or front walker, as Lou Cannon called him in the *Washington Post,* referring to the stately character of the Reagan effort—that the Republican race seemed all over except for Reagan's coronation. A coronation, however, was not what the press wanted, or the country needed (as the establishments saw it). For the press, campaign fights, horse races, and drama are thought to boost circulation (or raise TV ratings). But that is only a secondary matter. At the higher institutional circles of talk, the establishments had not make up their minds about Ronald Reagan. While these opinion makers were reflecting ABC (Anybody But Carter) feelings, they also felt ANRE (And Not Reagan Either). He was too old, too trigger happy, too conservative, too simplistic in his economic formulations and his nostalgia for a Norman Rockwell America. He was, moreover, an ex-actor (for Warner Brothers) and ex-public relations man (for General Electric). Verbal style and Buckleyian wit are one thing; reading lines written by someone else is quite another.

The results of the first Iowa caucuses in early 1980 appeared to save the campaign, the press, and the country, first, from the boredom of an early Reagan walkover and, second, from the uncertainties of a Reagan presidency. After Iowa the Republicans were all knotted up in a lively contest, thanks to the showing of George Bush, who seemed to make Reagan look not so much the front runner, or even the front walker, as the sleep walker.

The George Bush campaign promised to be not only fun but a familiar assignment; reporters could play handicapper, positioning the field of candidates.

No fewer than seven Republicans had announced that they were serious candidates. But campaign journalists did not take all of the candidates with equal seriousness. Columnists Jack Germond and Jules Witcover, for example, broke the field up into the heavyweights—Reagan, Bush, John Connally, and Howard Baker—and the middleweights—Philip Crane, Robert Dole, and John Anderson. Sometimes the field was called as "front-runner" Reagan against "the rest of the pack." Reagan, Bush, Connally, and Baker were also known as the big four; the little three, according to William Safire of the *New York Times,* were merely running for the exercise.

The category "others" is a familiar one in presidential politics. In 1976 Jimmy Carter's surprising show of strength in the Iowa caucuses effectively disentangled his candidacy from the pack—a feat duplicated by George Bush and his organization in 1980. Bush acknowledged that he had taken that page from Carter's book, or more precisely, that page from the book *Marathon,* Jules Witcover's account of the Carter presidential strategy. Bush's rewards for his mastery of history were the predictable headlines and the *Newsweek* cover, a picture of Bush jogging, with the line BUSH BREAKS OUT OF THE PACK. Bush was elevated to viable front-runner status.

John Connally, of course, had already broken fast from the press starting gate. He was the first of the Republican Magnificent Seven to appear on the cover of *Time* magazine. The conspiracy-minded thought that honor could be traced to the Temple crowd—Texas-based Temple Industries, the timber-holding and paperboard products manufacturer whose head, Arthur Temple, sits on the Time Inc. board. Many people are surprised to hear that the Temple family is the largest single stockholder in Time Inc., yet the Temples own about 15 percent of the company stock compared to 7.4 percent for the Henry

Luce Foundation, the next largest share holder. Arthur Temple's position led to the notion that Connally was benefiting from a Texas connection. Actually, the *Time* cover story was not all that kind to Connally, detailing as it did the Milk Fund case and other episodes of Big John's wheeling and dealing. If the Connally cover had to be traced to any one influence, the trial would lead to Henry Grunwald and Time Inc.'s sense of weakening American power and the need for strong leadership.

John Connally seemed to be that take-charge leader. He had a Texas-sized image; big money, tough, blunt talker. He rejected federal matching campaign funds and raised over $10 million on his own, far more than any other candidate. Meanwhile, Dole and Crane, and to a lesser extent Baker, remained largely indistinct, unfocused figures in the early stages of the primaries—images that may tell as much about their candidacies as about the press's habit of labeling. Connally, Reagan, Bush, and John Anderson came across quite clearly: their labels seemed to fit. They also attracted a great deal of press interest, an attention, in Bush's and Anderson's case, all out of proportion to their initial standings in the polls. In the press's eyes, Connally, Bush, and Anderson had earned special attention, and each became a focus of anti-Reagan hopes.

Reagan had earned the media spotlight as the candidate initially favored by his party. He was described as "Mr. Conservative" by Walter Cronkite on the *CBS Evening News*, the candidate that others had to be measured against. In the early primaries Reagan also received some attention for his nonrunning ways, for his advanced age, and for his apparent lack of fire. Thus the *Washington Post* reported: "The public part of a typical Reagan campaign day starts late in the morning or at noon, giving the sixty-eight-year-old candidate plenty of rest. Since he declared his candidacy, November 13, Reagan has visited seventeen states and made twenty speeches—about as many as his more active opponents make in a week and a half." And David Broder wrote: "Reagan is running a simulated campaign—a carefully staged set of mini-appearances composed of scripted television talks, stilted speeches, and brief, sketchy press conferences."

George Bush, by contrast, was frequently commended in stories for his hard running, exuberance, and enthusiasm. At first, journalists had a difficult time deciding on the correct political image for Bush. Was he old Eastern Establishment and a moderate? He had, after all, grown up in Connecticut and attended Phillips Exeter and Yale. Or was he on the New Republican-Conservative Right? He had made his big money in oil and served as a congressman from Texas. As Bush himself took hard-line positions on defense and foreign policy, the press at last came down on the side of the conservative image: "Bush has abandoned his Brooks Brothers wardrobe" (*Newsweek*); "He's a younger version of Reagan" (*Boston Globe*). Only William Loeb's *Union-Leader* (Manchester, New Hampshire) characteristically broke step, calling Bush the candidate of the leftist and liberal newspapers.

But most of all, Bush was judged a nice guy (Joseph Kraft) and vigorous (ABC News featured evening news footage of Bush running, running, running, plugging away). Bush, of course, knew what images he wanted to project. Anyone who has ever worked on a newspaper or magazine and has selected news photos for publication knows that you look for the picture that seems characteristic. Characteristic of what? Of the essential character you believe exists.

The Bush meteor probably got its most sympathetic sighting in the press for its style. Bush managed to combine the 1976 Carter campaign's sense of efficiency with the 1976 Udall campaign's sense of good humor—a heady combination for journalists. The attention given the John Anderson shooting star by the press, however, represented something fresh in press-candidate interactions. Journalists openly embraced the plodding Anderson for his alleged decency, intelligence, courage. "Why Not the Best?" asked the *New York Times* in an editorial approving of Anderson's support of a stiff gasoline tax. On television, CBS's

Roger Mudd did a bemused piece on Anderson as back runner. Anderson had been declared by America's political handicappers at 100-to-one shot when he announced in June, 1979, Mudd reported. "Today he's a 150-to-one shot. . . ." Mudd suggested that Anderson was the victim of a self-fulfilling prophecy: the press doesn't think Anderson has a chance, and so no reporters cover Anderson, and so he gets little air time or ink and so he can't win . . . . But the Mudd analysis missed the real point: Anderson's press-endowed extraordinary abilities combined with his low standing in the polls became a running story with its own momentum. The *New York Times* noted:

The first thing people say when John Anderson's name comes up in talk about the 1980 election is something like, "You know, he may be the best man in the race, the one who appeals to Republicans and Democrats at that." Invariably, the next sentence is something like, "Too bad he doesn't have a chance."

The *Times* deplored that attitude, as if a rejection of Anderson would call into question the goodness of the American people and of our political system. Enter the "viable" Anderson candidacy—someone not "inept" like Carter, or "simplistic" like Reagan. Columnists and opinion makers took to milling around Anderson—"rallying around" would be too strong a term—and Anderson himself achieved recognition for having low recognition. His certification as a serious candidate appeared in the velvet-gloved, iron-fist attention given him by columnists Rowland Evans and Robert Novak. Card-carrying liberals Stewart Mott and Stanley Sheinbaum, the columnists noted, had organized fund-raising events for Anderson, making the Illinois congressman not so much the candidate of the dessicated Republican left as of the frustrated Democratic left.

Anderson became the darling of the leftists, and the target of Evans and Novak, for opposing the MX missile system and for supporting ERA and public funding of abortions. Anderson's embarassing previous life as a supporter of the Vietnam War and author of "Christian Nation" resolutions in the Congress was lost in the false radiance of his meteor campaign. One column's liberal leftist is another's pragmatic Republican, as David Broder characterized Anderson. Political reporters, as much as the rest of us, see what they want to see. Only a few reporters—Robert Sherrill, that valuable resource, was one— discerned that Anderson really combined Carter's ineptness and Reagan's simplicities. (Sherrill praised Anderson for keeping alive the maverick candidate tradition but added that Anderson has described himself as a plain, old-fashioned, orthodox Republican on economic matters. Said Sherrill, "I don't think our economy can stand much more 'plain, old-fashioned, orthodox' anything.")

Press selective perception was most noticeable when the handicappers had some race results to interpret, such as the Iowa Republican candidates' forum. Looking in on the two-hour television show, the commentators saw their own inclinations mirrored on the platform. Courtly James J. Kilpatrick, the thinking man's conservative, thought he had witnessed a class act—he said everyone won. Practical David Broder found Anderson the winner for sheer eloquence and awarded Anderson the high Broder honor "pragmatist." The *New York Times'* William Safire, a veteran of the Nixon White House, found Howard Baker the winner; Baker "looked the most at ease and showed an old pro's capacity to speak sensibly and act likably." Serious-minded Joseph Kraft declared that the Iowa voters were the big winners at the forum, gaining access to needed information. Everyone agreed, though, on one point: Ronald Reagan had lost by not appearing at the Iowa candidates' forum.

Reagan's Press Pass

The reality, we know now, was quite the opposite. Connally, Bush, Anderson, Baker, and all the other early meteor candidates arched across our media visions and burned out. Again with hindsight we can see that Reagan had steadily fastened onto the hearts and minds—and wallets—of the Republican-

Conservative Right, while the press was gawking at sky shows and writing about momentum. That, as it happened, was exactly the way the Reagan campaign wanted it, for Ronald Reagan not only won the contests for the Republican nomination and for the presidency, he also won the battle for the press during the primaries and general campaign.

Reagan began the campaign with the support of a plurality of the Republican voters. As early as October 1979 Joseph M. Margiotta, the Republican leader in Nassau County, New York, and a long-time loyal aide of New York Governor Nelson Rockefeller, concluded that the Reagan nomination was inevitable and began acting accordingly. Margiotta jumped the moderate GOP ship and talked to Reagan about a unity vice-presidential candidate. No one paid much attention to this extraordinary development. Margiotta runs the best political organization in the country, but, because reporters are used to looking for machine bosses in the Democratic big cities, few people had bothered to study how Margiotta produced huge Republican suburban pluralities without benefit of myth. Joe Margiotta, of course, doesn't get his political information from *Time* or ABC, so he wasn't impressed by blustery John Connally or excited by the vigor of the George Bush candidacy. Reagan, and Margiotta, had long since concluded that Reagan didn't have to win the nomination and the presidency; he had to stay remote and cordial—and to avoid losing it.

Accordingly, the Reagan campaign had to be outwardly correct and pleasant to the press while not allowing it to get too close. In the small details as well as in the grand strategies, the Reagan campaign worked over the press, as all campaigns aspire to do. There were the jelly beans and candy Ron and Nancy handed out to traveling reporters, the long preparations for Reagan's big interview with the *Wall Street Journal,* the two-man Reagan blooper squad on hand to explain away the candidate's frequent pie-eyed assertions on matters of fact or policy. And overall, there was the candidate's aw shucks demeanor in his relations with reporters, as he turned aside his misstatements with a grin and a disarming, "Did I really say that?"

To those with long memories it was reminiscent of Eisenhower, the smiling Ike who was liked by everyone. The private Ike, of course, was known to have a fierce temper and a contempt for the press. Reagan, too, could be found on occasion without his sugary, jelly-bean manner. Once, campaigning in Connecticut, he leafed through the *New York Times* to see what "these bastards" in the eastern press were saying about him. During a Washington appearance before the American Society of Newspaper Editors convention, he faced a panel of senior executives and nervously joked before the questioning began, "Do I get a cigarette and a blindfold?" The notion that his establishment interrogators would muss even one postmaturely brown hair on his head was funnier than the line itself. Afterward, like little boys in the playground, the editors murmured that the candidate wouldn't be so lucky the next time—in the general election campaign. They would be tougher. They were not.

Reagan's misstatements, misquotes, and misapprehensions were mind boggling as he read from his 3-by-5 index cards the materials he had gleaned from old *Reader's Digests* and other reading on a thousand and one airplane trips as General Electric's PR man. If the natural gas and oil industries were not regulated by the government, he would say, America would in five years not have to import oil from OPEC. This claim was based on the statement, which he attributed to the U.S. Geological Survey, that there is more oil in Alaska, than in Saudi Arabia. The survey figures show a reserve of 165 billion barrels in Saudi Arabia, while the Alaskan fields may at the most prove to have between 12 and 40 billion barrels. No matter: the idea was embedded in Reagan's brain pan.

From the beginning Reagan's chief strategist John Sears wanted to keep the candidate above the battle and free of any reporters' questioning. Even after Sears was dumped by Reagan, the campaign proceeded on Searism without Sears. The press, flying around aimlessly, without Joe Margiotta's hard-eyed vision, helped this strategy along by refusing for the longest time to acknowledge the inevitability of Ronald Reagan's nomination. Perversely, the stories about Connally and Bush aided Reagan, occupying newspaper space and air time that might have gone for more thorough examinations of his own statements and positions. After looking at the primary race coverage of Reagan in the period of November 1979 to June 1980, Vivian Reifberg of the MIT News Study Group concluded: "It's not that the coverage of Reagan was 'too soft' or 'too hard'—it's that there wasn't enough coverage."

The coverage that did appear, she found, tended to focus on the reasons Reagan couldn't win. First there was the age issue. For example, in the February 11, 1980, *Newsweek*, the article on Reagan began:

> The crowd cheered, and Ronald Reagan beamed as 89-year-old Dorothy S. Rollins kicked off a campaign rally in Gilford, New Hampshire, last week—and in the aftermath of his embarrassing loss to George Bush in the Iowa caucuses, he is determined to prove that he is neither too old nor too complacent to win the Republican presidential nomination.

A few days later, in the *New York Times*, Adam Clymer reported from New Hampshire that across the state the age issue comes through as a dominant theme. In an interview with Reagan on CBS's *60 Minutes*, Dan Rather closed the questioning by asking: "You'd be the oldest American president at age 70, would you not?" But, by the time of the southern primaries, Reagan, according to *Newsweek*, "seemed finally to have overcome the age issue." What the press taketh, it also giveth.

Belatedly, when Reagan established himself as the press's front runner, journalists began showing a mild interest in what he was saying. The argument against Reagan was no longer that he was too old for the nomination. Instead it became an argument that he was too extreme to win a general election. This was the time of And Not Reagan Either, and the press sighted some more campaign meteors—the Gerald Ford candidacy, an effort run almost wholly on paper and television—and the Anderson appeal. On ABC's *Issues and Answers* on March 16, one of Bob Clark's first questions to Reagan was: "Aren't you going to have to do something to alter the course of your campaign to attract some of the Independents and Democrats and young voters that are swarming to John Anderson here in Illinois for instance?" Aw shucks, Mr. Clark, things are going just fine, thank you.

"But Can Reagan Be Elected?" asked *Time* in its March 31 issue, awakening to the possibility that there, in fact, was no Connally momentum, no Bush viability, no Gerald Ford candidacy and that Ronald Reagan, indeed, has a chance to be elected as the 40th president of the United States. The article began:

> For several decades, it has been an article of faith among politicians and political analysts that no candidate can win a U.S. presidential election unless he can dominate the broad center of the spectrum, that all candidates on the edges of the left or right are doomed. Barry Goldwater's 'extremism . . . is no vice' campaign of 1964 provides the classic evidence, reinforced by George McGovern's 1972 defeat in 49 out of 50 states. And since GOP front runner Ronald Reagan relies upon a base of support that is on the far-right wing of the Republican party, some experts have long declared that, if he wins the nomination, the GOP would simply be repeating the suicidal Goldwater campaign. . . .
> But last week, after Ford gave up his own ambitions and Reagan's nomination took on a look of inevitability, a reassessment was under way across the country.

Robert Healy in the *Boston Globe* caught the press's feeling of revelation when he wrote on March 12, "He [Ronald Reagan] is an entirely plausible candidate."

The Republican electorate had decided that Reagan was neither too old nor too extreme, and with each primary Reagan moved closer to the nomination. Obstacles to the inevitable were raised but never examined. Lou Cannon of the *Washington Post* wrote mildly about "the seeming paradox of a candidate who can outdebate rivals in candidate forums and outmaneuver contentious reporters in press conferences, yet still kindle questions about his intellectual capacities. . . ." Cannon, the best of the Reagan watchers, replaced the earlier question about Reagan— Is he too old and conservative to be elected President?—with another: "Does Ronald Reagan know what he is talking about?" Cannon questioned Reagan's statements of farm parity, waste and fraud in government, the oil potential in Alaska, U.S. weapons systems, American steel productivity, deregulation, General Motors employee figures, and more. According to Cannon, "Once a statistic finds a haven in a Reagan speech, it generally stays there despite the best efforts to dislodge it. This is the product of Reagan's photographic memory, which stores a lot of information but often doesn't discriminate about the quality." The same theme was later picked up by Steven Rattner in the *New York Times* ("Reaganomics," April 13), the *Los Angeles Times* ("Record Doesn't Always Support Reagan's Claims," April 12), *Newsweek* ("How's That Again Ronnie?") and by CBS News' Bill Plante and NBC News' Don Oliver. Reagan complained he was a victim of journalistic incest. But the campaign reporting was merely awakening from its own somnambulatory state. There was one problem with its arousal: the campaign was over.

FUTURES

PART IV

TED TURNER:
THE NEWS CONTINUES,
FOREVER

CHAPTER 17

After watching the start-up of Ted Turner's twenty-four-hour-a-day, seven-days-a-week Cable News Network (CNN), one conclusion seems inescapable to me: I've seen the future, and it doesn't work—yet.

The technology clearly exists: CNN demonstrates that it can use satellite hookups, live remotes, split screens, videofonts, and chromakeys just like the older, established network news organizations and that it can do this around the clock. "The news continues, from now on and forever," CNN anchorwoman Lois Hart pledged on opening night in June, 1980. The inspired will to succeed is evident, too. Entrepreneur Ted Turner, who is always described as flamboyant in stories about him, has assembled an equally hard-working crew to run CNN, a kind of expansion team with veterans from ABC, CBS, and NBC as well as local-station talent up for the first time before a national audience. Throughout 1980, and into 1981, they have been putting on ten times more news than the big three networks with a tenth or less of the resources. There is even a crazy group of viewers out there, news freaks like me and many of the people I know, who like the idea of a news channel that brings headlines, political talk, or west coast late sports scores at the flip of the dial at four in the morning. Equally important, CNN has attracted an audience of receptive advertising people. Michael Drexler, senior vice president at Doyle Dane Bernbach, calls CNN "a viable ad medium with good CPMs and upper demographics involving a small out-of-pocket investment." In standard language this translates: CNN commercial minutes sell at relatively cheap rates and reach the younger professional men and women that advertisers covet for their products.

The space age hardware, the boldness, the economic potential, are all there. CNN, in theory, could run forever. Even the current down-to-earth obstacles it faces could be overcome in theory. By mid-1981 CNN was in some 3 million households in thirty-three states through the local cable systems that subscribe to its service. CNN works like any one of the dozen existing cable networks (for sports, children's programs, or whatever). CNN's income comes from the fees charged the systems and from the ad revenues. Currently, this falls short of the $3 million a month it costs Turner to operate CNN. It is a chicken-and-egg relationship. As more homes get cable in the 1980s, more sets may tune to CNN, and CNN can grow stronger. Or, the other way: as CNN grows stronger, more homes will be attracted to tune to CNN.

But yet, after pulling for the CNN idea and watching its performance with some care, I've developed some serious reservations about it, a nagging doubt as insistent as the electronic humming that CNN used as its signature between items and commercials in its initial months. The reservation is that CNN is not very good journalistically. And the basic question is: Can anyone, even with unlimited resources, offer intelligent, useful, ultimately clarifying, news and information around the clock?

Can twenty-four-hour all-news television be made to work, not as some abstract demonstration of hardware but as a service to people?[1]

I know that there is around-the-clock all-news radio done very well by CBS, and there are the all-the-news-forever wire services, Associated Press, United Press International, and Reuters. But neither medium involves the much more complex task of producing continuous news with pictures. Newspapers manage once-a-day publication with perhaps two or three editions allowing minimum replating (changing) of half a dozen pages, achieving day-in-day-out quality in at most five or six cities. The weekly news magazines take progressively more time for presumably clearer, more comprehensive information and interpretation. CNN comes across as a mixed, or mixed-up, media. As Tom Wheeler, president of the National Cable Television Association, explained it, CNN is a "tele-publishing event . . . it offers all the information the print media provide in the medium the people like best."

Judging the effectiveness of CNN—does it work?—becomes complicated for the critic. Ted Turner expansively claims he is offering CNN as an alternative to the big three network news, about which he concocts provocative statements for the benefit of print reporters. "The network nightly news is nothing more than a headline service," he likes to say. "They don't offer business news, or sports news, and there's hardly any international news. I don't watch it." So, CNN, if for no other reason than Turner's words, has to be judged in comparison to ABC, CBS, and NBC newscasts. And, as a "tele-publishing" form it has to be compared, at least in part, to newspapers, radio, and the wire service texts it replaced on cable channels (on my cable set in New York, the moving type or crawl from the previous tenant, Reuters, has been periodically breaking into the CNN picture when some technician punches the wrong button—a ghost of cable news past haunting Ted Turner).

How well does CNN cover the news? Using videotape play-back technology and with the help of the MIT News Study Group, I compared two weeks of programming on CNN, ABC, CBS, and NBC. It was apparent before the start that, in one sense, there was no contest. CNN, not surprisingly, does more than the networks in every category—more headlines, more hard news, more features, more sports and weather, more financial news, more commentary. While Walter Cronkite or John Chancellor or Max Robinson was giving the price of gold and the Dow Jones averages in thirty seconds, CNN at the same time was offering almost thirty minutes of financial news with anchor Lou Dobbs, editor Myron Kandel, and commentator Dan Dorfman. Sheer quantity, however, cannot be the measure of comparison. Rather, such qualities as clarity (is this news understandable?), freshness (is this really news or information?), and usefulness (why am I being told this?) have to be employed. Looking for these qualities, here is what we found, category by category, comparing CNN with the big three networks:

Hard News

The first qualitative impression that jumps out of the set is the photocopy sameness of the three networks' news shows, from the hard news portions of the morning news shows right down to the same film bites of speeches, news conferences, and visual events. You can take that as testimony to the steady-eyed, objective journalistic judgment of ABC, CBS, and NBC—the news is the news is the news, and all news people recognize the important stories. Or you can agree with Turner that the big three networks are just headline services with little to choose from. Either way, no matter when you look at ABC, CBS, and NBC you tend to see the same hard-news stories. On a Wednesday night in June 1980 of our monitoring period, for example, the rundown went:

ABC	CBS	NBC
Frank Reynolds/ Max Robinson	Dan Rather	John Chancellor
1. Tease: Carter–Kennedy summit then into midwest tornado and trailer item on volcano activity	1. Carter gas tax defeat in House	1. Carter–Kennedy summit
2. Carter–Kennedy summit	2. Carter–Kennedy summit	2. Reagan's plans
3. Kennedy plans	3. California voter survey	3. John Anderson campaign
4. Iran developments	4. Midwest tornado, volcano activity	4. Primary season wrap-up
5. Violence round-up	5. Financial round-up	5. Midwest tornado
6. Carter gas tax defeat	6. Iran developments with violence round-up	6. Vernon Jordan shooting update
7. Airline woes (special report by Jules Bergman)	7. Preakness inquiry (Pimlico race track)	7. Carter gas tax defeat
8. Sports items, including Preakness	8. Domestic shorts	8. Iran developments
	9. KKK man on California ballot	9. Preakness inquiry

The second unavoidable impression is that there's no similar "that's-the-way-it-is" news package on CNN and that we miss the sense of order such a packaging imposes. While the evening news is on, CNN is consciously avoiding these major stories and counterprogramming with thirty minutes of financial news, followed by twenty minutes of sports news. One night the CNN financial news might center on the price of gold; another night on interest rates. Experts Mike Kandel and Dan Dorfman, both good print journalists, came across as knowledgeable resources; but the centerpieces, like the gold story, took a long time to tell the obvious, for example, about why gold was rising. It was too much for the nonspecialist and too rudimentary for the insider.

The same was true for the sports segment. On its first Sunday night CNN showed videotape of a Reggie Jackson home run that won an extra-inning game for the New York Yankees, followed by a report that Jackson had been in a shooting incident on a Manhattan street a few hours after the game. CNN offered more than the networks; Ed Bradley on CBS News later that night made no mention of the Jackson story. But a viewer who stayed tuned for the local CBS News heard Jackson talking about the incident and advancing the story beyond CNN. CBS TV had gotten the Jackson audio from CBS Radio sports, which has its own extensive news sources—one of the advantages of being a network in business for fifty years before CNN was born.

The same network factor gave the established news organization the advantage during another breaking story. Cuban refugees at Fort Chafee, Arkansas, rioted and burned a barracks, news that CNN naturally was able to report well ahead of the networks, as soon as it came over the wires; but CBS again had the better story when its broadcast came on the air—with videotape of the rioting supplied by a CBS affiliate station in Arkansas. CNN also has reciprocal news arrangements with some local stations, but nowhere near CBS's 200-odd affiliates.

Newspapers have a page one to organize the news; magazines a table of contents, radio its top-of-the-hour newscasts; TV a

Rather or a Chancellor whose presence says, this is what you should know about, at a minimum. CNN's headlines are everywhere, thus nowhere. A CNN showcase news comes on at 8 P.M., a good counterprogramming move—the networks are doing prime-time entertainment then—but not too helpful to the viewer seeking the ordering that journalism traditionally provides. If you arrive home right before the 7 P.M. network shows and dial CNN for the news, you might get, as I did, a kite-flying contest (6:55 P.M.); if you arrive later, eager for news, and tune to CNN, you might hear about the world's biggest egg cream (9:42 P.M.). In a newspaper, readers can flip the page past the egg cream; in a car listening to all-news radio, listeners can dial out filler items until the hourly newscasts. With CNN, viewers need patience for hard news—and then get short, snappy items that really are headlines, and tabloid-style heads at that.

For example, when Jimmy Carter visited the black areas of Miami where the major rioting of May 1980, had occurred, bottles were thrown at his motorcade. Here is how it played on CNN:

9:43 P.M.—Feature on the Tony theatrical awards (of night before) . . .

9:46—Tease: Sports scores ahead . . .

Commercial break

9:48—Anchor: Bottles were thrown at Jimmy Carter's motorcade. We have unedited film of what it looked like aboard the bus. Here's the film . . . (Unsteady camera records through bus window as crowd surges forward . . . shouts inside bus . . . *Stay down! Stay down!* . . . Bus speeds up . . . Crowds left behind . . . *It's safe! We're okay!* . . .)

9:50—Back live to anchor: Now a report on the single-handed Atlantic ocean sailing race. . . .

That was it. The anchor presented the unedited film as a plus, something CNN would take pride in. There was no further immediate explanation, no sense of the importance or unimportance of the episode. Were we watching the beginning of a Dallas, 1963, with the street crowds, the shouting, and the sud-

denly accelerating presidential motorcade? CNN's instant news
didn't tell us. In fact, it was the 11 P.M. network broadcasts that
supplied a context in the form of an edited tape piece on the
Miami episode. It was not Dallas, 1963.

Reese Schoenfeld, president of CNN, turns aside complaints
about the lack of an organized CNN front page and about its
tabloid news style. He argues that life isn't organized, that traditional network news gives an undesirable illusion of omniscience,
and that CNN is not here to do in-depth stories. This may be
good alternative programming theory, but it makes for mediocre hard-news coverage. CNN is not the newszak that some
critics feared, but it too often comes close to being background
sound.[2]

Live news

Because CNN is on forever, it doesn't have to wait until 7 P.M. or
11 P.M. or 7 A.M. to do its news. It can go live at anytime. That
capability, however, can also explode in CNN's face, like a booby
trap. For example, putting its very best foot forward on its
premiere night, CNN produced (1) a live report of Jimmy
Carter visiting Vernon Jordan's hospital room in Fort Wayne,
Indiana, (2) an Intelsat connection from Jerusalem, and (3) a
microwave-satellite link to Lee Leonard, an entertainment columnist in Los Angeles. The trouble was, no one had much to
say. It would have been far different for CNN, of course, if
Carter had stepped forward to announce that the FBI had
solved the Jordan shooting. That is news. But under what conceivable circumstances would Lee Leonard ever have any stop-
press news to tell us about, say, Burt Reynolds or Sally Fields?
CNN's admirable but eventually so-what demonstration of technological prowess then and on subsequent nights was reminiscent of some muscle beach weightlifter who has magnificent
biceps but who can't write his name; technology is of little use if
there is nothing to say.

Worse, the live news form can be a kind of video Bermuda Triangle, into which intelligent journalism disappears. CNN stationed correspondent Mike Boettcher on the Key West waterfront for a series of live reports on the Cuban freedom flotilla. Boettcher had the unenviable job of glancing over his shoulder seaward and reporting: "No boats are in sight . . . the flotilla has stopped. Eight-foot seas are stopping the boats. . . ." But CNN producers persisted, flexing their satellite muscles, and went back again to Boettcher. Forlornly, he reported: "It's the quietest night of the month here." Not even the reporter's personable, hard-charging manner could conceal the fact that CNN was the one at sea . . . and slipping right into a *Saturday Night Live* style News Update parody.

Live television, in theory, can be memorable television. It's hard to make it work in practice.

Soft News

Off-the-news stories, backgrounders on health or politics or gardening, movie and art reviews, and other features constitute one area where CNN should clearly beat the networks. ABC, CBS, and NBC usually confine features to an occasional multipart series and a two-minute story at the end of the newscasts, with perhaps a longer heartwarmer on Friday nights to send viewers away into prime time, and for the weekend, with reasonably benign feelings. During our monitoring period, in addition to the ABC News report on airplane safety, the networks offered an NBC special segment on American Mafia leader Carlos Marcellos, and a CBS report on workers who bought up a Youngstown, Ohio, plant after it was shut by bankruptcy and were trying to make it run through old-fashioned initiative. As its Friday sweetener CBS offered a story on pigs that jog for the sake of science at Arizona State University, while NBC's Jack Reynolds in Shanghai found a Chinese millionaire who survived the cultural revolution.

None of these qualify as Peabody Award winners. But light as the network efforts were, the CNN features seemed so fluffy they threatened to float away. After one such CNN piece, a split-screen interview with Kermit the Frog of the Muppets, the capable but apologetic-looking anchorman, ex-ABC News correspondent Bill Zimmerman, said gamely, "We give you all the news, folks."

When CNN features turned serious, however, Kermit the Frog would have been welcome. During our monitoring period, for example, CNN heavily promoted a series about a Denver area police sting operation (obtained through CNN arrangements with a local Denver station). The sting operation, essentially a stake-out and entrapment scheme with police posing as fences, was melodramatically played over six days on *Take Two*, the CNN midday program with the husband-wife anchor team of Don Farmer and Chris Curle. "We have real film of a burglary in progress . . . a crime actually being committed," Farmer declared, looking only slightly less uncomfortable than Zimmerman had. The Denver hidden camera piece looked much like other hidden camera pieces we've all sat through; but CNN had something more in mind than just cops and robbers stories. Such sting operations, Farmer said, are made possible by money from the Law Enforcement Assistance Agency, and LEAA's future was in doubt because of the Carter Administration and the Congress. Thus cuts in the LEAA budget would hurt crime-busting efforts across the country. To drive home the point, the Atlanta public safety commissioner came into the CNN studio for a gentle interview in which he described all the police good works LEAA had made possible.

In theory, again, there is nothing wrong with features that make editorial points; it is just not the sort of stance that the traditional objective network newscasts bring to features. While CBS features cheer on abstract mom-and-apple-pie ideals like Initiative (the Youngstown story), CNN lobbies for the cause of a specific government agency (and one with a questionable record of spending money to advance our understanding of crime).

CNN has a platoon of commentators and critics, from A (Bella Abzug on politics) to Z (fitness expert Arden Zinn). They make up the softest of CNN's soft features, and the biggest disappointment. Commentators aren't seen or heard enough on the big three's evening news. But CNN's commentators are so badly coached, poorly lighted, and indifferently directed that they might as well be invisible. The CNN film man, Fred Saxon, is a Rex Reed look-alike, his only evident qualification. He doesn't criticize or review movies as much as narrate clips from the movie. Running clips of Stanley Kubrick's *The Shining,* one of the big disappointments of the year, Saxon allowed that some people would be scared while others wouldn't be . . . and the movie is opening next week around the country. . . . (Reviewing the same film on local New York television in the same one-minute-thirty-second format, critic Judith Crist offered insights that viewers could think about for days after seeing the movie.)

Sports and Weather

These categories only make the big three network programs when they become breaking hard news: the Mount St. Helens volcano, killer tornadoes, major sporting events like the Preakness or the Superbowl. On CNN, by contrast, we clocked two to three hours of sports in most twenty-four-hour periods, and national weather checks about as frequently as on all-news radio. Sport and weather, then, play big on CNN, as they do on local newscasts around the country (as if in anticipation of CNN's emphasis of these audience pleasers, all of the big three seemed to do more sports and weather than usual during the first weeks after CNN started up).

Mostly, CNN sports and weather reports look and sound as they do at local stations. Yet, for all the attention CNN gives these reports, embarrassing gaps appear. CNN's national weather outlook typically isn't specific enough for a local viewer. One morning, when CNN talked of rain in New York, it was partly cloudy; the network morning news shows, with half-hour cut-ins by local affiliates, managed more precise weather news.

The sports coverage also left a lot uncovered. During the running of the Belmont stakes—telecast live on CBS—CNN offered its weekly Washington review of politics, intelligent enough counterprogramming. But after the Washington program, and after the Belmont run, a feature on Famous Amos the cookie maker came up, with no thought of even a ten-second race results item—not-so-intelligent news judgment. The sportscasters themselves appear as pleasant, enthusiastic cheerleaders for the home team and the visitors. One night CNN's sports desk called the release of Minnesota Twins relief pitcher, Mike Marshall, "the big story of the hour." Marshall had posted fifty-three saves for the Twins in the previous two seasons, and only one this year—a deteriorating record. But the better story, left untouched by CNN, was off the field: Marshall served as the Twins player representative, and his aggressive union activities displeased a team management known as one of the cheapest in all of sports. The newspapers told that story in businesslike detail. CNN, to allay any conflict of interest suspicion about its own management—Turner owns the Atlanta Braves—might have done much more than it did.

Geography of the News

This category occurred to us only after we had watched the big three and CNN intensively. By geography of news we mean the effects of location on selection of stories. The ABC, CBS, and NBC newscasts originate in New York and have heavy Washington orientation, national news, the president, the Congress. There is a New York–Washington news axis, with regional stories plugged in—midwest and southern natural disasters, far west life styles. At CNN, the balance has shifted visibly; its

Atlanta base gives it a tilt southward. The Cuban refugees, for example, command more attention. When expert sources are needed, they often come from Atlanta—the police official talking about LEAA, a Georgia State University specialist on the economy. The local story of Jack Potts, a Georgia prisoner then on death row, received more attention on CNN than on the big three. At CNN, Washington and New York are bureau towns subordinate to Atlanta, even though far stronger in talent and still at the headwaters of the national news. Daniel Schorr of the CNN Washington bureau is the most instantly recognizable of the on-camera correspondents and also the best-connected in Washington. When he is on CNN, there is a feeling of knowledgeable authority. Yet CNN appears uncomfortable with Schorr, as if he's too identified with the traditional newscasts from which it's trying to distance itself. For an interview with Senator Kennedy, CNN teamed Schorr with an assertive talk-show host named Sandi Freeman, a spectacular bit of miscasting.

Editorially, our scorecard shows Ted Turner's CNN operation scores no higher against its big three major-league competitors than his Atlanta Braves or Atlanta Hawks teams in their leagues. CNN's writing never rises above the bread-and-butter level of wire-service copy. Its reporting lacks depth; even in CNN's own backyard, National Public Radio did a series of far-superior reports on the Cubans during our monitoring period. Its journalistic judgments can be staggeringly wrong; a feature on the drug habit known as free basing, pegged to the accident involving the comedian Richard Pryor, became a how-to-do-it for any viewers who wanted to follow CNN's demonstration and cook up some cocaine with ether.

For better and worse, CNN's editorial direction bears the stamp of three untraditional men. Foremost, there is Ted Turner, who recalls that he wanted to be a missionary when he was sixteen and now wants to save America by, he says, "saving television from the networks." Next, there are Reese Schoenfeld, with his background in wire-service television news, and

Ted Kavenau, CNN senior producer for news and the man widely credited with being the father of tabloid television when he worked for independent stations channels 5 and 11 in New York several years back. Fortunately for the audience, in my view, there is a fourth man, executive producer John Baker, a very skilled hand at putting together a well-paced program. By design, by error, by geography, one way or the other, the Cable News Network has managed to set itself apart from the networks it likes to think of as its rivals. CNN can claim to be different. Nowhere has it been engraved in stone that all television news must, now and forever, look like the *CBS Evening News* with Walter Cronkite; even the Cronkite news will be changing as Dan Rather takes hold. Forever, we're all finding out, can be a very long time. Fred Friendly, the former president of CBS News and an adviser on communications at the Ford Foundation, believes specialized channels for news are inevitable, with the present big three right there on top as now. "There will be ABC 1, 2, and 3 and CBS 1, 2, and 3 and NBC 1, 2, and 3 with each broadcaster having a different cable network for news, culture, sports, and probably business," Friendly says.

While Turner's well-publicized cash-flow problems may take him out of the final competition, the around-the-clock news idea will certainly survive. If I had to guess what it will look like editorially, I'd say it would be something combining the reporting and editorial strengths of the big three traditional news with the verve and audacity of the Turner idea. In a way that would make a happy medium.

WAITING FOR GODOT?

CHAPTER 18

In politics, it's said, the voters get the kinds of leaders they deserve. A lot of people thought the choices in recent years showed we've not been too deserving. Yet who can say that the 1980 presidential candidates were any less inspiring than, say, John W. Davis and Calvin Coolidge in 1924?

So it is also with the media. We get the press we deserve, which is another way of saying that television, magazines, newspapers, and radio, like politics and presidential candidates, reflect the state of society at any given time. Society nurtures or stifles creativity; it provides—through education—an attentive, or illiterate, audience; it plunks down its $1.50 (or its vote) at the point of sale. If the future of broadcasting lies in cable, the future of print may lie in magazines, which also can appeal to special interests. And to understand where the magazine business is going, we have to look at magazines in relationship to our society over the span of the last thirty years. As usual, it's easier to see where we've been and where we are now than where we're going, but it's not impossible.[1]

The first important date to look back on is 1950. It was a
simpler time. Magazines like *Life, Look, Collier's,* and the *Saturday
Evening Post* rode high in 1950. Television was an infant on
flickering black-and-white, eight-inch screens. Computers like
Univac required bookcase-high rows of circuitry. The United
States had probably the strongest hard currency in the world
and certainly the most important nuclear enforcement power.
Most important of all, America became a high-school-equivalent
society at mid-century—half the adult population had at least a
high school diploma. Not so long before as societies go, around
1920, the United States was a grammar-school-equivalent society, and daily newspapers were the dominant information form.

Most people tend to think of the 1950s and early 1960s as the
era of the general-interest magazine, by way of contrast with our
current era of special-interest magazines. But memory, especially nostalgic memory, often plays tricks. *Life, Look, Collier's,*
and the *Post* had general circulations—with readers up in the
millions—but their interests were quite focused for a mid-brow
audience. *Life,* for example, was, for any middle-class white over
forty today, "our television." The 1950s *Life* story line-ups were
not too different from the story line-ups on the *CBS Evening
News. Life* like Walter Cronkite offered the illustrated national
and international news, plus human-interest features, done in
twenty-three minutes.

Also there always have been specialized magazines around,
devoted to sports, shelter, home improvement, science, and
health. The *Cosmopolitan* girl may look very contemporary, but
her magazine has been around since 1886; *Ladies' Home Journal*
(started 1883), and *McCall's* (1876) are even older. The so-called
women's service magazines—hot right now because they tell the
busy woman ten ways to fix hamburger and five ways to fix her
hair—have been around longer than many of their readers
(*Family Circle* is forty-eight years old, *Woman's Day,* forty-three).
The basic point about the magazine business at any given time,
however, is societal and not editorial; 1950 was a threshold year,

with a significant part of the audience growing more sophisticated and demanding just as traditional political, economic, and communications systems were about to change.

The results of these changes are still being felt in the magazine business. Beginning in the 1960s, a general sorting out of the middle-class audience occurred, with television winning away the allegiances of middle-class consumers, and the advertisers who wanted them, from *Life* and the other high-circulation magazines. The growth of the Great Society state at home and abroad, the complexities of a new multipower international society created new information needs. Life in reality, not the magazine, was growing more complex. Television, the new mass medium, was unable or unwilling to meet the new needs for explanatory and analytical information. Most newspapers also failed to respond, or responded tardily. Instead of becoming more information packed and interpretive—to keep pace with the demands of society and the needs of better-educated readers—many newspapers lost sight of their real franchise. They sought instead to emulate television: big pictures, little stories, and lots of celebrities and white space became the newspaper format of the 1960s and 1970s. So fixed were mongoose newspapers on the beady eye of television that they failed to see the threshold event of 1970—the arrival of a college-equivalent readership in the United States.

With the information field thus so underpopulated, magazines pushed in. *Time, Newsweek,* and *U.S. News and World Report,* seeming competitors fighting to survive in one tight corner of the magazine business, all grew steadily throughout the 1960s and 1970s. By the end of the decade *Time* and *Newsweek* alone, with their departmental approach to the news, could claim a total readership of 40 million, with perhaps 10 million of that overlap (people reading both magazines). That number represented just about a sweep of the educated, upper-income audience, as well as a measure of the hunger for the semblance of organized information.

Time Inc.'s editors understood this perhaps better than anyone else. The magazine-publishing success of our era is Time Inc.'s *Sports Illustrated*, which treats men's and women's games with the same journalistic attention that the news magazines give to politics or economics. *Sports Illustrated* held pages for Sunday results, used expensive color reproduction, got off the news mark fast—and did it every week. Time Inc.'s *People* magazine, the second publishing success of the era, has much the same newsy style, but it's executed on the cheap, Rona Barrett or Tom Snyder rather than Walter Cronkite or Lesley Stahl.

Our present stage of development, and especially the years of the 1960s and early 1970s, represents something else besides an information society in our national history, and in the magazine business. It has also been a time for the release of awesome social energies. In the 1960s particularly, there seemed to be so many of us doing so many audacious things, whether it was marching for peace and justice, or making rock music or trying new print forms. It was a time of social challenge, both politically and artistically. The noted graphics designer Milton Glaser refers to this time as a period of "cultural arrogance"—the arrogance that assumes "you know something even if you can't prove it, the arrogance that works out of a passion to change the world because it believes the world can be changed."

Out of that arrogance, and the ferment of the times, a number of brilliant editors started new magazines using putatively unworkable formats. Jann Wenner, for example, started *Rolling Stone* for a youthful generation that supposedly would not read anything in print that was longer than a record label. Clay Felker's *New York* breathed vibrant life into the moribund city magazine format and became the most imitated magazine of the 1970s.

That brings us to the early 1980s, and possibly the next era. After the energetic and apocalyptic years of the 1960s and early 1970s, we've seemed to reach a kind of leveling off—a plateau in our national life, and a flat stretch in creativity and innovation.

For the media, and for magazines, as Clay Felker observes, "it is a plateau that is often profitable and certainly professional in what it does but is nevertheless increasingly arid of ideas and passion." No one is taking our collective breaths away in any field of artistic imagination. "Just as there are no really great novelists writing today as measured by past giants," Felker says, "there are no truly great artists, musicians, playwrights, or any other practitioner of the arts who can match the heights of past achievements. The popular arts are equally impoverished."

Periods of consolidation typically follow spasms of innovation, in politics as well as art. For magazines, the present plateau may have been signaled as early as 1970, the year that marked the birth of *Smithsonian* and the *National Lampoon*. While entirely different in subject matter and sensibility, both magazines are implicitly about our pasts, in *Smithsonian* the past as collective heritage, in the *Lampoon* the past as personal Joe College life.

Over the last few years caution has replaced experimentation in the magazine business. With everything costing more these days, it's no wonder that only the publishing giants seem to have the resources for new ventures. But the bigger they are, the harder it is for them to move. Time Inc.'s *People* magazine was a play-it-safe venture, taking the most popular department of *Time* magazine, the celebrity page, and spreading it over an entire issue. Rival Newsweek Inc. sat on its considerable assets and finally labored in the late 1970s to produce *Inside Sports*, a monthly sports magazine. Hardly what the world needed (the magazine was put up for sale in late 1981).

Other publishing giants have been equally conservative in their efforts. *The Reader's Digest*, born 1922, has just brought out *Families*. Like the *Digest*, *Families* is a compilation of articles from other places. The New York Times company tried, unsuccessfully, to imitate *People* with *Us* (born, 1977, put out to adoption, 1980). The Hearst Corporation is fussing with a standard-sized edition of its *Reader's Digest* size *Science Digest*. Conde Nast's *Self* (three years old) joins the already crowded sorority of women's magazines, including Conde Nast's *Glamour* (born, 1939). *Self* is the all too predictable product of market research that named physical and mental health as hot topics among women.

Market research, of course, is supposed to tell us what good editors intuitively hunch. Good editors know that major continuing stories ultimately create audiences for good journalism. Richard Nixon's Watergate, to take a familiar recent example, helped sell magazines. But not all news is stories as melodrama (good guys vs. bad buys), and not all stories are newsy.

A major ambiguous theme of our time is how to live intelligently. This can be approached as an economic story of inflation, OPEC, productivity, unemployment. *Business Week, Forbes,* and *Fortune* magazines, among others, do just this, and as the news about business gets grimmer and grimmer, the business magazines that cover the news seem to be doing better and better. "It's a terrific, wonderful time to be writing about business and the economy because things are so terrible," says a cheerful Sheldon Zalaznick, managing editor at *Forbes. Forbes,* for example, predicted in a recent issue that the grim times New York City has gone through are a "preview and foretaste of what the entire nation faces in the 80s." A similar business magazine success story is Judith Daniel's *Savvy,* a handsome new magazine for business and professional women who need something more than hamburgers and hairdo advice (for example, advice on how to make out expense accounts or draw up a personal will).

We are not just economic men, or economic women. The need to work out ways to live intelligently suited to our personal styles has created a whole area of self-interest, with the trendy name "lifestyles." Commentators claim they've detected a certain turning inward of concerns in the privatist late 1970s compared to the collectivist 1960s. But every generation, if you think about it, worries about its own self-interests (the idealism of the 1930s was in part related to the depression, just as the idealism of the 1960s was in part related to the draft and to the denial of equal opportunities). In the past only the very wealthy and worldly could think about embarking on classical psychoanalysis treatment. Today, with wider affluence and education, literally millions of people can search out psychotherapies to fit their needs and can pay other people to listen to their private stories.

The special-interest magazine may not be all that new, but the existence of a large and expanding, well-off, college-trained, self-interested audience means that many more special-interest magazines can find suport, even magazines that are poorly conceived and poorly executed. Moreover some things have not gone up in price, relatively speaking. New communications technologies, such as photocomposition, cold type, and computer production, help make possible modest press runs for selectively distributed publications. Today we have a magazine for every conceivable taste. Some 37,000 periodicals regularly move through the U.S. mails. Is it *World Tennis*, anyone, or perhaps *Polo? Country Living* or *Colonial Homes? The American Beagle* or *Full Cry* (the magazine for hunting dogs)? *Car and Driver* or *Pick up Van 4WD? Adweek* or *Ad Age? Washington Journalism Review* or *Iron Age?*

Tom Zito of the *Washington Post* probably captured the far outer shores of the special-interest magazine world with a list that included *Wet:* "The Magazine of Gourmet Bathing"; *The Razor's Edge,* which concerns itself with women sporting shaved heads; *The Pick-Up Times,* a self-spoofing guide to meeting women; *Bikini Girl,* a sporadically published report on the punk scene; *The Chocolate News,* a bimonthly about every imaginable form of chocolate, printed on paper that smells like its subject; *Zero,* a review of contemporary Buddhist life and thought; *Paraphernalia Digest,* which catalogues every new piece of hardware created by the drug culture.

None of the magazines on Zito's list existed ten years ago; ten years from now—ten months from now?—none may still exist. But others will take their place. According to the Magazine Publishers Association, some 200 new magazine ventures were started in 1981. This suggests that a lot of entrepreneurial talent is around. In truth, however, there is a fairly well-established formula around for the magazine start-up these days:

1. Get editorial idea.

2. Invest $75,000 in a direct mail test to, say, 200,000 likely readers. If the response is positive—if 3 to 5 percent say they will subscribe on the basis of your description—then go ahead. Otherwise, quit while you're behind.

3. Make up a color dummy and do an editorial line-up of a half dozen issues to be sent to potential investors.

4. Plan to spend at least a year talking to these potential investors in order to raise $1 million. If you're planning a nationally circulated magazine, try for $3 to $4 million.

5. Now spend another year raising more millions, or seek out an established publisher with the resources to sustain a new publication anywhere from the three to six years it takes to break even.

None of this is easy, and step one is the most deceptive of all. Of the 200 start-ups annually, only 20 magazines survive the first year. The obvious questions are, Which ones? What's next?

If we hold constant the publishing plan—that is, assume direct mail, marketing, and big money are all in place and adequate— then it comes down to ideas, editors, and to society's shape over the next five to fifty years. Societally, it's possible to conceive of a near future (until the 1990s) and to speculate about a far future (beyond 2001).

Economic fears, international turmoil, and squeezes on the dollar, it seems clear, will be with us the rest of this decade. So will social unrest, group conflict, and violence. At the same time the intelligent audience is expected to continue to grow; 18 million more college-educated adults should be around in 1990, and they'll have money in their jump suits. Two out of three women probably will be working, many contributing to two-paycheck households. Hard news and useful information probably will be in demand, so the news-oriented and business-oriented magazines will continue to do well.

Given this scenario, other magazines with marginal current resources may be able to compete technologically. In theory, magazines should be able to look better graphically and react faster to developments with the use of web offset, better color keys, laser photoscanners, copy mergers, computer production, and satellite transmissions. The magazines that use these techniques will find an audience that appreciates—indeed, expects—high-quality graphics and up-to-date information.

Organizationally, magazines with tax advantages will also do better—again, if they have intelligent, distinct editorial content. The Congress and the federal government, for a number of reasons—noble (the diffusion of knowledge) and not so noble (cozying up to potential critics)—have historically granted tax advantages to organizations that use their profits for socially useful purposes. Such nonprofit publications are exempt from most taxes and save up to 50 percent on postal rates—a big edge over for-profit magazines, whose postal bills have increased some 450 percent since 1971. Magazines enjoying these subsidies range from shoestring religious and labor newsletters to the *National Geographic* (circ. 10.4 million) from the National Geographic Society, *Smithsonian* (circ. 1.8 million) from the Smithsonian Institution, *Natural History* (circ. 478,000) from the American Museum of Natural History, *Mother Jones* (circ. 222,000) from the Foundation for National Progress, *Science* (circ. 151,000), and *Science 80* (estimated circ. 400,000) both from the American Association for the Advancement of Science. Other magazines have converted to nonprofit status when, as *Time* magazine put it, "market forces threatened their existence." *Ms.* magazine (circ. 491,000) made the switch in 1980 after convincing IRS and postal authorities that the monthly's role in combating antifemale biases entitled it to federal support. *Harper's* (circ. 325,000) was saved from extinction recently when it was bought by two nonprofit foundations. William

Buckley's conservative *National Review* (circ. 86,000) and the liberal *New Republic* (circ. 75,000) have formed the Corporation for Maintaining Editorial Diversity to solicit tax deductible contributions to help pay mailing costs. (The two magazines will continue as for-profit enterprises.)

Beyond the 1990s, the crystal ball clouds up. Lewis Lapham, who was editor of *Harper's*, worried that general magazines like his own may suffer as our national discourse breaks up into beagle owners talking to other beagle owners. Twenty years ago, he pointed out, "an issue of *Harper's* might have contained articles or essays on topics as miscellaneous as marine biology, toy railroads, the failures of U.S. foreign policy, the ecology of Yellowstone National Park, and the unhappiness of women. Now, each of these topics commands a magazine of its own."

Lapham, as well as others who share his vision, may be in for a surprise, and a pleasant one at that. In demanding times demanding readers may reach for the wise guidance of a demanding editor, one who publishes magazines of liveliness and usefulness—concentrated skills all applied to a broad range of topics. I for one would read a magazine whose articles included Yellowstone Park and unhappy women if they were the work of a central editorial intelligence with an important point of view. Nobody may be reading such a magazine today because no one is editing such a magazine today.

The point of view offered by the successful magazines of the far future may surprise some of us. Clay Felker sees a turn from politics, with its disillusionments, to a concern for traditional and/or spiritual values (consider, for example, the born-again Christians in the United States and the militant Islamic movement in the Middle East). "People," Felker says, "want something to believe in, something greater than themselves. The next great creative burst in magazines could possibly come from the spiritual world, the realm of religion."

Perhaps a new breed of magazines has already begun to respond to that need to believe, which like self-interest is hardly confined to any one generation or era. Science/technology has been our post-modern religion, appropriately for the century of Freud, Einstein, Ochoa, Kettering and Ford. Sci/tech, we are told in *Omni, Science Digest, Science 80,* and *Discover,* will solve the problems that sci/tech has created. We're often assured in these magazines of a serene future above the clash and clamor of our conflicted, OPEC-spooked daily lives. Directly or subliminally, the sci/tech magazines offer us a future dreamscape of salvation with peace and a good sex life. "Man: He Makes Hope in His Own Image," *Omni* assures us. "Inherit the Sun: We Can Capture Its Fire," says *Science Digest.* "Fighting Cancer with Cancer," promises *Science 80.* "Mount St. Helen's Spectacular Show Enables Science to Learn How to Predict Eruptions," according to *Discover. Next* magazine rhapsodizes on a recent cover: "Have We Got A Future For You." In fairness, *Next* countered its own euphoria in a later issue with a chilling analysis of the future-obliterating possibilities of nuclear war.

Three magazine people can't gather anywhere today without one of them dropping what's supposed to be the print equivalent of the atomic bomb: What about the coming telecommunications revolution? And what are the chances that people will be getting video magazines on their television screens by punching up commands on their key pads? Well, what about it? There's a program on invention and innovation at MIT, and one day I am going to assign a project: design a communications system that is lightweight and easily portable yet has a 60,000 to 100,000 word capacity. Display screen should be no more than 9 by 12 and fit flat on a desk top. System should have easy access, so even an eight-year-old can plug in. It should also be storable and recall-able in seconds. If needed, system should be usable in airplanes, autos, and canoes. Keep the cost under $2 a unit.

The seminar would have to invent the magazine.

THE VIEWERS' DECLARATION OF INDEPENDENCE

CHAPTER 19

A serious thing happened to American television viewers on the way to supposed inanity. They have become more demanding, and more active, in their television watching. In fact, television-watching habits have changed fundamentally in the United States while the critics and experts were looking the other way.

Some intellectuals may still put down television as the boob tube, or the idiot box. Textbooks and communications courses may still talk about the passivity of the television viewer, the homogeneity of television fare dictated by the big three networks and the dominance of audience-flow theory—the notion that viewers are sitting inertly in front of their television sets all evening as one network show succeeds another like so much electronic wallpaper. Actually, the theorists' image of the typical telefixed family was always an exaggeration. Now it is clear that the passive audience is being displaced by viewers who interact consciously with their television sets.

These viewers take an active role in programming, picking,

and choosing from among the week's offerings. Newspaper television pages have belatedly acknowledged the existence of this new audience in the past few years by providing serious previews of noteworthy programs and "tonight's choice" features. Magazines like *TV Guide* long ago understood what the newspapers have been discovering. The regular coverage of television in the news magazines confirms again television's new-found status as an art-and-commerce form worth reading about seriously, as well as watching actively.

The most obvious vehicles of the viewers' new interaction with television are the cable-television systems and the various video disc and video cassette recording machines (VCRs). About one in every five television households in the United States now receives extra non-network channels via cable television. Ten years ago the figure was one in every thirteen households; some analysts believe that ten years from now a majority of homes will have multiple channels. The VCR units are selling at a rate of around half a million units a year, despite the relatively high price (between $800 and $1,300) and the lack of a standard system. A recent marketing study by the Arthur D. Little Company of Cambridge, Massachusetts, concluded that by the mid-1980s one in every 10 U.S. households will have a VCR unit. When a family pays $1,000 for its VCR player and $5 to $10 a month for its cable hookup, that's not the price of wallpaper; the cable/VCR family is going to take a closer, more active interest in its television fare than it did before.

The cable/VCR technology, of course, means more choice. In New York City, my cable system brings me twenty-six channels—the three networks plus three independent stations, plus three public stations (if one doesn't carry a certain PBS program, the others usually do), plus multiple sports events, including most of the New York home teams and selected Philadelphia and Boston games, plus several foreign-language channels (permitting Chinese and Hispanics to enjoy certain programs and some of us to brush up on French during a Simone Signoret film festival), plus experimental video and soft-core *Midnight Blue* and other minority taste programming. For a few dollars more a month I can get a subscription service, Home Box Office (HBO) or Showtime. About 4 million U.S. households already are paying for these channels, which typically offer recent-issue motion pictures—more home choice.

With the addition of my VCR unit, as the nearly one million Americans who own one can testify, I pay more attention to my programming choices from among these channels. VCR owners can record certain programs they want to save. Because a device permits time shifting—recording a program while they are out of the house—VCR owners can have their cake and eat it too: they can go out to dinner and still see the evening news with Rather, Chancellor, or Reynolds.

Technology succeeds best when it meets unfilled needs, rather than trying to create new wants. Sensurround and 3-D movies never caught on because nobody needed them to enjoy made-for-theater films. Cable and VCRs—and the newer videodiscs—meet an important social need. Today, as always, Americans are opting for freedom of choice and for mobility in their lives. Roger Williams began it when he left the Bay Colony for Rhode Island. We heirs to this tradition live in an age of education and affluence (despite inflation). While very few of us can affect the outcome of the SALT II treaty or the energy crisis, many of us have the knowledge and the means to take control of our personal time and our lives, as Americans historically have sought to do.

Applied to our leisure hours, this control means that the audience increasingly chooses to watch television at its own convenience just as it quilted, pitched horseshoes, or danced to its own rhythms in earlier days. Equally important, the audience wants to watch specific programs, not *tv qua tv*. The active viewers seek out what they want—old movies, sports events, quality productions, reliable news, pure escape, soap operas, or grand opera—without regard for channel, network, lead-in, or lead-out. The independent, active viewer has established an eclectic sovereignty throughout the broadcast schedule. In the 1979–80 season NBC's *Today* show dominated in the early mornings, ABC's soap operas led in the daytime. The dials then switched to CBS and the *CBS Evening News*, then ABC and CBS won the prime-time hours before the dials changed to NBC's Johnny Carson or *Saturday Night Live* in the late-night hours. With a new season, the individual program ratings may change, but the pattern of excellence prevails. The qualitatively best of breed—*Today*, CBS News, Carson—win. So much for audience flow theory.

One of the best places to observe the independent, active viewer is among younger urban men and women in their twenties. They were supposed to be the lost television generation, made passive by prolonged exposure to the tube. In fact many of them have developed a lively, sophisticated view of television and film. They own VCRs just as they own stereos, and they collect video tapes of favorite vintage movies, Bogart or Kubrick, and of classic television programs like *The Honeymooners*. Peter De Forest, a member of our News Study Group at MIT, has observed this developing video culture at firsthand. As he reports: "They trade off-the-air videotapes of movies, television programs, and sporting events. They are members of informal video-trading clubs, whose sole purpose seems to be the non-profit trading (no money changes hands, just tapes) of tapes for personal-entertainment purposes. The various law-enforcement agencies ranging from the FBI to local police do not attempt to prosecute videotaping of copyrighted material off the air for personal use and so members of these clubs think they are not violating the law."

(There is also, obviously, the illegal selling of copyright-protected material, currently released movies being the most popular, by video pirates, who operate in much the same manner as drug dealers. These pirates manage to steal and videotape copies of popular movies, duplicate them and sell them for from anywhere near $50 to $100).

The marvel is that the present but fading system of standard television fare lasted as long as it did in the face of these individualistic currents of American society. As the public-opinion analyst Louis Harris observed, television may be our hearth, but it has been too confining for our contemporary mood. The new technology of VCRs, cable, and videodiscs merely recognizes the inevitable. Surveys suggest that television viewing, after years of uninterrupted growth, has leveled off over the last few years. Over-the-air broadcasters argue that a leveling has occurred because everyone has a television set now, maybe two or three. But while the broadcasters always boast of the 80 to 100 million people turned to television sets nightly, they conveniently overlook the obverse: while two-thirds of all households are tuned in, nevertheless, one-third aren't.[1]

The independent active viewer comes from both sides—the "ons" and the "offs." When the Alex Haley docudrama *Roots* (Part I) was broadcast in January 1977, and achieved one of the largest audience ratings ever—36 million homes or 80 million viewers tuned to the last episode—the program managed something else in addition to high ratings. A significant percentage of those sets had been dark; people tuned on as well as tuned over from other fare. Whenever quality programming or special programming is presented, the results are the same. Television's daytime coverage of the solar eclipse of 1979 drew higher ratings than the regularly scheduled programs it competed against. Independent-station offerings of *Edward the King,* a British dramatic series, and *Scared Straight,* a documentary made in a New Jersey state prison, topped their network opposition in many areas. NBC's *Holocaust* and ABC's second *Roots* series attracted people who are normally light or infrequent viewers.

But no one should conclude that the new viewers are some kind of an elite, small in number and therefore easy to dismiss.

A recent analysis of the purchasers of VCR units suggests that they tend to be heavy television viewers as well as frequent moviegoers. Not surprisingly, then, motion pictures are among the most recorded television fare by unit owners. Also not so surprisingly, when the television networks, in their scramble for ratings, schedule blockbuster movies against each other, such as CBS's *Gone With the Wind* vs. NBC's *One Flew Over the Cuckoo's Nest* one night in February 1980, the programmers succeed in driving more viewers to the VCR solution: watch one, record the other; or watch none, record one.

There is the problem of another kind of elitism. Cable, VCRs, Home Box Office, and videodiscs all cost money; will only the relatively affluent be able to afford them? Yes, we will have to pay for our independence and our freedom of choice. But the most innocent among us understand that no television is ever free; those advertisers who support the present on-the-air broadcast system collect hidden fees as part of the price of the goods that they sell. Public television depends on federal tax dollars or underwriting grants from corporations (also passed on to the consumer). With cablevision, the payments for our programming at least will be aboveboard. Also, with cassettes and discs, royalty or pooling arrangements are necessary so that the performers/artists/producers are recompensed for their efforts to some degree. I, for one, willingly pay for my independence and choice. Judging by the growth rates for cable households and home recording equipment, millions of others of active viewers are making their own declaration of independence.

LIBERAL PRESS, LACKEY PRESS (CHOOSE ONE)

CHAPTER 20

Liberals

Back in America's time of the troubles—the Vietnam 1960s and the Nixon 1970s—John Chancellor of NBC News suggested that journalists belonged to the extreme middle. From the right, the Nixon-Agnewites complained that the media gave too much attention to the antiwar forces and others who were always tearing down America. On the left, the same journalists were excoriated for being lackeys of the capitalist class.

Todd Gitlin and Kevin Phillips were emblematic of these two extreme attacks on the middle. Phillips, the columnist and writer, thundered from the right; we'll come to him in awhile. Todd Gitlin stood on the left, or new left, in the sixties, as president of Students for a Democratic Society (SDS). Today he's still on the left, but his current tools of new Marxist political analysis are more sophisticated than the SDS slogans that young radicals shouted. Gitlin is now an assistant professor of sociology and the director of the mass communications program at the University of California, Berkeley. In 1980 he published a book, part evocative memoir of the SDS years and part earnest thesis along the Ph.D. obstacle course, called *The Whole World Is Watching*.[1] Gitlin wrestles with the crazy, paradoxical nature of the extreme middle—that is, how the new left and the Nixonites could both be right about the news in America, how journalism can tear down American institutions while being a major mediating part and marketing arm of these same capitalist institutions. Gitlin doesn't quite win this wrestling match. One of his hands—guess which?—is effectively tied behind his back, but he puts on a good, provocative exhibition: Karl Marx versus Dan Rather, two falls out of three.

What makes Gitlin's study well worth reading, out of most of the usual preliminary-card gropings that pass for media research, is his stance of sixties radical activist and seventies-going-on-eighties radical academic. He uses two analytic tools in particular, one from the American sociologist Erving Goffman, the other from Antonio Gramsci, the Italian Marxist whose prison notebooks from four decades ago are being studied these days by younger American academics. Each of these tools is helpful to an understanding of the media.

Goffman proposed that in everyday life we frame reality in order to negotiate it, manage it, comprehend it, and choose appropriate repertories of cognition and action. Gitlin moves this idea forward by suggesting that media frames organize the world for journalists and for all the rest of us who rely on their reports. Media frames, says Gitlin, are largely unspoken, unacknowledged, persistent; they help process large amounts of information quickly, and they help us package reality.

All true. Journalists with no more experience than their first two weeks at a wire service or newspaper will recognize that media frame is another way of saying news routines. All news coverage involves some principles of selection and rejection, or superordination and subordination of the chaotic, blooming,

buzzing cosmos of events into the relatively neat world of news:
we do this on page one, we skip that, we plan this with pictures,
we balance this with that, we wait and do this differently next
week, and so on.

Because of their framing power, Gitlin says, the media play
key roles in the rise and fall of political movements in America,
another not unfamiliar point. A good part of Gitlin's book traces
how two of our best and brightest news organizations, the *New
York Times* and CBS News, handled the SDS of Gitlin's youth in a
news cycle swinging from indifference, through attention and
celebrity status, back to indifference again. Gitlin is not the first
to complain about how events get mangled as they are turned
into hot news, big news, old news, and non-news.

Gramsci's idea of hegemony helps Gitlin explain to his own
satisfaction just why the media behave the way they do—why the
press screws up. It's not just lack of time or our dumbness or the
superficiality of the routines. Those are all factors, but the explanation goes deeper. Hegemony is the name Gramsci gave to the
ruling class's domination through ideology, through the shaping
of popular consent. Ruling class hegemony, in Gitlin's view,
explains away the contemporary Marxist dilemma. Why, if western advanced capitalism is so bad, do the people continue to
support it, indeed to embrace it? The hegemonic answer: Because the people have been tricked by the media, those ink-
stained, wretched servants of the ruling class. The people, bless
them, have only repackaged media versions of reality to read or
watch. Capitalism still lives, not because, in its lurching, unjust
way, it still manages to provide some opportunities and justice
for the people, but because the dominant elite imposes its definition of the situation—its frames—upon those it rules. If capitalism, through its lackeys in the press, doesn't "usurp the whole of
ideological space," it still "significantly limits what it thought
throughout society."

But wait a minute: if the hegemonists and their media framers
rule so pervasively, how are we able to hear about any dissidents

or radical ideas at all? Gitlin has to poke two escape hatches in his hegemonic structure. First, the ruling elites may disagree among themselves—for example, about Vietnam, and therefore permit media coverage of antiwar dissent. Or, alternatively, some of the dissidents can get coverage inside sympathetic media frames if their aims are liberal reformist (Stop the War!) rather than truly revolutionary (Two, Three, Many Vietnams, and Here at Home!). Thus in Gitlin's world Ralph Nader becomes an elite-media favorite because he talks about consumers rather than the workers. Soft-headed environmentalists worried about the nuclear plant at Three Mile Island get attention but not those Rocky Flats radical demonstrations against the production of nuclear weapons. It seems that the ruling elites aren't sure as yet which way to go on electrical power energy paths, but they know their minds on A-bombs: they want more bucks for more bangs.

But Gitlin the radical SDSer is too smart to believe that the real world is as modeled as Gitlin the Ph.D. candidate tries to make it. He says so himself, as early as page 16 in his study, effectively dismissing his own central assumption that political movements and the people are merely passive objects being acted upon by elites and their media. Gitlin knows that there are many media including the movement's own. The people aren't a supine field of video-raised vegetables. Who, these days, relies solely on CBS or the *New York Times* for their thoughts? It's not us, of course, who believe what the media says, but always them, some dopes out in Queens or Iowa some place. When you get out there, however, "them" aren't dummies, either.

The hegemonic model trips and falls over everyday life, where activist groups of all kinds, some more or less radical, others racial, sexual, economic, or political, pull along both a semi-inert, easily distracted press and a huffing, puffing elite. The press, were it to be observed unblinkered by either Goffman or Gramsci, would resemble nothing as much as Frank

Morgan's fake wizard in *The Wizard of Oz*—a bumbling operation bolstered mostly by a voice machine and phony visual effects.

Gitlin's frame analysis is much more useful. Yes, all news judgments or framings involve certain principles of selection. A number of critical studies, for example, my own work and the work of Herbert Gans, have shown how the press emphasizes the values of liberal reform and entertainment and excitement in deciding what events become news. Gitlin is just wrong in thinking that the media's function solely is usurping ideological space. The media do that, but they also play many other roles: reformer, lackey, entertainer, educator, adversarialist, just as the constitution has provided. The press also does what Gitlin would have it do; in fact, the press is at its best when it de-stabilizes, when it makes viewers and readers think about and *question*—if you please—accepted truths and settled practices, including the practices of the elites.

Gitlin spends considerable time analyzing a simple news item on the *CBS Evening News* of May 8, 1976. Dan Rather reports on FBI burglaries and wiretaps that had their beginnings in the 1930s, continued through World War II and the cold war and reached a peak during civil disturbances of the sixties. Gitlin makes much of the subliminal messages he believes Rather is conveying: ". . . With a clipped, no-nonsense manner and a tough-but-gentle, trustworthy, Watergate-certified voice of tech-nocracy [Rather] was deploring this law that brought it to the surface, and now proposed to stop it, and affirming that the media are integral to this self-correcting system as a whole."

That's a mighty arabesque on a slim point of reality. Rather was actually reading from copy some CBS bracero had typed out, copy which had come in turn from a wire-service report representing the processing work of even lower-ranking proles. And anyway, how many people in the world are attending, let alone listening, their academic notebooks open, their minds unformed, to CBS's characterization of the 1960s in May, 1976? Media influence is a slippery subject to trace. But Gitlin maintains that the black and student opposition movements of the sixties would have looked different with a different media frame, that is, a sympthetic frame. Gitlin thinks they should have been called "movements for peace and justice," so as not to reduce them to a "nasty little thing." But who judged them so, solely or mainly on the basis of media frames?

It is true that different frames suggest different pictures. Lyndon Johnson had his own clamps. He objected to one CBS News report that, he said, "shat on the American flag." Christian fundamentalism is another clamp. The Reverend Jerry Falwell would like us to use his frames on the world. Framers as diverse as Alexander Solzhenitsyn and Ted Turner have clamps to push. Those of us in the middle can only say: let them, let a hundred frames bloom, allowing space for every one.[2]

The ideologues of the left and the right usually meet in the same place. They powerfully want their clamps used, and no one else's. This desire is so powerful that, when it conflicts with ideology, then the ideology must be bent. For example, not too long ago columnist-ideologue Kevin Phillips startled a number of people who thought they knew their left from their right when he declared in *TV Guide* that there is too great a public interest in television news and programming "to permit exclusively private decision-making." Added Phillips, jabbing like Ralph Nader, "we are talking about the 'public airwaves.'"

Phillips's statements reflected how the debate over the kind of system we have in the United States has scrambled the traditional liberal and conservative positions. Vastly simplified, the debate is between the principles of a free press and the principles of a fair press. Sounding like Republicans, many liberals want the government—specifically the Federal Communications Commission, but other Washington agencies as well—out of its present role of regulating television and radio in the public good. From the other corner, conservatives have charged out ducking and feinting like old statists, talking about more direct government control of broadcasting.

The shift in the liberal position has been evolving for several years now. While liberals have been traditionally inclined to oppose governmental intrusions on the press's First Amendment rights, they, nevertheless, have been willing to make some trade-offs in the public interest. Liberals have tended to go along, for example, with court-imposed restrictions on the press, gag orders intended to reduce pre-trial publicity; the ACLU, for instance, has publicly expressed its preference for the individual's right to a fair trial over the public's right to know.

But the Nixon years scared liberals and reinforced their First Amendment fervor. It was a couple of *Washington Post* newspaper reporters who helped keep the Watergate story alive; and it was, after all, the *Washington Post*'s television properties that the Nixon gang calculated would be vulnerable to counterattack, through the television-licensing procedures of the FCC. The *Washington Post*'s company newspapers need no government license to publish; such a requirement would be contrary to the First Amendment. But television stations, the *Post*'s and everyone else's, do not enjoy such full First Amendment protections.

One of the reasons historically offered in defense of this second-class status has been the so-called spectrum scarcity argument; since only a limited amount of voices can go out over the air, the government has a duty to regulate broadcasters to make sure they use the people's airwaves in the public interest. The classic liberal statement of this argument was made by Supreme Court Justice Felix Frankfurter speaking for the court majority back in 1943. Referring to the Federal Communications Act, he wrote:

The act itself establishes that the commission's powers are not limited to the engineering and technical aspects of regulation or radio communication. Yet, we are asked to regard the commission as a kind of traffic officer, policing the wavelengths to prevent stations from interfering with each other. But the act does not restrict the commission merely to supervision of the traffic. *It puts upon the commission the burden of determining the composition of that traffic.*

As liberals have gradually moved away from this activist position, conservatives have rushed in to embrace it. To hear Kevin Phillips talking about more direct governmental control of television news is like being told that the sun rises in the west and sets in the east. It can mean only one thing: he has made one of those sightings that conservatives are prone to make: he has spotted eastern radical lib bias in the news. As with UFO landings and reports of Big Foot only true believers ever have close encounters or make contact with this alien force. The rest of us only see the normal confusions, delusions of objectivity, and foul-ups of journalism. No matter, Phillips is as much a stranger to media reality as Gitlin. Phillips wants more conservative influences in the news. His argument is that the mass media, especially the television networks, are an information utility. As Phillips writes:

Throughout U.S. history, when "private" businesses of a certain sort—from banks and railroads to public utilities—have achieved a critical public importance, they have been subjected to increasing regulation in the national interest. Now it would seem that the information-and-opinion industry is coming under the same guns, notwithstanding self-interested assertions that it ought to be untouchable under the First Amendment. Growing public demand for media access—whether from conservatives, gays, blacks, women, or just concerned citizens—is based on growing public appreciation of the pivotal role of the media. It's just about that simple.

Not quite so simple. Phillips himself sees the irony in a situation in which conservatives, in other cases the first to support and maximize private-property rights, are arguing for interfering with the private prerogatives of the networks. His argument also skips over the major part of the information and opinion industry—1,750 daily newspapers, 37,000 magazines, and scores of thousands of other print outlets. Are they to be regulated by government in the national interest as well? The word "access" in these discussions usually means the right to reply—to get on the air or in print—or to have standing air time or column space.

Do conservatives really believe that the public—not otherwise defined—should have routine access to the pages of the *New York Times,* or to the columns of *TV Guide,* or to Kevin Phillips's own newsletter, *Media Report?* Changing the name of the "press" to "information utility" may make the *Washington Post* or *Time* magazine or CBS News sound, to some ears, like Bell Telephone. But the framers of the First Amendment, and the courts through the years, treated the press as something more than an information and opinion industry; the press also was—or was supposed to be—a counterforce and check on government. In the Tornillo case, the Supreme Court overturned a Florida statute requiring newspapers to allow the right of reply. And Chief Justice Burger, a Nixon appointee, no less, defended the broadcaster's right to make day-to-day decisions when he declared in a 1973 decision, "editing is what editors are for."

The principle battle in the free press versus fair press (or access press) debate has centered around federal communications law. The so-called Fairness Doctrine, an FCC rule that has been incorporated into congressional law, says that broadcasters have to allocate a reasonable amount of time to the discussion of controversial issues and that they have to do this in a fair and balanced manner in order to allow reasonable opportunities for the expression of opposing viewpoints. The Fairness Doctrine ought not to be confused with the so-called Equal Time Doctrine (though it often is). The Equal Time provision of the communications law applies specifically to the treatment of candidates for public office and to the broadcasters' obligations to make air time available to candidates so that the rich or the incumbent do not monopolize all the broadcast time.

The Equal Time Doctrine should not create too much trouble for anyone, liberal or conservative. A stop watch can determine how much time Ronald Reagan, or Senator Phogbound, gets on television, and how much their opponents are due. This is a traffic cop regulation, a bearable minimum of government intervention in broadcasting. But how much harder it is for everyone—liberal or conservative—to agree on what constitutes fair news treatment of a given subject, or to agree on what is balance in public affairs programming. While the courts historically have been among the better friends of the press, print and broadcasting, in this area they have also been sympathetic at times to the idea of an activist FCC. Because of the Fairness Doctrine, the FCC has been called upon by allegedly aggrieved parties to decide, among other things, on the fairness or unfairness of an NBC News report on pension plans and on a CBS News report on the Pentagon. Are these topics we want the political appointees of the FCC to judge?

My own answer is, No. Liberals have been wise to abandon the position that conservatives are now so foolishly rushing to occupy. If conservatives are serious about embracing more direct government regulation of broadcasting, then they are playing Cuba in Angola; it's their quagmire, and welcome to it.

Just about all the justifications put forth for an activist FCC are shaky and/or silly—or out of date. First of all, critics like Phillips still talk about the awesome concentration of network power. But the real news these days is the prospective break-up of the present broadcast system, as cable TV, two-way television, satellite networks, home recording devices (videocassettes and video discs), computer-assisted retrieval systems, and other new developments begin to fragment the old mass audience and create new special-interest viewing groups. New communications technology, as well as new private enterprise arrangements, will effectively destroy the scarcity arguments. They will be producing access and rights of reply without government. Second, Phillips still talks about further governmental incursions into broadcasters' rights when the long-term judicial trend, despite occasional back-sliding, has been to lift broadcasting from second-class citizenship toward full First Amendment status.

One argument to save the FCC, I admit, causes me some disquiet. If the Fairness Doctrine and government regulation of broadcasting were abolished, wouldn't it mean that only the rich and the powerful could be heard on the air? Who would give the little people—consumers, conservationists, women, blacks, and other minorities—a chance to be heard? We need the government to act as a referee, in the old liberal sense, don't we? My answer is that the powerful, such as the oil companies and the banks, are heard so loudly and clearly now under the present system, that de-regulation won't make any noticeable difference in the decibel level. The remedy for unequal, entrenched power in America lies elsewhere, not at the expense of the First Amendment.

Television, radio, cable, satellite broadcasting, all should be deregulated because the courts can go only so far in getting government out of broadcasting. The broadcast establishment, like other enlightened capitalists in other industries, powerfully prefers a certain kind of federal regulation—the kind they can control. Most of the push will have to come from conservatives (old style) and liberals (new style) in the Congress. I expect it will come in the 1980s as the new technologies finally undercut the old scarcity-based arrangements. Or perhaps more precisely, government will be pushed out of broadcasting when the broadcasters no longer require regulatory protection from their economic rivals—when ABC, CBS, and NBC complete the switch of their interests to the new cable-satellite-home-communications systems, probably by the late 1980s.

"Government out of Broadcasting" has a stirring bumper sticker emphasis to it. The television audience, however, may not notice very much at first, or even after a time. Free television will probably be no better—and no worse—than free print. Some of the new unregulated networks and station groups will pursue expediency as well as profits; others will not. Some will be community minded and public spirited; others will not, just as with unregulated newspapers, magazines, or newsletters. The

constraints on newspaper publishers and broadcast station owners take many forms other than government regulation; the
audience (viewers/readers), the advertisers, competitors, special-
interest groups, peer tastes and pressures, the staff's tastes, all
influence the final outcomes of media organizations, as they
should in a free society. Free broadcasting may not immediately
make the world a better place or a more just place. But by now
liberals have learned to know better than to expect that hap-
piness can be guaranteed by government any more than by the
marketplace.

NOTES

Notes to the Introduction

1. The big three networks, for public consumption, usually picture themselves as near-invulnerable to challenge from cable TV. For example, the then NBC President Fred Silverman, speaking to the NBC affiliates convention in Los Angeles, May 19, 1981:

> . . . we and the broadcasting industry will continue to be successful as we meet the challenge from the new technologies. To be sure, the mature technologies may be somewhat less dominant than in the past, but they will still have by far the lion's share of the electronic marketplace. In fact, while our percentage of the total marketplace may be somewhat smaller than it is now, the absolute number of our viewers will increase. . . . I see no reason to fear the new technologies. They are "add-ons," not replacements, for what we already do. I know some of you are investigating and investing in the new technologies. NBC is making its plans. Our parent, RCA, as you know, is too. But the present system of broadcasting remains central to the future of each one of us.

2. As of May, 1981, no fewer than twenty cable and satellite networks were accepting advertising.

Notes to Chapter 1

1. George Herbert Mead, "The Nature of Aesthetic Experience," *International Journal of Ethics,* 36 (July 1926). For a lively discussion of

American journalism's social history see Michael Schudson, *Discovering the News* (New York: Basic Books, 1978).

2. For a round-up of the "shock and dismay" of editors after the Cooke case—and a similar sad episode involving the writer Michael Daly of the New York *Daily News*—see Jonathan Friendly, "Disclosures of Two Fabricated Articles Cause Papers to Re-examine Their Rules," *New York Times*, May 25, 1981, p. A7.

3. For the full background, see "Complaint number 150" and "Complaint number 165" both on file at the National News Council, 1 Lincoln Plaza, New York City, 10023.

Notes to Chapter 2

1. Hype, a common word around newsrooms, is defined as "implying excess or exaggeration" (*Random House Dictionary*). The word probably derives from hypodermic needle: to hype is to shoot up a story, to give it a shot of color, excitement, drama. The writer who does this is known as a hype artist; it is not intended as a compliment.

2. Fred Friendly, the former CBS News president now on the faculty of Columbia University, calls this "the selling of the news." Friendly writes: "Controversy and brutality are high priority sells. It is like a daily auction in which the sensational is hawked and the deadly serious ignored." Personal communication, October 11, 1979.

3. Fast slipping and falling. In April 1979 Howard K. Smith announced his resignation from ABC News, where he had served with distinction since 1961. Smith had been doing three-times-weekly commentary— the serious analysis the critics urge on television—on ABC's *World News Tonight*; when management told him they planned to cut down on his commentary—in order "to lighten the show," Smith reports—he decided to leave.

4. The findings of the Surgeon General's Scientific Advisory Committee on Television and Social Behavior, *Television and Growing Up: The Surgeon General's Report*, U.S. Public Health Service (Washington, D.C.: Government Printing Office, 1972).

Notes to Chapter 3

1. Studies by William Martin of Rice and by Jeffrey Hadden and Charles Swann have punctured the picture of a vast, lockstep audience for the televangelists. Their figures show considerably smaller audiences than the numbers claimed. See Martin, "The Birth of a Media

Myth," *Atlantic,* June, 1981 and Hadden-Swann, *Prime Time Preachers: The Power of Televangelism* (Reading, Mass.: Addison-Wesley, 1981).

2. Well before the 1980 campaign, the writer Elizabeth Hardwick was among the first critics to pay attention to the electronic church. See her comments on Schuller, Roberts, et al., in her review of Marshall Frady's book on the Reverend Billy Graham, *New York Review,* August 16, 1979, pp. 3–6. Stuart Zanger of WMC-TV, Memphis, Scripps Howard Broadcasting company, also became interested about this time in the intersection of television, religion, business, and politics. Personal communication, August 23, 1979.

3. The Reverend William F. Fore, communications director, National Council of Churches, New York, argued in *TV Guide* that "There is no such thing as a TV Pastor"—that is, the warm, loving, dynamic figure on the screen is not available to baptize children, comfort the sick, or bury the dead. He received a flood of letters, mostly in disagreement. He had thought the electronic church audience was lonely and alienated; he didn't realize how much until he read the letters. New York *Daily News,* May 12, 1981, p. M2.

4. John Lawrence, professor of philosophy at Morningside College, has also been following these developments. He says:

> I have tried to think about telereligion some myself and have come to the conclusion that apart from the appeals based upon the peculiar kinds of content that you describe, we are also seeing the process of religious reshaping. It is the form of television and the cultural power of its established genres that is remaking the traditional content of religion. Preacher becomes talk-show host, restorative ritual becomes commodity giveaway, etc. What the new religious leaders seem to understand so well is the source of secular power and they are remaking their religious content so as to share in it. [Personal communication, June 27, 1980]

5. *Newsweek,* September 15, 1980, p. 28. See also *Time,* February 4, 1980, p. 64; *New York Times,* December 2, 1979; *Forbes,* July 7, 1980, p. 118.

Notes to Chapter 4

1. Elizabeth J. Roberts is at the Harvard Graduate School of Education. Her work is gratefully acknowledged, especially Roberts, "Television and Sexual Learning in Childhood," in *Television and Behavior: Ten Years of Scientific Progress and Implications for the Eighties,* Pearl, Lazar, and Bouthilet, eds. (Washington, D.C.: Government Printing Office, 1981).

2. Soapland is the world of the daytime soap operas, so-called because detergent makers are among the biggest advertisers. This territory has only been occasionally explored by critics. James Thurber, confined to a

hospital room, wrote memorably about radio soaps in 1948 for *The New Yorker*. These essays were collected in The Beast in Me and Other Animals (New York: Harcourt Brace Jovanovich, 1948). More recently, Anthony Astrachan looked at the soaps at their moment of transition toward real-world concerns such as abortion, race relations, and feminism. "Life can be beautiful/relevant" *New York Times Magazine*, March 23, 1975, p. 12.

Notes to Chapter 5

1. Max Robinson went public in a major way with some of his criticism of white television's presentation of black America in February 1981, during a speech at Smith College. According to newspaper reports, "Robinson called the media 'a crooked mirror' through which 'white America' views itself and said it is time for black America to make itself known. He said ABC wants him to speak like 'any old white boy' and not incorporate his history, culture, or views 'and certainly not speak out of experience.' " Quoted by John Carmody, *Washington Post*, February 10, 1981, p. E1.

2. A year after the Miami riots, the conclusions of a Ford Foundation-sponsored report was released. The report found the Miami riots not only unlike the ghetto riots of the 1960s but perhaps "unprecedented in this century." According to the Ford report, the 1960s riots were warnings of the underlying hostility blacks felt about whites, while the Miami riot was the outpouring of the hostility itself—the sole purpose was the beating and killing of whites. *New York Times*, May 17, 1981, p. 28.

3. What stories would black America like to see covered? The subject is not opaque to white journalists. A great deal of material has been collected by the Newspaper Readership Project, sponsored by the American Society of Newspaper Editors and the American Newspaper Publishers Association. See, for example, "News Sources and Interests of Blacks and Whites" (Newspaper Advertising Bureau, New York).

Notes to Chapter 6

1. The Annenberg School of Communications, University of Pennsylvania, under the direction of Prof. George Gerbner, did a ten-year study of over 1,300 programs and some 16,600 characters to measure how aging is depicted on television. Among the findings: The over 65s, actually constituting 11 percent of Americans, appear to be hardly more than 2 percent of the TV population. Older people are shown as

eccentric, stubborn, nonsexual, ineffectual, and often silly. A report on the study, "Aging with Television," appeared in the winter 1980 issue of the *Journal of Communication.*
2. *The Washington Post,* September 23, 1979, p. G1.

Notes to Chapter 7

1. Television gets especially tongue tied when covering technology matters. About the same time our News Study Group looked at Three Mile Island, we also studied television's treatment of energy and the oil companies. See Edwin Diamond, "Is Television Out to Get Big Oil?" *TV Guide,* May 17, 1980. My answer was, No. For another answer, see the speech of Herbert Schmertz, vice president, public affairs, Mobil Oil Corporation, to the Business International Chief Executive's Round Table. Schmertz' speech, plus five case histories of what Mobil regards as press mishandling of energy stories, are in a booklet "The Energy Crisis and the Media: Some Case Histories," which can be obtained from Mobil's public affairs department, 150 East 42nd Street, New York, 10017.

Notes to Chapter 8

1. The working man's alleged hatred of the national media has been the subject of several essays by Michael Novak. Television can indeed be remote from the concerns of "ordinary people." During a New York City transit strike a few years ago, as a local television reporter finished his late night update, the anchorman asked if he would make it home. Not to worry, said the reporter: The company was putting him up in a convenient midtown hotel.
2. The Media Institute, which is funded by corporations, looked at how businessmen are portrayed in prime-time programming. Its survey is called "Crooks, Conmen, and Clowns." About a year earlier, the machinists' union did a somewhat similar survey of how work and unions were presented with the news programs on national and local television.
3. See, for example, William Serrin, "The Changing Nature of Work," *New York Times,* January 12, 1980, p. 1.

Notes to Chapter 9

1. Ezer Weizman, *The Battle for Peace* (New York: Bantam Books, 1981).
2. Marbrook is quoted by Jack Shaheen, "The Arab Stereotype on Television" in *The Link,* April/May 1980. *The Link,* a publication of

Americans for Middle East Understanding, gives a pro-Arab perspective on the American media.

Notes to Chapter 10

1. Here is how NBC reconstructed and justified the negotiations for the Gallegos interview:

Saturday, December 8, 1979. The Iranians approach three American television networks for a pooled Monday night broadcast, under editorial control of the Iranians. All three networks reject the proposal. Sunday Morning, December 9. The Iranians offer a slightly altered second plan to networks. Also rejected. Sunday Afternoon, December 9. NBC News returns to the Iranians with a counter proposal. That NBC correspondents alone would conduct the interview with the hostage and that no questions would be submitted in advance. That NBC News would retain journalistic control, including editing, and would broadcast the interview in prime time, at an hour selected by NBC News. Sunday Evening, December 9. The Iranians agreed, provided they could make a brief statement. NBC felt that such a statement would show the intensity and depth of Iranian feeling and, more important, show what the Iranians are saying to the hostages. Anchorman John Chancellor would make that point on the air. Monday Morning, December 10. At approximately 7 A.M., EST, NBC News Correspondents George Lewis and Fred Francis talk with Corporal William Gallegos, in an interview taped by an Iranian crew. Monday Evening, 9.47 P.M. EST. NBC News presents "Hostage! First TV Interview."

As NBC News said on the air, the interview with Cpl. Gallegos raised some new questions. Why was he the one selected by his captors? What about the condition of the other hostages? What else is going on behind the embassy gates? We think the interview provided new information about the questions every American has been asking. We believe the American public can judge for itself which questions are still unanswered. We will continue to pursue those answers. [From NBC News Press Department]

2. See "The Ayatollah and the Election," remarks by Bill Leonard, president, CBS News, to the California Broadcasters Association, Palm Springs, Calif., January 14, 1980.

3. The question persists: Did ABC News act out of concern for an informed public, or out of self-interest? We know the Iranian crisis was good for the ratings. Here is an internal memo from ABC's public relations division:

To: The Staff
From: Roann Levinsohn
Date: December 14, 1979
Subject: ABC News Late-Night Iran Specials

ABC News' late-night specials, "The Iranian Crisis: America Held Hostage," are continuing to draw sizable audiences. According to the latest available data, the 18 late-night specials which aired from Thursday, November 8th, through Friday, December 7th, averaged a 9.5 rating and a 28 share. The 9.5 rating translates into 7,250,000 households per average minute. An average of 12,150,000 viewers have watched some or all of each telecast. . . . Of further interest is a comparison of total available audience (for network affiliates and independent stations) in the 11:30–midnight time period during the last half of November, this year versus last year. This year, 43,430,000 people were watching television during this time period, compared to 39,500,000 people a year ago. This represents a 10% increase in available audience for the 11:30–midnight time period, with ABC News' coverage of the Iran crisis contributing significantly to this increase.

Notes to Chapter 11

1. The members of the News Study Group who shared in the reporting and analysis of the events of January 20 were Bill Meyers in New York and Clive Smith in Cambridge.

2. Two correspondents in particular managed to step back far enough to see what we also saw. George Will in his Sunday column, February 1, 1981, began:

The movable feast of celebration about the hostages has abated a bit, so perhaps it will not seem intolerably churlish to ask what, precisely, people have been celebrating. Clearly, more is involved than just gratification about the hostages' deliverance. At the risk of seeming stone hearted, I suggest this: The crisis that began because of weakness, and was prolonged by confusion, and ended in extortion, has been followed by a national celebration: "America 52, Iran 0." When calamity is translated into the idiom of sport and christened a victory, when victims are called heroes and turned into props for telegenic celebrations of triumph, then it is time to recall George Orwell's axiom that the great enemy of clear language is insincerity.

Critic Marvin Kitman in *Newday*, February 2, 1981, was also on the mark:

This could be Day 1 of television without the hostage story, a welcome change, a relief from the intense emotions of the last 10 days which have left me all hostaged out. There were times when I wished they would be given a day off to finalize their book deals, and whatever other merchandising is ahead. The emotional story left me with mixed feelings that I have been too cowardly to write.

Notes to Chapter 12

1. Tim Wicker, *On Press* (New York: Viking, 1978).

2. Suzannah Lessard, "Kennedy's Women Problem, Women's Kennedy Problem," *Washington Monthly,* December, 1979.

3. James David Barber made the case for "life histories" of the candidates in his essay "This Year, Why Not the Facts?" *New York Times,* March 17, 1980, p. A19. My own effort at life history, written with Bruce Mazlish, was *Jimmy Carter: An Interpretive Biography* (New York: Simon and Schuster, 1980). See also Doris Kearns, *Lyndon Johnson and the American Dream* (New York: Harper and Row, 1976).

Notes to Chapter 13

1. Steward Weiner, "*Lou Grant:* Staff in Rebellion," *Los Angeles Magazine,* February 1980.

2. Frank Van Riper, "How Hollywood Views the Press . . .," *Neiman Reports,* Harvard University, Winter 1979.

Notes to Chapter 14

1. See also, for example, Reeves's comments in "Lights, Cameras . . . Politics," an ABC News *Close-up Report* broadcast on Friday, July 11, 1980 8–9 P.M.

2. F. Christopher Arterton et al. *Race for the Presidency: the Media and the Nominating Process* (Englewood Cliffs, N.J.: Prentice-Hall, 1978).

Notes to Chapter 15

1. Most of the candidates' advisors were kind enough to supply us with videotapes of their handiwork in 1980, in particular Gerald Rafshoon of the Carter campaign. A number of broadcast journalists were also helpful, especially Bill Aber of KYW-TV in Philadelphia and Sasha Norkin of WNAC-TV in Boston.

2. There were two journalists who watched and wrote astutely about the effects of political commercials in the 1980 campaign: Robert G. Kaiser of the *Washington Post* and Len Zeidenberg of *Broadcasting* magazine. See in particular Kaiser's article "TV Ads: An Aid To Some Candidates But Not Others," *Washington Post,* May 2, 1980, p. A2, and Zeidenberg's "Reflections on the Media and the Campaigns," *Broadcasting,* November 24, 1980, p. 54. Also see *Broadcasting,* April 14 and 28, 1980.

Notes to Chapter 16

1. David Broder, Lou Cannon, Richard Harwood, et al., *The Pursuit of the Presidency* (New York: The Washington Post/Berkley, 1980). For the

record, a New York Times political team produced its own account of the 1980 campaign. Hedrick Smith, Adam Clymer, et al., *Reagan the Man, the President* (New York: Macmillan, 1980).

Notes to Chapter 17

1. It's dangerous to count Turner out too soon. As television critic David Bianculli of the Fort Lauderdale (Fla.) News has said, "Ted Turner is no fool." As evidence, Bianculli points out in the Television Critics Association Newsletter (Fall 1980):

In 1970 Turner invested his family fortune in Atlanta's Ch. 17, a last-place UHF station with little or no future. . . . Turner outlasted his independent competition simply by his willingness to lose money; a year later, the other independent station folded, leaving Turner to take on the affiliates single-handed. He paid the Braves for TV rights, then bought the team outright, to give WTCG credence as the southeast's finest independent sports station. When local affiliates preempted network shows, Turner eagerly contacted the networks and ran the shows on WTCG—anything to get his station noticed. In 1976 WTCG began transmitting its signal by satellite to cable companies nationwide, even though most companies had no earth stations with which to receive it. . . . In less than a decade, Turner would turn WTCG (later renamed WTBS, for Turner Broadcasting System) from a fifth-rate Atlanta independent into a national cable "alternative" with millions of potential viewers.

2. The most important kind of hard news that television does is the documentary. This is an honored form, but through its first year of operations CNN produced no documentaries at all. Mary Alice Williams, the able head of CNN's New York bureau, in an interview with us, explained: "Setting up sources, doing heavy research and investigative work takes up a lot of time. . . . Our mandate is to tell the news as it's happening. . . . Newspapers can spend six months doing investigative research for people who want to know the in-depth story."

Notes to Chapter 18

1. In this chapter I concentrate on magazines, and in particular special-interest magazines, for two reasons: first, because magazines are important information sources and, second, because the cable television of the future will probably resemble special-interest magazines in content and audience appeal. For two accounts of the state of the American magazine today, see "Turbulent Times in the Magazine Business," *Adweek*, February 1981, and "Magazines in the '80's," *Adweek*, March 1980.

Notes to Chapter 19

1. In the fall of 1978 the *Washington Post* did a national telephone survey of television-watching habits under the direction of editor Barry Sussman. According to Sussman's report (February 28, 1979, p. B1): "In all, 53 percent of those interviewed said they are watching less TV than they did five years ago, compared to 32 percent who say they are watching more now. If those figures are correct, they represent a striking reversal in the nation's entertainment and leisure habits. From the inception of TV until the mid-1970s, viewership had been reported as increasing year after year."

Notes to Chapter 20

1. Todd Gitlin, *The Whole World Is Watching* (Berkeley: University of California Press, 1980).
2. The idea of media frames is hardly new. Walter Lippmann, sixty years ago, wrote about the news-processing machinery in *Public Opinion,* a book still fresh in its statements. Civil liberty and a free press, Lippmann pointed out, "does not guarantee public opinion in the modern world. For it always assumes, either that truth is spontaneous, or that the means of securing truth exist when there is no external interference. But when you are dealing with an invisible environment, the assumption is false. The truth about distant or complex matters is not self-evident, and the machinery for assembling information is technical and expensive."

INDEX